MW01204791

Architecture 101

Architecture 101

A Guide to the Design Studio

Andy Pressman, A.I.A.

John Wiley & Sons, Inc.

New York / Chichester / Brisbane / Toronto / Singapore

Library of Congress Cataloging in Publication Data:

Pressman, Andy.
   Architecture 101 : a guide to the design studio / Andy Pressman.
      p.   cm.
   Includes bibliographical references and index.
   ISBN 0-471-57318-3 (paper)
   1. Architectural design. I. Title.
NA2750.P695 1993   92-40504
729—dc20

Printed in the United States of America

10 9 8 7 6 5 4 3 2 1

To my brother Peter;
To Elie K. Mangoubi, M.D., a true professional role model;
and
To architecture students, who deserve as much support as
possible

Foreword

There's little in a normal primary and secondary education, or even in a prior college degree, that prepares a student for the singular experience of the architectural design studio. My own story is similar to many others. I came to architecture school with two years of university under my belt and a record of solid academic achievement that stretched all the way back to first grade. I *knew* I was going to do well. But my first studio almost undid me. On the first of an initial string of two-week design projects, I got a C. Not nearly good enough. I resolved to try harder. My second project brought a B. Aha! I was catching on! My third project fetched an A-minus. Almost back on track, I told myself. Just try a little harder yet. The fourth project? F. Failure. Desolation! Obviously I had no idea what my studio teachers expected of me. Should I give up architecture and return to my engineering studies? I yearned for those physics and math exercises where every problem had a right answer. Studio problems didn't seem to have right answers. There were eighty others in my class, most of them as clueless as I. Later I realized that the beginning students in a hundred other schools were also suffering the same self-doubt at the same time, puzzled about what was expected of them, uncertain how to go about achieving it. And each new class of students, generation after generation, have had to work their individual ways through the same agonies.

Finally, help has arrived. Andy Pressman has created the book that everybody has always known we need but that nobody thought could be done: A guide to the uniquely provocative and often puzzling culture of the design studio in architectural education. It's a book to be read, re-read, and read again; a book whose pages will gradually become dog-eared and graphite-smudged; a comforting companion both in times of trouble and times of success. For the student it is an indispensible source of information on how to interpret what is going on in the studio, how to react to it, and what to do next. For the seasoned practitioner it refreshes the memory, helps resharpen one's tools, puts temporary troubles in perspective, and assists in recalling the worthy dream that we all began studio with, that of designing wonderful, even magical buildings.

Wisely, Pressman has not attempted his task alone. Dozens of architects, teachers, and students have contributed valuable insights into their particular specialties and the studio experience in general. Despite the diversity of their backgrounds and opinions, there is an impressive unanimity regarding the underlying principles of successful performance in studio. Students, listen up: This is an authoritative volume. You can believe what it tells you. Keep it by your side. Read it well and understand it. It will spare you much pain, and it will help you get much more out of your design education.

The design studio is a miraculous educational device. Looking back on my experiences as a student, and contemplating the many studios I have taught since that time, I marvel at its power and audacity. It attempts nothing less than to teach what would seem to be unteachable: How to use the mind, eye, and hand in concert to create useful and beautiful objects of the most complex kind. By the time of graduation every student of architecture has come to realize that the design studios comprise a gift of inestimable value. Now I regret only that the studio concept has not permeated more deeply into our educational system in general, teaching kids from kindergarten through every kind of graduate school to be creative—not just to throw out bright ideas, but to do the hard work and critical analysis necessary to develop them and bring them to fruition.

Thoreau observed that education often makes a straight-cut ditch of a free meandering brook. Today the most obvious and joyous exception to this observation is the architectural design studio, a place where students learn once again to be spontaneous and creative. This book makes it easier to overcome the inhibitions that one has acquired involuntarily during a dozen or more years of prior education, and to go on to a successful career in architecture.

EDWARD ALLEN, A.I.A.

Preface

Architecture 101 is a design primer for beginning- and intermediate-level students. It is intended to help with the sometimes epic struggle through early design studios. The design process, from programming to presenting, is clarified, perhaps caricatured, and analyzed. Approaches to various aspects of the entire process are illuminated in "Supplements" (contributed by prominent professionals and educators) and summarized in "Take-Home Messages" that appear throughout the text. In short, there is explicit guidance on how to view, attack, or accomplish particular tasks.

Successfully completing design projects and maximizing learning in the studio are the fundamental objectives of this book. In light of the overall challenge of architectural education, *Architecture 101* is designed to be easy to read, accessible, and entertaining. Immediate personal meaning for the student reader is paramount.

More specifically, *Architecture 101* seeks to promote activation of talent by (1) addressing basics, thus lowering anxiety, and (2) providing insights from professional practice. Relevancy to professional practice is a recurring theme throughout the book. Apart from the interest intrinsic to an "applications" format, there is an effort at preparation for professional life. An understanding of the roles of the various players and the bigger forces involved in the planning and design of the built environment can only inform and enrich design projects. Anecdotes from actual situations focusing on clients, engineering consultants, contractors, and others exemplify selected ideas and issues, and provide windows on achieving design excellence.

Among the special Supplements from a wide range of guest experts are mini-consultations on the values that are important in the design of buildings; the impact of structural and mechanical engineering on preliminary design; acoustics; daylighting; computers; landscape architecture; color; the role of history; graphic communication; accessibility; building codes; interviewing clients; and landing a first job in an architect's office.

Finally, *Architecture 101* implicitly tries to suggest something about a life in architecture. It will be apparent that, at its most grand, architecture may have rich and enduring effects on society. At its most mundane, architecture may have an influence on the quality of a day—and to paraphrase Thoreau, that may be the highest of arts. Since a life in architecture begins in the design studio, it seems a natural place to explore, not only routinized and objective methods, but the more abstract images of people and the world that fire the imaginations and inspirations that transform the student into a designer.

Architecture 101 attempts to unravel some of the mystery of creating beautiful, responsive, and responsible architectural design.

ANDY PRESSMAN, A.I.A.

Chicago, Illinois
November 1992

To the Student

Among my chief concerns was the need to make this book concise and portable. You should be able to read it in departure lounges, on airplanes, and on trains, as well as in the studio. Coverage of topics strives to be **comprehensive but digestible**, and contributed Supplements are varied and lively. My hope is that even with little or no background, and not much time, you will pick up *Architecture 101: A Guide to the Design Studio* and acquire a framework for learning and doing design. I expect that at least a few of the contributions will serve to tease, tantalize, or otherwise provoke more in-depth exploration of a particular area. Chapters are intended to be read in sequence, but you should not hesitate to consult them as self-contained units.

While this book is a primer and a reference, it certainly does not represent the *only* way to approach projects in the studio. It does try to capture what helped *me* most in developing as a student, and more recently as a practicing architect and teacher.

Acknowledgments

This book is a direct result of my teaching experiences in the School of Architecture and Urban Planning at the University of Wisconsin–Milwaukee from 1987 through 1991. I would like to express appreciation to all my students and my colleagues for providing a stimulating and enjoyable environment.

Tom Hubka is due special thanks for his valuable insight and support.

I am greatly indebted to all the gifted people who so generously agreed to participate in writing the Supplements, contributing material, or talking into my tape recorder. They include (in alphabetical order): Teri Appel, William Brinkman, Blair Brown, Rick Buckley, Ernest Burden, Marvin Cantor, Virginia Cartwright, Caren Connolly, James Diaz, Arthur Erickson, Paul Friedberg, Catherine Gawlik, Scott Gordon, Robert Greenstreet, Lawrence Halprin, David Hoedemaker, Hugh Newell Jacobsen, Helmut Jahn, Chris Jofeh, William Keeley, Eugene Kohn, George Kousoulas, William Lam, Kent Larson, Norbert Lechner, Pat Lemmons, Charles Linn, David Linton, William Kirby Lockard, Ruth Lusher, John Lyons, Jim Maitland, William McDonough, Norman McGrath, Denis McMullan, Charles Moore, Raymond Novitske, Fred Ordway, Terry Patterson, William Peña, Peter Pfau, Norman Rosenfeld, Mark Roth, Douglas Ryhn, Lawrence Schnuck, Gary Siebein, Robert Singleton, Iris Slikerman, Michael Sobczak, Lydia Soo, Bryan Strube, Deborah Sussman, Jeri Vaughn, Gerald Weisman, Mary Woolever, and Raymond Worley.

Appreciation is extended to Eleanor Pressman, who discovered *The New Yorker* drawing for the chapter on presentations.

Finally, I wish to thank Everett Smethurst, Senior Editor, and the staff (especially Linda Bathgate) at Wiley for their guidance and professionalism.

Credits

COVER PHOTO: Design Studio of Paul Segal Associates NYC © Norman McGrath.

CHAPTER 1: "Catherine G." and "Bryan S." are Catherine Gawlik and Bryan Strube, quoted during interviews with the author.

CHAPTER 2: Subtitle quote from *The TIBs of Bill Caudill* © 1984 by CRS Sirrine, Inc., Roseanne Terry Elisei, Editor; Norman Foster quote reprinted with permission of *Progressive Architecture*, Penton Publishing; Supplement 2-6 and Supplement 2-7 adapted from articles by the author, reprinted from *Commercial Renovation*.

CHAPTER 3: Subtitle quote by William P. Miles from a speech in the House of Representatives, March 31, 1858.

CHAPTER 4: Annie Hall quote from screenplay by Woody Allen and Marshall Brickman. Screenplay © 1977 by United Artists Corporation, from *Four Films of Woody Allen* © 1982 by Random House, Inc., New York.

CHAPTER 6: Subtitle quote by Sir Winston S. Churchill, from a speech at the Lord Mayor's Day Luncheon, London, November 10, 1942.

Contents

Foreword   vii

Preface   ix

To the Student   xi

Acknowledgments   xiii

Credits   xv

Chapter 1   **The Initiation**   1
"A journey of a thousand miles must begin with a single step."

Welcome to the Studio / 2

Seeking Criticism / 3

Time Management / 4

Read the Journals / 6

Desk Crits and Pinups / 7

Mentors / 9

Grades / 9

Equipment / 10

Rewards / 11

Advice from the Stars / 13
    Helmut Jahn / 13
    Hugh Newell Jacobsen / 14
    Arthur Erickson / 15
    Charles Moore / 16

Chapter 2   The Program   **17**
"The genes of a building are determined before a sketch is made."

Approach / 18

Information Gathering / 19
    Primary Data / 19
    Secondary Data / 22
    Construction Costs / 23
    Building Codes and Standards / 25
    Accessibility / 27

Analysis and Interpretation of Information / 30
    Diagrams / 30

Concept Development / 35
    Scheduling Note / 35

Social Responsibility / 37
    Environment/Behavior Factors / 37

Chapter 3   The Site   **41**
Like voting in Chicago, go "early and often."

Appreciating the Environment / 42
    Landscape Architecture / 42

Examples of Site Influences on Design / 46

The Inventory / 50
    Start with the Big Picture / 50
    Zero-in on Your Site: Preparation / 52
    Zero-in on Your Site: Record Data / 52

Diagramming the Data / 55

Marrying Program and Site / 56

Entry Sequence / 58

Daylighting / 60

Miscellaneous Considerations / 62
    Indoor/Outdoor Transitions / 62
    Understanding Contours / 62
    Parking / 63
    The Site Context Model and Drawings / 65

Globalization of Architecture / 65
　　Metrication / 66

Chapter 4　**The Design**　　　　　　　　　　　　　　　**71**
*How to avoid having your work seen as "artificially inseminated
rather than passionately conceived."*

The Magical Synthesis Myth / 72

Facilitating Design / 72
　　Examples of Organizing Elements / 73
　　Three-Dimensional Considerations / 74
　　History / 76
　　Aesthetic Issues / 79
　　Brainstorming Tips / 82
　　Common Mistakes / 83

Tools / 84
　　Drawings / 84
　　Models / 87
　　Computers / 90

Construction Technology / 92
　　Detailing / 95
　　Working with Constructors / 98

Materials / 101

Color / 103

Who 'Ya Gonna Call? / 104
　　Structures / 105
　　Mechanical Systems / 110
　　Lighting / 113
　　Acoustics / 118

Orchestrating Design / 120
　　The Symphony / 120

Chapter 5　**The Presentation**　　　　　　　　　　　　　**127**
"You look mahvelous!"

Another Design Problem / 128

The Dog and Pony Show / 132
　　Responding to Criticism / 134

Quick Tips / 138
　　Art Supplies and Reprographics / 141

Three-Dimensional Vehicles / 147

An Addendum on Juries / 149

Chapter 6   The Future   **151**
            "There is no room now for the dilettante, the weakling, for the
            shirker, or the sluggard."

            Getting in the Door / 152

            In the Trenches / 157
               Your First Job / 157

            Continuing Education and Development / 162
               Travel / 163
               Portfolio / 164
               Define Your Role / 165

Appendixes   **167**

            Appendix A: Reading List / 169
               Books for a Professional Collection / 169
               Books for Reference / 170

            Appendix B: Assessing Architectural Photographs / 171

Index   **173**

1

The Initiation

"A journey of a thousand miles must begin with a single step."—Lao-tzu

A second-year design studio at Rensselaer Polytechnic Institute.
Photo credit: *The Transit* (The Rensselaer Yearbook).

Catherine G. (senior): Just starting is the worst thing. And fear of failure. You just have to jump in, just do it.

Bryan S. (third-year student): Having seen the lights on *all* the time in the architecture building, and hearing the rumors about no sleep, I expected it to require a big time commitment. And it *is* all encompassing, everything else gets shoved away—I mean everything. One of the hardest things is to be able to turn that off and say, "Okay, I'm not going to do that, I'm going to relax . . . I'm going to sleep. . . ."

WELCOME TO THE STUDIO

Educational traditions such as basic training in the military, gross anatomy lab in medical school, and moot court in law school have an importance far beyond that of simply learning course material. The design studio in the school of architecture is no different; it is perhaps the most intense and multidimensional "classroom" experience in all of higher education. In what is really a very short span of time, the studio becomes the matrix within which a student develops the habit of thinking and talking both as a design professional and as a member of a team. The routines, the beliefs, and the standards associated with the studio all help to form a professional self-image. This occurs at personal and collective levels: How the individual sees him/herself as a distinctive member of a profession, and how the emerging group begins to see the nature and value of the profession in which they are being trained. Thus, in the studio, a student will begin to absorb and respond to the culture of the architectural profession.

Then, of course, there is the manifest content: The more obvious and concrete things you do in studio. Through assigned projects, you develop considerable skill in identifying and solving problems. Your prowess in assessing a creative challenge, integrating and synthesizing available data, conducting your own research, applying material from other courses, and responding to an array of forces and constraints with a three-dimensional solution will be quite amazing. Your ability to communicate verbally as well as graphically will grow enormously. Your capacity to listen and observe will grow in equally profound fashion. Like the Eskimo who is said to visually discriminate many grades of snow where most of us see only a few, you will actually *see* more; a new world of awareness is a heady place. And your resources for absorbing and reacting to the inevitable criticism you will receive from colleagues, teachers, critics, and above all, from clients, will mature.

Design studio is probably the only common element among the one hundred or so diverse NAAB accredited programs in architecture in the country. As such, it is not as important *where* you are as it is *what* you personally make of the studio experience. Understand that at this stage of development, you will have to begin to discern good pedagogical content and style from bad. I believe that in architecture perhaps more than in any other field, students must become progressively independent and responsible for their own education at an extremely early phase.

You will come to know the architecture building intimately, but you will know it with eyes sensitive to such concepts as form, space, proportion, and plan. The architecture building will serve as a kind of daily (and often nightly) field trip to a new world. The building comprises the framework for a culture so rich and full of creative potential that it leaves little doubt about its association with one of the great professions. If this sounds a bit romanticized, I plead guilty. I would assert that architectural design can indeed be visionary, idealistic, hopeful, and full of passion—in essence, quite romantic.

SEEKING CRITICISM

Receiving criticism from both colleagues and faculty is a fundamental part of learning in the studio. *Make sure that your work is reviewed and discussed as often as possible.* This is your responsibility. If you feel you are being ignored by faculty, be aggressive about tracking them down during office hours or otherwise. Seek out specialists on the faculty (not necessarily your studio instructor) who may offer advice on a particular aspect of a project, such as structural design. Their job is talking to students, so make an appointment. You will be surprised at how pleased your teachers will be when given an opportunity to help.

Despite what many of us espouse about the merits of "constructive criticism," at some level it's all knives. Criticism is, however, a fact of professional life. So while there is unquestionably some utility in the intense evaluation of the merits and shortcomings of your work, it is never easy to take. When you invest so much of yourself in a project, it is impossible not to experience criticism as a personal assault. *The Take-Home Message here is to try to view criticism in terms of how well your work fits the expectations of the critic.* Ideally, in the studio, the instructor's expectations have to do with more objective standards of performance. With honest effort and some ability, these standards can be achieved. In contrast, in professional life, your client's expectations are more likely to involve many more personal preferences which may represent a spectrum of elusive factors. The point is this: Assume that revision of your work will always be demanded. Even when you just *know* that there could not be a more elegant solution, incorporation of instructor's or client's modifications *almost always translates to an opportunity to make the work even more potent.* Do not view change as compromise but as something that makes a project more sensitive and responsive to a special client need, instructor guidance, site circumstance, aesthetic priority, or the like. After all, architecture is a service profession. The image of Howard Roark (from *The Fountainhead*) dynamiting a building not in complete accordance with his design is antithetical to the image of any professional and all that term implies.

Talk to your classmates. Engage in dialogue about general issues and specific project strategies. Cultivate the habit of listening and talking about everything you hear, read, and see in the studios and in other architecture classes. This is obvious but important: If you're not in studio, these spontaneous and often very valuable interactions can't happen. Further, contact hours and repetition facilitate absorbing and understanding a whole new "architectural vocabulary"—which in turn promotes better communication with critics and faculty. In the course of one year of classes, you will hear hundreds of new terms; it is *in the studio* that you learn to apply these terms. There are some students who, for a variety of reasons, prefer to work at home rather than in studio. This is a BIG MISTAKE. It subverts a principal intent of the studio, and learning suffers as a result.

Take care of your peers; if you see a way around a design issue that has defeated the student next to you, share your view. By offering opinions about what is good and what is bad, you learn to *critique your own work* more objectively. Try to defeat

FIGURE 1-1 *The typical studio environment is in itself a vehicle for creativity and whimsy. However chaotic it may appear (crowded with drawing tables, tackboard panels, the ubiquitous tracing paper and cardboard), respect for classmates and a professional attitude must underlie all productive activity. Photo © SARUP, University of Wisconsin–Milwaukee.*

any feeling of competitiveness. *The Take-Home Message is that the moment you walk into the studio, you are a member of the profession. As a professional whose life will be committed to serving others with your specialized knowledge and skills, you must begin by serving and being considerate of your colleagues in exactly the same manner.* Imparting knowledge and helping where possible are hallmarks of the professional. The relatively superficial "walking the walk and talking the talk" is quickly outdistanced by actually thinking and behaving as an architect.

If you are in a large class with many sections of the same studio level, visit other studios periodically, and study the projects. "*If you see an idea on somebody else's desk, and it's great, ask to steal it! . . . do it better!*" says Caren M. Connolly, Visiting Professor at the University of Wisconsin–Milwaukee. She also comments: "In the studio, I try to get students to work in teams. In 'crit' situations, I'll assign two students to 'crit' another student, or get a student to present someone else's drawings so that another point of view is fully experienced."

Take advantage of the more advanced students in the school: They can be a wonderful resource. Some will be more approachable than others; some will be intimidating in their sophistication and talent. But you will undoubtedly find that a fantastic amount can be gleaned from all types. Visit as many desks as possible; attend public reviews; go to thesis presentations. Be attuned to what is going on at all levels, both graduate and undergraduate.

TIME MANAGEMENT

There is no question that it takes a long time to design a building thoughtfully. For most of us, the creative process is stimulating, boring, energizing, painful, filled with self-doubts, and satisfying—in varying degrees and sequences, depending on the particular project. Because creativity is so idiosyncratic and often quirky (even in the same person), it may be very difficult to manipulate all the variables and forces toward planned inspiration. But *plan you must* to promote, to the extent possible, a balanced, healthy, and successful school experience. The habit of struggling with "planned inspiration" inevitably results in the ability to "turn on" talent when it is demanded. One of the hallmarks of the professional is the discipline to perform in this way even if you wake up on the proverbial wrong side of the bed.

> *SUPPLEMENT 1-1:* Charles D. Linn, A.I.A., Editor at Large of *Architectural Record*, comments on the "all-nighter."
>
> Looking back, I think many of us in architecture school pursued very unhealthy lifestyles. The number of consecutive all-nighters was worn on our sleeves like a badge of honor, not as the badge of stupidity that it was.
>
> Still, working in the studio until we were exhausted wrought a sense of belonging and camaraderie among many of us—maybe it was the first time in our lives some of us ever felt that, I don't know. It was certainly the first time most of us had the thrill of creating spaces in models or in our minds, the first time some of us ever created hues with Magic Markers or ornament or typefaces. But it got out of hand. I think some people actually started thinking that the point of the thing was to stay up all night—that this was better somehow than a balanced, healthy life.
>
> During an all-nighter, there is the tendency of exhausted persons to stare at their drawings, unable to make more than a few decisions in an hour, all the time believing that they are jamming full speed. These people are better off in bed. There is also the tendency to spill bottles of ink on just-completed renderings at 4:00 A.M.—these people would definitely be better off in bed.

Staying up all night is inefficient. Careful planning to avoid a time crunch at the end of projects is critically important to achieve success. Consider developing a schedule as another *design problem*: Lay out and prioritize all the tasks and requirements for each project of the semester, and attach an estimated time to each. Be sure to factor in work in all classes, along with other obligations. Catherine Gawlik, a senior architecture student, says: "I mark up all due dates in a diary. If you can learn how to plan effectively, the stress is definitely reduced. One of the problems when just starting out is accurately estimating the time it takes to get design tasks done: Whether to allow two days or five days for presentation drawings. (Ask your instructor for help with this.) You have to be rigid and structured in the beginning to complete projects. You have to be dogmatic about it; there's no other way."

Chip away! If at first things seem overwhelming, just chip away one small bit at a time. Try a quick and simple bar chart for the first design exercise to help visualize project milestones (see Figure 1-2). Use them for each project or for all courses, including design studio. They are graphic—a perfect tool for the architect! Be good to yourself as you reach goals—celebrate!

One last note about deadlines. If you believe that you will not be able to finish on time, see your professor as early as possible. There are legitimate reasons for incomplete projects, so negotiation is usually possible. Alternatively, submit everything you have in a coherent way, and complete the work at a later time. The worst thing a student can do is not show up without prior warning. Deadlines are extremely important in the real world, so learn to respect them.

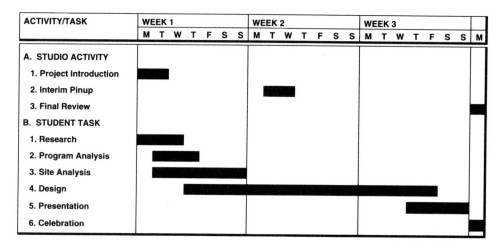

ACTIVITY/TASK	WEEK 1							WEEK 2							WEEK 3							
	M	T	W	T	F	S	S	M	T	W	T	F	S	S	M	T	W	T	F	S	S	M
A. STUDIO ACTIVITY																						
1. Project Introduction		▆																				
2. Interim Pinup									▆													
3. Final Review																						▆
B. STUDENT TASK																						
1. Research		▆																				
2. Program Analysis			▆																			
3. Site Analysis			▆																			
4. Design				▆																		
5. Presentation																			▆			
6. Celebration																						▆

FIGURE 1-2   *Bar chart/timeline for a "typical" design project. Note overlapping of tasks—be flexible and responsive to special project demands. Mac graphic by Raymond Novitske, A.I.A.*

Between semesters or during summer break, I recommend scheduling time to complete any unfinished design work. It makes sense for two reasons: Personal satisfaction (achieving a feeling of closure) and for the best possible portfolio. Further design exploration is a luxury and may clarify a specific criticism or simply lead to a better result.

READ THE JOURNALS

Architecture, Progressive Architecture, and *Architectural Record* are the Big Three journals and the most readily available. Short of visiting important works of architecture (*which is highly recommended*—see "Travel" in Chapter 6), reading about them, or at the very least looking at the pictures, is the next best thing. The importance of studying examples of good architecture cannot be overemphasized. Take lunch with a current journal twice a week. Make it a routine part of your schedule (regardless of pressing deadlines in the studio). Note what is appealing to you; *if something in a photo catches your eye, analyze and determine the relationship of the photo to the accompanying plans. This is a great exercise in developing the capacity to think three-dimensionally. However, it does require effort and practice.*

Another benefit of reading the journals is becoming familiar with, and understanding, new terminology. However, at times, depending on who is writing or being quoted, material can be quite unintelligible, even laughable, in its arrogant, convoluted verbosity. Don't despair; many experienced, practicing architects (and academics) don't have a clue about the meaning behind some of the theoretical silliness we all occasionally enjoy a bit too much. Hyperbole and metaphor may flow—projects are described as "coyly asserting" some quality, inanimate structure is seen as "mute" or in terms of "colliding" systems of philosophical and political belief. Certainly, buildings can and often should symbolize something greater. The point is that sometimes a gas station is just a gas station.

This section on journals is not meant to imply that every published project is sacred. There are many reasons (apart from design quality) why projects are published in journals. Terrence G. Heinlein, A.I.A., elaborates this point: [It is important to] "clarify that architectural journals illustrate a minority of work that is judged by a few with limited evaluation criteria, and that architecture is viewed and evaluated differently by those who build, buy, use, maintain, and watch architecture." *The Take-Home Message is to get exposed to a lot of buildings; get a sense of what is good conceptually and in detail, and why. Read, but know that it is not necessarily the gold standard.*

Journals can be a source of inspiration for even the most blocked students and practitioners. Intriguing design features that trigger ideas may come from projects completely unrelated to current work. If someone owes you a favor and wants to give you a gift that genuinely keeps on giving, ask for a subscription to *Architectural Record* or *Architecture*, the major national publication of the American Institute of Architects. Or go to a local architect's office and ask for back issues of any magazine with the word *Progressive* in it. (See Appendix B for information on reading architectural photographs.)

DESK CRITS AND PINUPS

Student: My car broke down, my dog ate one of my drawings, my girlfriend surprised me with a visit, and my boss at the pizza place wanted me to work overtime, so what do you think of this scheme?

Teacher: It has possibilities [NOT!], but have you tried X, Y, and Z? Look up the ramp detail and use of natural light on the new wing of the Schmoolowitz Museum in Frankfurt. For next class, let me see how you apply this principle to two new alternatives.

This is the desk crit, the most important event during studio class. It's where the student has the opportunity to go one-on-one with the teacher. *Make the best possible use of this time by doing your homework: Have as much material (design sketches, concepts, analyses, precedents) as possible to discuss.* Depending on the organization of your studio, you may be seen by three or four other instructors or teaching assistants. They may contradict each other, give conflicting guidance, and confuse the student. This is good. As Hugh Jacobsen writes later in this chapter, there are indeed no correct solutions, only approaches. The more exposure to diversity in points of view, the more possibilities become evident. Within this pluralism, it is ostensibly up to the student to distinguish the approach most compatible with personal values, and appropriate for the specific circumstance.

Studio is a hands-on exercise. Ask to be shown how to do something. If references are too oblique or the vocabulary is mystifying, ask for clarification. Make your studio critics earn their minimum wage. Take time to reflect on and respond to each critique. There should be constant feedback and therefore no surprises at the end of each project or semester.

> "Wrestling with the idea of change is the hardest thing for me about the whole studio experience. Not being locked-in to a design, looking at different sides of a problem, that's hard to do. But you've got to at least listen to the critics."—Student Bryan Strube's words of wisdom.

SUPPLEMENT 1-2: Charles D. Linn, A.I.A., contributes an anecdote about a pinup in one of his first design studios. [The pinup is a group interim review. These are conducted occasionally during the course of the project, prior to final review.]

Designing good spaces takes talent, but even that must be developed. So difficult is designing space, that what often marks the neophyte is not knowing the difference between great spaces and average spaces—or mistaking average spaces with lavish, trendy decoration for great spaces.

I clearly remember when I began to understand the difference between the kind of thinking that produces average spaces and the kind of thinking it takes to design great spaces. I was in a third-year design studio that was made up of a series of one- and two-week sketch problems. We had just finished a four-hour marathon session of about eighteen student presentations, which had all of the usual problems: We had grabbed every visual idea from a year's worth of P/As and jammed them onto our impossible structural situations. We had daring facades that omitted or misplaced critical fenestration. We created buildings that totally ignored parking, grading, and drainage problems.

Our professor, who had a gift for metaphor, took a deep drag off his black cheroot and gave this assessment of our work (the expletives have been deleted):

"Ladies and gentlemen, these buildings do not represent three-dimensional thinking. The 'buildings' we see here are merely *extrusions* of floor plans with roof structures attached. You have made buildings of Play-Doh walls squeezed out of toy extrusion machines! This is not architecture. You do not simply cut off the extrusion when it reaches the proper wall height and pinch doors in where they are required. Your extruded floor plans have been produced with a template, and their ornament applied like frosting. It is Hostess Cupcake architecture.

"Look at the richness of buildings designed by Eero Saarinen, Bruce Goff, Arthur Erickson, Charles Moore. Great spaces cannot come out of an extrusion machine, nor are they simply the product of extrusion machinery with frosting decorations applied. They are conceived and developed in totality. Don't become obsessed with ornament at the expense of developing great spaces that work for people."

From then on that semester, we worked on all of our buildings stripped of the preoccupation of ornament, using models, perspectives, cutaway axonometrics—anything it took to remind ourselves that buildings are three-dimensional objects, and that buildings must first work for people. We focused on creating spaces—not merely enclosing volumes of space within flat planes.

This eliminated a lot of mistakes. Gone were windows drawn on elevations that had no relationship to floor-to-floor heights or interior partitions. No more did steel beams accidentally project waist-high through corridors. No more stairways to heaven. We cleaned out our Rapidographs and rolled up our vellum. Everything was done in ebony pencil on yellow tracing paper—this was very uncommon then—more the rule was drawing-in every brick by hand in ink, and renderings made of billions of tiny dots. But changing our rendering method was the only way to finish our design problems within two weeks. Instead of allocating the second week for rendering, the last two days of the problem were budgeted for it. The notion that design of great spaces is more complex than squishing Play-Doh out of an extruder made a deep impression on me.

Pinups and final reviews are addressed in greater detail in Chapter 5.

MENTORS

A mentor is an instructor or professor who can be a friend and advisor, someone who brings out the best in you and with whom you feel comfortable and confident. The mentor will come to know you so well that he/she will be your strongest, most effective teacher and most insightful critic. The mentor will be able to sit on your thesis committee and write you meaningful letters of recommendation that will be especially important in obtaining summer work in a firm, scholarship or grant funding, and if applicable, admission to a graduate program. The social and economic roller coaster with which all the professions currently struggle makes it all the more valuable to have someone who you can look to and count on as a constant and strong ally. So as you sit in classes and work in studio, consider each faculty member as a possible mentor, and don't hesitate to visit the more approachable people in their offices. It is this sort of informal discussion which leads to a mentoring relationship that is most gratifying for both parties; and it is desirable to have more than one.

A possible side effect of closer teacher/student relationships may be characterized as favoritism. Favoritism is unusual but does appear in the course of studio life; instructors are human and for a variety of reasons, may not end up giving equal time to everyone. It therefore makes sense to become somewhat political, in the best sense of the word. Again, the issue centers around active listening and talking in studio. Students probably develop "political skills" as their comfort with routine communication increases. Purposeful effort to be ingratiating with peers or teachers never supports anything of value. Initiating questions, asking for help, and responding with courtesy, enthusiasm, and generosity all translate to the best political presence in any arena, that which minimizes any resentment by other students and faculty.

GRADES

Grading is an issue on which emotions run high and deep. In an ideal world, this wouldn't be the case. Grading is important only if it helps the student to reflect on what was good and bad about a project. In practice, you may be the only professional around who can evaluate your own designs. You're not always going to have someone to look over your shoulder. *So the Take-Home Message is that grades (whether you agree with them or not) should be used to achieve another vital capability in doing design: The art of self-correction.* This can only make projects better and support more effective decision making.

No matter what objective criteria exist and no matter how fair instructors want to be, there will *always* be an element of subjective judgment. This means that instructors will occasionally make mistakes. In my experience, students are sometimes quite unhappy about the grades they receive. While they are important (for financial aid or graduate school admission), students must not lose sight of the bottom line, that is, the work itself. Most employers are interested in looking at portfolios, not grades (I have yet to hear about a firm requiring an applicant to submit a transcript), and satisfaction comes from the inherent qualities of the design, not one person's view of it. Like taking criticism, it is hard to accept a bad grade. But remember, one bad grade or even a failed course is not going to change a career track. *Acknowledge and discuss the reasons behind uneven performance. Move ahead. Continue to grow toward and identify your optimal rhythm and niche.*

Every student should get a *bad grade* at some point in the design studio. The list of famous (and good) architects who received Cs or worse in design would shock. This does not mean if you get a C, you will become famous. It does mean that everyone learns at his/her own pace. It is all too easy to be obsessed with grades to the point where it distracts from the goals of the studio. Architects must learn how to handle negative feedback and rejection from clients. "*Alas, you just didn't capture JoAnne's imagination,*" was the stated reason I was fired by my client's husband. Turn it into a positive experience; "design" an appropriate response. I'm still getting publicity today for JoAnne's unbuilt project (but obviously the experience still hurts). As Helmut Jahn suggests later in this chapter, work to maintain self-confidence, and use any frustration and emotional energy to drive the next project. "Can you learn from the mistakes?" is not the question; the question is, "How much can you learn?" There are few temperamental artists who are effective architects.

Every student should get a *good grade* at some point in the design studio. There should be recognition of talent and ability. It cannot be stressed enough that some students require more time to mature professionally; poor or average grades through early studios do not necessarily mean there is no potential to be good or even great. In the presence of talent, desire and strong emotion about the work virtually guarantee terrific final results.

EQUIPMENT

A basic inventory of equipment is necessary in order to properly execute projects in the studio. See Chapter 5 for more details. Here are some recommendations for getting started.

Work Surface. There should be a smooth surface for drawing. Typically, students buy a vinyl board cover (mount on desk with double-sided tape). More economical and less durable are laminated graph paper (the grid lines can be helpful or distracting), or smooth and dense illustration board, which would require frequent changing.

Sketching. Thin, transparent, yellow trace (or "tissue") is a classic in the architect's office, and for good reason. It's both cheap and easy on the eyes. Buy 12-inch rolls—you won't feel guilty about ripping off huge lengths, and it's a comfortable size to work with. Obviously, wider rolls may be necessary for bigger drawings. The trace also comes in cream and white—aside from personal taste, the lighter colors produce better copies (less background) from photocopiers. Sketchbooks are a popular and traditional accessory; there are blank pages, hardbound, for recording sketches and just about anything else—good for bringing to the site.

Thick marking pens and soft pencils are perfect for sketching—since it's hard to be precise with these instruments, they're great for the rough–ambiguous–brainstorming kind of drawing. Again personal preference applies; I use the Pentel Sign Pen, Flair, Sanford's Sharpie, and Pilot Razor Point.

Drafting. The parallel rule is another staple in the architect's office and design studio. It's a big initial investment, but it will last a long time. (I'm still using mine from college, after fifteen years of practice.) The T-square is the alternative, not recommended for the serious student but workable if your financial empire is crumbling.

Acrylic triangles are part of the drafting ensemble. Get an adjustable one, in addition to the standard 30°–60° and 45°, if budget allows. An inking triangle has raised edges to avoid smearing while the ink dries. Scales, both architectural and engineering (and perhaps metric) are critical. The gradations on the engineering scale will be important for studying and developing smaller-scale drawings such as site plans. Automatic mechanical pencils (with a variety of lead sizes and degrees of hardness) save time since they obviate the need for sharpening. For presentation drawings, you may be asked to do precise ink drawings. A good set of technical pens such as Rapidographs will do the job (be sure to get a range of point sizes), and good-quality tracing paper, vellum, or Mylar may be used: Depends on the project and instructor. Other ancillary equipment includes a circle template, french curves, a large bow compass, colored pencils and markers, erasers, an erasing shield, a brush for dusting off drawings, and tape.

Model Making. A metal straightedge, a knife (there are many types—X-Acto is a good brand that is widely available), scissors, Spray Mount (by 3M), Elmer's glue, and possibly clay are the basics. A surface on which to cut is important. If one is not available in the studio, scrap cardboard will do (be sure you don't cut through to your drawing board!), and expensive cutting surfaces are also available. See Chapter 4 for a complete discussion of models.

Don't necessarily purchase everything at once—and what you do buy should be of good quality—it's an investment in your future! (Equipment and supplies for the sketching basics are most important.) See what the specific projects for the semester call for in terms of presentation. That will have an impact on graphic supplies beyond the basics listed here. Frequently, secondhand equipment may be available from upper-class students, so ask around or look on bulletin boards. Sharing on some of the big-ticket items may be another option.

REWARDS

The design studio is an incredibly full experience. As we peel off the layers of arduous training, we discover a place of personal and social importance. In the course of a few years, you are certainly going to evolve as a person as well as a professional. As the profession begins to shape you, you will shape the profession as one of its newest members.

Is it worth it? What do you get out of an architectural education? John S. Lyons, Ph.D., Associate Professor of Psychiatry, Psychology and Medicine at Northwestern University Medical School, advises students on how to think about the relevance or ultimate importance of what one "does":

"The process I always invoke has to do with defining the IMPACT of the work. I ask: What are the specific effects, and what is the maximum potential? Of course, you have to prioritize some—order the dimensions you want to impact the most. So, whether you are talking about social effects, or aesthetic, or even economic effects, you must define these as specifically as possible, and then you're well on your way. When you decide exactly what you want to achieve, it is much easier to go out and fulfill the prophecy."

It is all too easy to view architecture school as a means of learning how to design great buildings. Indeed, one does learn a good deal about designing buildings. This goal is celebrated both directly and indirectly by the professional literature and by popular culture. A concern of mine has long been the extent to which a sometimes exaggerated focus on producing superb objects contributes to a skewed view of what an architectural education is all about. With a proper but often exclusive enthusiasm about what we design, we risk ignoring other important rewards obtained in school and in routine professional practice as well.

Other avenues of reward are encompassed at least in part by terms such as *process* and *approach*. Throughout a life in architecture, one learns and then refines a certain way of making sense of, and then addressing, problems. This learned and progressively personalized way of working becomes internalized as a "process." Even as students, you will find this process valuable not only as it promotes the making of buildings, but in approaching abstract and/or nonarchitectural problems. Assessment of a problem from all possible angles, critical evaluation of relevant information, and development of alternative solutions culminating in the implementation of one judged optimal are all "habits" one acquires in architecture school.

FIGURE 1-3   *The fully outfitted workstation. Note such touches as a task light (reducing eye strain is a worthy goal), and note the flowers on the left, a reminder to at least dream about a balanced lifestyle. Photo © SARUP, University of Wisconsin–Milwaukee.*

Another aspect of the rewards of architectural education involves a benefit of preparation for any profession—serving people. In the next section, Charles Moore refers to "inhabitants" of buildings, and he speaks of making their lives fuller. Moore's language uses such terms as *support systems*, *dignity*, and *values*. Arthur Erickson implores that we back away from the "artifice of the mercantile world" and challenges us to examine other ways of considering what is important. Again, "value" and "meaning" in cultural, social, and personal human context is emphasized. The point is that from earliest civilized times, people have wanted, utilized, and sometimes depended on architects. Learning how to respond both creatively and with maximum appreciation of human needs ultimately yields perhaps the greatest reward—the manifest pleasure and improved quality of life of building users.

ADVICE FROM THE STARS

Several of the most prominent practitioners and educators in North America agreed to speak to student readers. While many other "stars" generously contributed their expertise in subsequent chapters, this first distinguished group was chosen to respond to the more general aspects of beginning in school. In open letters, the following three questions were addressed:

1. What *values* do you feel students should consciously strive to incorporate and practice?
2. What should students know or do, or what preparation might they undertake to minimize the anxieties of starting out?
3. What advice/message would you offer beginning students to support successful performance in the design studio?

Helmut Jahn

With respect to values, perseverance, integrity, and consistency would rank among the highest, given the status of the time in which we live. *PERSEVERANCE* is obvious. *INTEGRITY*, because difficult times create difficult situations. *CONSISTENCY* in work, in attitude, and in approach. To me it is obvious that there is no difference between the personal values one has and the architecture one produces; both have the same qualities.

Anxiety was present for me when I started out and it will be present for all others as well; it can't be eliminated but it certainly can be controlled. *SELF-CONFIDENCE* and a *POSITIVE PLAN* of action for achieving your goals will go a long way toward minimizing anxiety. Doubt and a lack of self-confidence not only fuel anxieties but produce a negative image that may exist even after early anxieties have subsided.

With respect to work in the design studio, I feel the choice of terminology ("design studio") itself sends the wrong message to the student. The student's goals should be to be the best all-around *ARCHITECT*, not the best in design or any *ONE* aspect of architecture. In the beginning, the student should want to learn everything. *HIS TOP PRIORITY SHOULD BE HIS WORK*. His approach should be one of total *FLEXIBILITY*. The student should do any task given with the same level of enthusiasm and effort. Each task has a learning curve but the payback is experience.

My response is like my architecture—matter of fact. Good luck with your book, the students should benefit from its use.

Regards,

Helmut Jahn

Helmut Jahn

What I especially appreciate about Helmut Jahn's comments is the point he makes about *work in general* as a priority, in contrast to a singular or premature focus on a specialty. Particularly at an introductory level, one is not striving to be "a designer," or "a historian," or "a technologist." Rather, the goal is to work hard at absorbing and integrating as many facets of architecture as possible. Whatever specialty interest a student eventually develops will be best served by the most comprehensive background.

Hugh Newell Jacobsen

Thank you for including my words in your forthcoming "Architecture 101"—the very title still secretes bile within.

Our profession is one of many facets. I do not believe that every professional is capable of design nor should he/she try to practice accordingly. Because I do believe that design is the most important facet, I will address your question with design in mind. Those few students who are encouraged by their training to understand the full meaning of architecture *and* design should endeavor to practice as a principal. Design is personal and private and from a committee it comes not.

When starting out the student or the beginning professional should never try to be original. It will be hard enough to learn how to build and keep a building dry inside without taking on Frank Gehry. It is far more important to be good. Architecture is an old persons' profession. Try to contribute.

To perform successfully in the design studio the student should:

1. Listen and ask questions.
2. Read and *reread* history. You can *never* know enough!
3. Know that there are no solutions, only approaches. Work hard to understand the problem, what it means, simplify, and *try* to solve it. Then try again.

I hope the above helps ~
— Hugh Newell Jacobsen

Hugh Jacobsen's feeling that not everybody is destined for design seems an important and natural extension of Jahn's comments. I don't think it can be overstated that the studio is a place in which all manner of specialists are born.

Whether in lighting, programming, marketing, computer applications—whatever the area—the studio provides the medium from which interests and properly informed choice grows.

Jacobsen's deemphasis on "originality" and "solutions" as goals in themselves is also noteworthy. It is implicit that tenacity and "approach" will lead to an innovative and effective solution.

Arthur Erickson

A student needs to have nourished an aesthetic sensibility. If he doesn't have it, he cannot develop it. It cannot be learned—if it is there—he can nourish, refine, expand it infinitely. Since architecture is a visual art, it is his visual sensitivity that must prevail over all other abilities. If that sensitivity exists, he can transfer it from one visual art to another—from the two-dimensional to the three-dimensional, the sculptural to the spatial. If he has an ability in any visual art, he is well ahead. He must only recognize and become practiced in the basic elements of architecture—space, structure, and place. I emphasize place because architecture is not conceived in a vacuum but always for a place and that place is inevitably part of its composition. If he is familiar with any art form he will recognize that at a certain point, the artist is no longer the creator but the midwife of a creature that from that point on takes over to determine itself on the basis of the compositional rules that you gave it in the first place.

Nor can he ever be satisfied fully with his work but anxious to go on exploring to satisfy his curiosity with the next challenge. He needs an endless curiosity, sense of wonderment, and love of craft. The greatest teacher is actual experience of architecture and art through personal contact with it in the widest possible context—the world itself—as well as nature in its endless creative response to challenge and delight in being. The student has to learn to distrust the intellect, letting it serve rather than lead the creative quest. Design is instinctual and must be felt by the inner perceptual sense and not thought out, for the mind can never be trusted in itself, only when it follows the conviction of the senses. *Perception* is the key.

Cultivate the eyes by looking—the senses by feeling through exposure to the arts—not through magazines or film unless the film is an artwork in itself—but through exposure to the real thing. The student needs to remove himself somehow from the artifice of the mercantile world and expose himself to other world cultures in their vivid interpretation of the issues of existence. Only then can he begin to see himself as part of a culture that wrestles with the same issues and needs his contribution to give value and meaning to those issues.

Don't give up. Struggle even if you don't seem to be getting anywhere. Often only when you are completely frustrated does a solution come. No one who creates finds it easy unless what they are doing is only superficial inventiveness. It is often necessary to get away from a challenge that you are struggling with to see it in a new light: Look at it upside down, backwards in a mirror, between your legs, standing on your head, or immerse yourself in something else enlightening and inspiring before coming back to it. Remember, it is not easy for anyone who is any good.

Yours sincerely,

Arthur Erickson

Arthur Erickson persuasively advocates active exploration of, and immersion in, the cultural and perceptual realms of human experience. "Instinctual" talent for design is a blessing, but it must be cultivated. Even then, as Erickson points out, creativity is not easy.

Erickson also wants us to prize other golden rules: Persistence is important, as is the habit of developing alternative ways of looking at a problem. Erickson's final caveat is worth repeating: "Remember, it is not easy for anyone who is any good."

Charles Moore

Students should strive toward an awareness of their own dignity and the dignity and worth of the inhabitants of their buildings.

To minimize the anxieties of starting out, students should have confidence in the place they come from and the values they cherish. They do not have to be remodeled in another image to be architects.

To perform successfully in the design studio, relax. Remember that the things you're designing are meant to be useful and to give the inhabitants of your designs the confidence to make their own lives fuller. You are designing a support system, not a hair shirt.

Sincerely,

Charles W. Moore, FAIA

Charles Moore's message is deceptively simple but contains a rather profound dual reminder. First, that each of us has a distinctive world view with particular priorities and tastes, and that maintaining a strong sense of what we prize somehow complements and motivates us. Second, there is the reminder that we serve others who are likely to have equally distinctive and different world views. If we are doing our jobs well, we will incorporate our personal priorities with an understanding of others'—the architecture we then produce for them is more likely to be successful.

2

The Program

"The genes of a building are determined before a sketch is made."—*Bill Caudill*

Even though the building user may be large, shaggy, and have a limited vocabulary, the architect is still obliged to try to understand his/her point of view and needs.
Photo credit: Andy Pressman.

"I went into architecture to solve problems for people. I will never sacrifice a client's program for my design objectives."—Susan Maxman, F.A.I.A. (1993 President of the American Institute of Architects)

"If there is one aspect that unifies all our buildings, it is the suitability of the building to the requirements. We do an unusual amount of research, not only into the technological systems that we eventually use, but also to develop the program, before we ever develop a physical image of the structure."—Norman Foster, of Foster Associates (reprinted with permission of *Progressive Architecture*, Penton Publishing)

"You can't just come up with great designs and shove them in the client's face and say, 'Here it is,' and that's it."—Scott Gordon, M.D. (on working with an architect for his new house)

Simply stated, *the program is the design problem*. It usually includes project goals; functional requirements, activities, and organizational relationships (general and sometimes very detailed); client and/or user preferences; a mandate for budget; future expansion, conversion, and phasing capabilities; utilization and scheduling of spaces; and any other criteria to facilitate the user's activities. Clients' wish lists and the architect's personal expectations for the project may all have an effect at this stage. It is easy to see why the program is the single most important element in shaping successful buildings: It is the foundation for design decisions.* *The program is what makes architecture one of the great professions, distinguishing it from pure art.*

Meaningful discussions with the client and with typical building users are invaluable in eliciting information that helps define the problem. Because the client often has difficulty in voicing needs and problems, the architect has an early opportunity to be a *creative* diagnostician. In practice, *continuing* dialogues and diagnoses through all design phases fine-tune (or in some cases redefine) the program to ensure an optimal design response. In fact, since programming and design are so interdependent, I have come to view programming as the initial stage of design.

The program can assume many forms. As a function of project scale and circumstance, a verbal command from client to designer may be sufficient ("I want a new Las Vegas-style bathroom with a hot tub and a skylight"), or something more comprehensive may be necessary (a five-pound document describing the special needs of inmates of a large urban correctional facility). The program can be the tool that "empowers" the client and users in shaping physical design. For complex projects, programming may be enhanced or performed by specialists, consultants who conduct sophisticated social, behavioral, and market research. A client's demands for specific building "components and systems" to minimize energy use, for example, may also be elicited and will have an impact on design. *The Take-Home Message is that a good rapport with client and/or building users will ensure ongoing communication. It is this communication that shapes the program. And it is the program, in turn, which very significantly drives the design.*

APPROACH

Students should be aware of the basic steps of approaching the program once a project is introduced in class. These steps are adjusted or prioritized as needed based on

*See David Haviland's section on "Predesign Services" in the A.I.A.'s *The Architect's Handbook of Professional Practice* for an elegant and detailed discussion of facilities planning and programming.

the faculty's objectives for the problem and the semester. Note that in practice, the programming process also varies with the client, project, and architectural firm. Generally, however, programming phases may be organized as follows (I have invoked much of the scheme endorsed by the A.I.A. in D. Haviland's "Predesign Services" section of *The Architect's Handbook*):

1. *Information Gathering.* This phase encompasses two types of research: Collecting primary data (personal contact with all the "players") and accumulating secondary data (looking at precedents—familiarization with what has been done before; identification of applicable codes and regulations; awareness of construction budget; observation of typical activity patterns in similar buildings; and study of existing condition surveys if the project is a renovation).

2. *Analysis and Interpretation of Information.* This phase involves laying out all material in order to define and inventory all problems, needs, and other program elements comprehensively and with the highest possible degree of resolution. Patterns of circulation are determined, and organizational requirements that may diverge from the norm are carefully documented and diagrammed. This exercise, in turn, helps the designer conceive of spatial qualities that represent the unique character and scale of the program elements.

3. *Concept Development.* The "soul" of the project may be born at this point. Suddenly there is a light in the designer's eye, stimulated by just about anything that might have evolved during the previous work. That the "functional" aspect of a solution emerges in this final phase of programming makes it potentially as exciting as the first design sketches.

This chapter describes what is included and how to execute the three broad phases of the programming process as outlined above. *A Take-Home Message is that the process is likely to become very personalized; the following approach is suggested only as an example of a rational basis upon which to develop what works best for you.*

INFORMATION GATHERING

The introduction to a design exercise typically begins with the distribution of a sparse program or brief for the proposed building type. There is usually a listing of all required spaces with their respective square footages (*net area*). Realize that *net area* does not include the sometimes significant space required by circulation, mechanical equipment, and servant spaces. Thus, *gross area* describes the sum of net area and the less circumscribed spaces listed above.

Also included within introductory material should be some background on the client and how the project came into being. Now is the crucial time to launch yourself into a full understanding of what the building is about: How it functions and its relationship to the community.

Primary Data

If not part of the agenda for the class, *take the initiative* to arrange interviews with mock clients and/or users. There is simply no substitute for getting out in the field and observing firsthand similar buildings and the people who use (or commission) them. Make time to do this—it is a small investment that can yield enormous benefit. Observe, listen, and talk. For example, at a fire station: Visit the fire chief and firefighters. Ask questions about special needs, preferences; ask for a wish list for a new facility. Review the program and ask about functional clarifications and equipment uses, and suggestions for improvement. Sit, sip a mug of coffee, share some of what you are about, and you are bound to get a great deal in return. *The Take-Home Message: Try to appreciate the client's and/or user's special point of view.* Effective assessment requires personal contact and connection. Discover the value of what is being said "between the lines," then check it out. Test any hypotheses you may form simply by asking, "Does this make sense?" Try to take notes privately, reflect *after* you've left the site. Writing while someone is taking the time to talk with you may be experienced as distancing or even rude. You will surprise yourself at the level of detail you can recall and meaningfully recreate from memory.

Apart from client/user issues, broader concerns should not be neglected. What social factors may influence or shape the project? Talk to influential people in the neighborhood. Solicit opinions in the local park and grocery store. Elicit reactions to the possibility of a proposed new structure. Ask what might be done to maximize community support. Ask about the pressing problems and the political exigencies in the area. Once again observe what is happening during the day (and night), and what seems positive together with what seems negative. Record your thoughts. Talk to potential builders in the area: General contractors (or even subcontractors) who specialize in the relevant building type. They can offer helpful suggestions on a variety of areas, including construction systems, materials, and detailing. It is almost conventional wisdom that sensitivity to community input will not only promote the ultimate success of a project, but is likely to enhance the probability of approvals from any public agencies, associations, or planning boards that have authority to review designs.

Typically, the university setting is a gold mine for discovering a diversity of populations (including students, faculty, and staff in various departments) as simulations of clients, users, and consultants. Take advantage of this primary resource group: If they are unable to provide insights directly, referral to someone more appropriate will be forthcoming in response to a simple, "Who can help me?"

One note of caution. Much tangential information is bound to result from your discussions. Try to avoid preoccupation with irrelevant factors, however colorful they may be. Keep the big picture in clear focus. In addition to obtaining answers to your standard or designed questions, do remain alert to valuable bits of information that may emerge spontaneously from conversations with clients and/or users.

> *SUPPLEMENT 2-1:* Peter Pressman, M.D., has taught interviewing at Northwestern University Medical School. He describes the "good interview."
>
> I believe it is very useful to think of interviewing in medical-clinical terms, that is, in terms of diagnostic and therapeutic value. The good interview is one in which stated problems are clarified, and unstated problems are discovered and given voice. A level of understanding is achieved, and this points the way toward the optimal therapy [or design].
>
> The good interview is one in which a trusting alliance is established with the client, and a common agenda is agreed upon. It is from this framework that open and unguarded (meaningful) communication ensues. Plunging into an encounter without

first carefully nurturing an alliance with a client is likely to yield little if anything of value. Of course, every situation and every client is different, but if there is such a thing as THE standard condition for engaging people, it is rapport. To have rapport with another, be yourself; do not affect some wooden formality you may believe is "professional," nor should you be excessively casual and familiar. Rather, simply be yourself and try to employ the following components:

1. Use a warm, appropriate greeting, introduce yourself, and summarize the purpose of the meeting. (Spontaneity and self-revelation occur only after an encounter is well under way.)
2. Maintain eye contact, and use gestures, smiles, and nods to encourage the client's conversation/responses.
3. Paraphrase (check) responses to your questions to invite clarification, correction, additional detail.
4. Repeat key words/phrases, again, to invite clarification and elaboration (i.e., "More space?" or "How do you mean?").
5. Use some open-ended questions, but give gentle direction to help keep the client focused on the issue at hand (i.e., "I'd like to hear more about that, but I was particularly intrigued by what you started to say about . . .").

Try to avoid:

1. Comments that may threaten the self-esteem of the client or which can be construed as confrontational challenges to his/her judgment or taste.
2. Questions that result in yes/no responses.
3. Leading questions that consciously or unconsciously elicit the response you want to hear—try not to manipulate your client!
4. Jargon.
5. False or premature promises (on the other hand, as an expert professional, your "therapeutic presence" should always inspire confidence and optimism).

Having stated all of the above, I'll conclude by quoting an old supervisor of mine, who said, "Now forget all the theory and go in there and try to understand your patient [or client]!"

Have fun, it's a rich, gratifying, and infinitely interesting task.

For a moment, let's further illustrate the benefits of architect/client dialogue. Consider an office project. If the designer invests the time to make him/herself visible and well known as a good and responsive listener, he or she is likely to be seen as a kind of employee advocate. This situation has the tendency to enhance employee morale and even productivity: Not only are employee needs given voice, but there is personal investment in the design process. Another less obvious question to explore is: How do *clients* perceive and engage the office? Meet with representative clients. This may not only reveal another point of view and stimulate new concepts, but may serve to deepen existing relationships and add to the firm's service reputation. *Take-Home Message: In practice, maximize the participatory element; enlist people connected with the project as **collaborators**. This will often yield a richer and more responsive architecture.*

Secondary Data

At the start of any project, it is necessary to become fully informed about the building type. Know what's been done before. Go to the library. Start with any general information or historic precedents. Then search the journals for similar projects, and note any common as well as distinguishing qualities. Try to ascertain and pay particular attention to the organizing principles. (*Hint*: For lack of other indexing, the December issues of *Architecture, Architectural Record*, and *Progressive Architecture* have annual indexes in which buildings are listed by architect's name, subject, or building type.) *Time Saver Standards for Building Types* is a good reference for a basic, very conventional "cookbook" view of the project. Typical functions, sizes, and spatial relationships are discussed. *Architectural Graphic Standards* (known as the "Bible" in architects' offices) has "General Planning and Design Data," in addition to specific data on everything from equipment, materials, construction, and furnishings to parking lots. A moderately priced student edition is available, and many public libraries stock this volume. Copy the material, and build a file for future reference. This is all quite important as a knowledge base, but since, by definition, architecture is circumstance specific, standard examples will not provide the best solution to a given problem. Only the architect can do that.

> *SUPPLEMENT 2-2:* Mary K. Woolever, Architecture Archivist and Reference Librarian at The Art Institute of Chicago, describes the range of special resources that may be available to architecture students.
>
> For some assignments in design studio classes, you will probably need to conduct research in a library, pursuing information about individual architects, historic styles, specific buildings, or building typologies. To ensure the most successful and efficient library research, ask the staff about scheduled tours of the library. It is best to familiarize yourself with its facilities and services as early in the year as possible, preferably before classes begin.
>
> The following outline of reference tools can serve as a base from which to begin your research.
>
> 1. *Biographical Data on Architects.* For better-known architects, the *Macmillan Encyclopedia of Architects* (Collier Macmillan, 1982) and *Contemporary Architects* (St. James Press, 1987) will provide biographical sketches, lists of projects, and bibliographies of writings by and about the architects. For lesser-known architects, you should consult the *American Architects Directory* (AIA, 1956, 1962, and 1970); *Avery Index to Architectural Periodicals* (available in paper copy, and additionally on-line since 1980); *Avery Obituary Index of Architects* (G.K. Hall, 1980); *The Burnham Index to Architectural Literature* (Garland Publications, 1989); and Withey, *Biographical Dictionary of American Architects (Deceased)* (Hennessey & Ingalls, 1970). You should always consult the card catalog for books and exhibition catalogs on the architect.
>
> 2. *Historic Styles.* In a single volume, *Sir Bannister Fletcher's A History of Architecture* (Butterworth, 1987) sets forth basic monuments and stylistic criteria. For the next level of detail, look at the fourteen-volume series *History of World Architecture* from Abrams Publishers, on the important general periods such as Roman, Renaissance, Neoclassical, and so on, as well as on non-Western architecture.
>
> 3. *Building Typologies and Specific Buildings.* Begin your search at the card catalog, using such access points as building type (e.g., school, shopping mall, bank); the name of the specific building; or the architect's name. For periodical articles, go to the *Avery*

Index, Architecture Index (the holdings of the Royal Institute of British Architects library on-line), and *Art Index*. For contemporaneous articles on nineteenth- and early twentieth-century buildings, see *Avery Index* and the *Burnham Index*. Older American buildings may be documented in *Historic America: Buildings, Structures, and Sites* (buildings included in the Historic American Building Survey), and *National Register of Historic Places.*

4. *Technical References.* Some of the handbooks and manuals commonly used in professional practice (with which you should be familiar) are the series *Time-Saver Standards*—for Building Types, for Residential Development, for Site Planning, and for Architectural Design Data (McGraw-Hill). *Architectural Graphic Standards* (Wiley and AIA, 1988, 1991), and *Interior Graphic and Design Standards* (Whitney Library of Design, 1986) offer many basic technical guidelines and data. Product descriptions and specifications are offered in the *Sweets Catalog File*, organized by product type and published annually.

When you seem to have exhausted your search options at the card catalog and in the indexes, never hesitate to review your search with a reference librarian. Often, the librarian will be able to direct you to photographs, drawing collections, and archival collections that will be pertinent.

We can employ a hypothetical design problem to work through the sources mentioned above. Your professor has asked you to design an addition to the Crow Island Elementary School, by Eliel and Eero Saarinen. Beginning your search in *Macmillan Encyclopedia of Architects*, you learn the date—1940—and the location—Winnetka, Illinois—and find a list of books and magazine articles on the Saarinens. The search continues in the *Burnham Index* and *Avery Index*, which produces several references to articles. An on-line Avery search (generally handled by the librarian) also locates several more recent articles on the building and its history, one on the building as it celebrates its fiftieth anniversary. In one article, the current partnership name of the architects originally associated with the Saarinens is published; you may decide to contact them for additional information *after* you complete the library search.

An Avery on-line search would also produce references to numerous articles on other contemporary elementary schools plus an *Architectural Record* building-types issue devoted to the design of schools.

At the card catalog you should also look for books on schools as a building type, to locate pertinent titles such as *Space Planning Guidelines for Elementary and Secondary Schools in the U.S. and Canada*, published in the 1980s by the Council of Educational Facility Planners International.

The manuals and handbooks—*Time-Saver Standards*, and others—will provide you with the elementary data for school design. *Sweets Catalog File* includes the product literature for the furniture, fixtures, and equipment for the classrooms, kitchen, cafeteria, gymnasium, and so on.

A good student will thoroughly search and assemble library materials from as many sources as possible. This admittedly large task will more than return the investment in time and effort and will undoubtedly become increasingly easy with successive projects.

Construction Costs

Cost is always the one big issue for all projects. In practice, from the first doodles on napkins (and from the first conversation with the client), there should be a growing awareness of priorities for allocating money available for the project (both initially and for the life of the building). In some instances it may be important to set forth clearly the savings of investing in superior materials or systems from the very beginning of a project. Although initial expenses may be higher, savings in reduced maintenance and operating costs over the long run will be significant.

In school, appreciation of budgetary issues should translate to a very rough (ballpark) sense of appropriateness of construction costs to the particular project. In terms of materials, for example, a rare South American hardwood paneling in a town supervisor's office probably doesn't represent the best use of taxpayer's money, not to mention the negative ecological implications. *The Take-Home Message for considering costs is to use common sense and prudence—that is, take a cue from the building type, client, and location.* **Be very cognizant of cost constraints, but do not allow the idea of budget limitations to in any way inhibit creativity or innovative ideas.** The apparent conflict intrinsic to this Take-Home Message is resolved in the following Supplement.

SUPPLEMENT 2-3: Architect and real estate developer Raymond A. Novitske, A.I.A., writes this very astute piece underscoring the implications of cost on creativity.

Cost is a real-world concern and one of the most important factors affecting design decisions. Financial decisions are often made by clients even before an architect is brought on board, leaving the architect with little input on a budget. Expenses for construction, fees, debt and interest, operations, and maintenance are all determined before the architect is hired, to allow the client to arrange financing for his endeavor. The role the architect is left with allows him to "divvy up" the construction budget according to the design.

Clients want value for their money—more bang for the buck! Architects may not be judged by their design talent, but by their ability to deliver the bang within the budget. To do this, materials, technologies, labor, equipment, time, and their relationships must be understood. Brick may cost more than wood in construction, but they cost less than wood in maintenance. Steel and concrete may have similar initial costs, but one may require more engineering, while another might require more time to erect.

Cost continues as a factor affecting design up until final completion. Modifications are always being made during construction, and easily increase cost. Thus, expenses are always considered in the evaluation of proposed changes. Here, cost forms the basis for the age-old conflict between contractor and architect.

On the other hand, restrictions in budget may actually improve an architect's work. With very affluent clients, creativity may unintentionally be discouraged. This is because a greater budget means more freedom of choice, and thus a reduced pressure to innovate. *Some architects' best work was produced on shoestring budgets because they were forced to be resourceful with what was available or affordable.* It is fine to think that the high-tech aesthetic came from cerebral designers wanting to strip away the bourgeois, but it is more realistic to believe it was developed by imaginative designers who could not afford finishes.

How should cost affect a student? Students in college already know how to "allocate funds" and squeeze a dollar. The kind of knowledge they lack comes only through experience and exposure. And let's face it: Many experienced architects still haven't mastered it.

Building Codes and Standards

Don't skip over this material! Building codes [and zoning ordinances (see Chapter 3)] have an impact on preliminary design. Your instructor may have already researched much of the code data for you (leaving more time for design), but it is important to know what they are and what they mean. Raymond Novitske, A.I.A., believes strongly in the importance of students' familiarity with building and life safety codes even if not explicitly designing with them. A knowledge of code concepts can help with an understanding of their application later in practice, and more immediately with how they relate to schematic design issues in school. Mr. Novitske cites an example. Consider the code requirement for exit stairs. One response is to place them as vertical elements on exterior facades. In contrast, in high-rise construction, exit stairs (along with elevator shafts, etc.) are typically located inside the structure, hence shaping core designs.

Codes can be quite complicated and vary between jurisdictions; an excellent reference that facilitates incorporating building code information simply and quickly into schematic designs is *The Architect's Studio Companion*, by Edward Allen and Joseph Iano. If you are still confused, telephone the local building department. The building inspector will probably be pleased to help a student.

SUPPLEMENT 2-4: Marvin J. Cantor, A.I.A., is the 1992 Chairperson of the American Institute of Architects Building Performance and Regulation Committee. In this Supplement, Mr. Cantor summarizes the intent and application of codes and standards.

Building codes have historically evolved in conjunction with responses to disasters in the built environment. Their primary charge has been to define the minimum standards construction must adhere to, below which there would be a significant detrimental impact on the public's health, welfare, and safety. More recently, the rights of the physically disabled have also been incorporated into the regulations governing the built environment.

In the process of preliminary design for a structure, one must balance the *size* of the structure with its *type of construction* and its primary *use*. Building codes establish a rational process for doing this. When more than one type of *use* exists in a structure, one must determine whether it is more cost-efficient to treat the entire structure under the regulations governing the most critical *use* involved, or whether the building can effectively be "compartmented" with fire separation structural elements for each *use* (virtually treating each such building *use* as a "separate" structure).

The steps outlined briefly below illustrate consideration of the building code (and other complementary regulatory steps) as the preliminary design evolves:

1. Determine if covenants pertaining to the site involved limit the size and uses of any structure erected on that site.
2. Determine the maximum envelope (length, width, height, and gross area above grade) of structures permitted by zoning regulations. [See item 8, zoning, in the Inventory in Chapter 3 for an example of zoning issues to consider.]
3. Evaluate the particular topography of the site and of surrounding adjacent site areas to see if such an "envelope" can in fact be accommodated.

4. Evaluate the client's needs in terms of area required. This summary step (encompassing steps 1, 2, and 3 above) establishes the desired maximum building envelope for the design.

5. Classify the building by its use (B—business, M—mercantile, I—industrial, A—assembly, S—storage, etc.).

6. Using the code's *"height and area"* table, determine the maximum size of building permitted as it relates to the structural type being used. Here, alternate types of structure (1—fire resistant, 2—incombustible, 3—combustible protected, 4—mill, 5—wood frame) will be considered to arrive at the optimum structure/building area to be designed.

7. Moving next to the *"structural elements"* table, one can determine the fire resistivity required for the particular structure involved with respect to the major elements in the building (exterior walls, columns, floors, ceilings, shafts, stairways, etc.). These are measured in hours that a particular element can resist a fire before failing [according to testing established by the American Society for Testing and Materials (ASTM), and carried out by testing laboratories such as Underwriters' Laboratories, Factory Mutual, etc.].

Having established the maximum permitted size, the type of structure that will be used, and the basic structural elements' fire-resistive requirements, one can address the other significant items in the code as the preliminary design progresses:

1. *Egress.* Normally, two remote means of appropriate egress (or exit) are required for the typical structure (remoteness is defined in the code). Keep in mind that one of the required means of egress should be usable by the physically disabled (which means having an "area of refuge" near one of the required stairs unless an approved acceptable elevator for egress has been incorporated; at this time, no such elevator construction has been certified to my knowledge as meeting the code's requirements for an acceptable emergency egress).

2. *Accessibility.* All parts of the structure's "primary" use areas must be accessible to the physically disabled (this includes those with impairments in mobility, sensory function, and cognitive development). Accessibility should be achieved without extraordinary auxiliary aids. In particular, one should look at the building's primary entrance, corridor routes to various parts of the structure, the primary use areas, toilets, drinking fountains, and egress.

3. *Miscellaneous Code Requirements.* These cover a broad range of elements, including:

A. Stair construction

B. Minimum room heights and areas

C. Railing (guard and stair) requirements

D. Roofing and general building waterproofing requirements

E. Sprinklers and other requirements for fire-resistive items

F. Structural, seismic, wind, and snow load requirements

G. Building occupancy design factors

H. Energy conservation factors

Finally, if a project involves the adaptive *reuse* of an existing structure, one should become familiar with the code chapter that deals with this item; certain "trade-offs" are permitted. For example, where it is economically impractical to install certain code required items, they may sometimes be omitted if in other areas additional protective measures are incorporated (i.e., "compartmenting" a structure may permit longer egress corridors than otherwise mandated in new construction).

Keeping the code in mind as the preliminary design evolves makes the resulting structure's compliance with legal building regulations much easier, and reduces the probability of embarrassing moments between the designer and the client and the building official at a point when the design has been largely finalized.

Accessibility

Barrier-free design should be so thoroughly integrated into the preliminary design process that it is second nature, does not assume visual prominence, and certainly does not occur *after* the design is established. Good designers have always thought about this; generally, accessible buildings are better buildings for everyone. Now with the recent promulgation of the Americans with Disabilities Act (ADA) and other codes, accessibility is required by law.

The American National Standards Institute (ANSI) developed (and is continuing to revise and update) a very useful resource for design specifications (including many graphic explanations)—ANSI A117.1—to achieve barrier-free design. This standard has been referenced in many building codes and federal design standards. *Review a copy to become familiar with the basics.*

> *SUPPLEMENT 2-5:* Civil rights, medicine, and sociology have all intersected to forge the Americans with Disabilities Act of 1990. Ruth Hall Lusher discusses this crucial development in public policy and its major implications for the architect.
>
> Ms. Lusher is currently working in the Office of the Americans with Disabilities Act, Department of Justice, Washington, DC. She was previously the Director, Office of Technical Services, United States Architectural and Transportation Barriers Compliance Board.

DESIGN FOR THE LIFESPAN

Barrier-free design, accessible design, and universal design or design for all people are all related concepts which aim to ensure that the built environment will accommodate all people, including those with disabilities, younger people, older people, smaller people, and bigger people.

Whatever design approach a student takes, the built environment must first work for people. And, virtually everyone experiences disability at some point in his or her life. During each person's lifespan, from birth to old age, each of us experiences both the development and the loss of abilities. Sometimes the loss is only temporary, but the important thing to remember is that disability is part of the "normal" human experience.

How Many People at Any Point in Time Need Accessible Design?

The estimates of the numbers of persons with permanent disabilities at a point in time range upward to 43 million Americans. A 1986 study by the Bureau of the Census* con-

---

Disability, Functional Limitation and Health Insurance Coverage 1984/1985, Bureau of the Census, Washington, DC, 1986, Series P-70, No. 8.

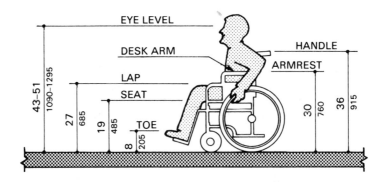

NOTE: Footrests may extend further for very large people.

Fig. A3
Dimensions of Adult-Sized Wheelchairs

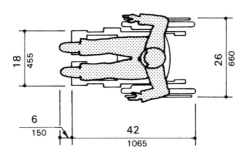

4.8 Ramps

4.8.1* General. Any part of an accessible route with a slope greater than 1:20 shall be considered a ramp and shall comply with 4.8.

4.8.2* Slope and Rise. The least possible slope shall be used for any ramp. The maximum slope of a ramp in new construction shall be 1:12. The maximum rise for any ramp run shall be 30 in (760 mm) (see Fig. 16). Curb ramps and ramps to be constructed on existing sites or in existing buildings or facilities may have slopes and rises as shown in Table 3 if space limitations prohibit the use of a 1:12 slope or less.

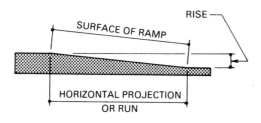

	Maximum Rise		Maximum Horizontal Projection	
Slope	in	mm	ft	m
1:12 to 1:15	30	760	30	9
1:16 to 1:19	30	760	40	12
1:20	30	760	50	15

Fig. 16
Components of a Single Ramp Run and
Sample Ramp Dimensions

FIGURE 2-1 *Examples of written and graphic material excerpted from the ANSI standard. This material is reproduced with permission from* American National Standard for Buildings and Facilities—Providing Accessibility and Usability for Physically Handicapped People, *ANSI A117.1, copyright 1986 by the American National Standards Institute. Copies of this standard may be purchased from the American National Standards Institute at 11 West 42nd Street, New York, NY 10036.*

cluded that more than 37 million people, out of a population of 181 million non-institutionalized people age 15 or older, had functional limitations; of this group, 13.5 million people had severe limitations. Of those with severe limitations, 6 million were under 65, and 7.5 million were 65 or older.

Of the 37 million people who were termed functionally limited, approximately one-fifth of the population, 19.2 million, had difficulty walking a quarter of a mile; 18.1 million, one-tenth of the population, had difficulty walking up a flight of stairs without resting. The number of people unable to walk a quarter of a mile was 8 million; 5.2 million could not walk up a flight of stairs. Approximately 7.7 million people had difficulty hearing what was said in a normal conversation, and 0.5 million were completely unable to hear such a conversation. The number of people who experienced difficulty seeing words and letters in ordinary newsprint (even with corrective lenses) was 12.8 million; 1.7 million were unable to see words or letters at all.

These startling numbers don't include many others who need or benefit from accessible design. These people include children, parents who push strollers, and virtually everyone who finds accessible environments easier to use. In Europe, accessibility is more the norm; lever door hardware, for example, is easier to use than the American doorknob. Curb ramps accommodate delivery people and bicyclists as well as people with mobility limitations.

The Law

Accessible design is no longer simply an option for architects and designers. It is the law of the land. The Americans with Disabilities Act (ADA) of 1990 extends to people with disabilities the civil rights protections that have long been provided to individuals on the basis of race, sex, and religion. The ADA is landmark civil rights legislation that promises to open up the mainstream of American life to full participation by people with disabilities. As such, it strives to overcome our past failures to eliminate attitudinal barriers, architectural barriers, communication barriers in employment, public accommodations and commercial facilities, public services, transportation, and telecommunications.

Under the ADA, Congress has made it discriminatory to design and build or to alter most buildings and facilities without providing accessibility and usability for persons with disabilities. State and local government buildings, public transportation facilities, public accommodations, and commercial facilities must all comply with standards issued under the act.

Many state and local laws [i.e., building codes] also require buildings and facilities to be accessible.

"Good" Design

Although architects and designers must follow accessibility standards, simply applying the standards to a design that is virtually complete will not generally result in good design. In general, accessibility should be carefully integrated with the design so as to be unnoticeable. Like HVAC systems, accessibility elements should almost automatically be present to ensure that the space is comfortable and usable.

This is not to imply that ramps and other accessibility elements should be hidden. Quite the contrary. Where it is not possible to provide a level entry or access to a level without a ramp, the ramp should be carefully integrated into the design.

Examples of "good" accessible design surround you but you will need to look closely to see them. Two examples I would like to share are the Copley Place Marriott in Boston, MA and the historic Mayflower Hotel in Washington, DC.

When the Copley Place Marriott (The Stubbins Associates, Architects) won the "Best of Accessible Boston" competition in 1985, the most common comment was, "It doesn't look accessible." Because accessibility was so well integrated, it was not obvious. Everyone could use the building in essentially the same manner.

When the historic Mayflower Hotel was renovated in the mid-1980s (Vlastimil Koubek, A.I.A., Architect), ramps were installed to connect the main lobby with the grand promenade where ballrooms and meeting rooms were located. The ramps were so well designed, integrated, and detailed that they have become an integral part of the space, and it is easy to forget that they were not part of the original design.

However, such "good" design is not effortless and can often be challenging. To be successful, students must carefully consider the purpose of the space they are designing. They must further remember and understand the variation in the abilities of the people who will be using the space and how best to accommodate their needs through design. This is where the knowledge of design standards is essential. It is also essential to learn about people by observing how they use space and by talking with them about their needs.

To promote full integration of accessibility into the design, careful thought and consideration must occur at each step in the design process. From programming and conceptual design phases through design development and the completion of working drawings and specifications, the architect must think about spaces that support employment and independent living for all people as they move through the lifespan.

[Ms. Lusher adds that there are two valuable references in the Code of Federal Regulations (CFR), U.S. Department of Justice, that graphically illustrate how to apply standards and technical requirements to new construction and renovation projects:

1. Non-Discrimination on the Basis of Disability by Public Accommodation in Commercial Facilities; Final Rule 28, CFR, Part 36. U.S. Department of Justice, Washington, DC. July 26, 1991.
2. Non-Discrimination on the Basis of Disability in State and Local Government Services; Final Rule 28, CFR, Part 35. U.S. Department of Justice, Washington, DC. July 26, 1991.]

ANALYSIS AND INTERPRETATION OF INFORMATION

The next phase after information gathering is to convert the raw data into a form that is analytically illuminating. Analysis is a meaningful prerequisite for designing; it results in a clear and fine-grained view of the problem, and as previously suggested, may provoke the designer's creativity. For example, following discussions with management and employees for an office project, desired conference rooms are projected as underutilized. The architect is in the position to suggest a dual function: Meeting room and employee lounge/library. With careful scheduling, multipurpose utilization can save space and improve overall efficiency. Note that this is an *administrative* action, with the only formal result being the potential reduction of space required.

Diagrams

Visual depiction of data invariably helps us to understand more clearly. Graphic techniques allow designers to organize efficiently and perceive relationships between program elements; assess ideal patterns of use; suggest zoning or grouping of like functions with respective adjacency and access requirements; and develop and reveal a sense of scale, area, and volume or mass.

Bubble diagrams are abstract graphic representations of the program spaces and their layout. (See Figure 2-2 for an example.) They are quickly drawn and lend themselves to a variety of arrangements simply by ease of manipulation. Over the years, many students have found it is useful to imagine themselves as building users who "walk through" the bubbles to explore the validity of proposed relationships. (The path that is traced becomes a circulation diagram, and represents a good way to start thinking about arranging bubbles.) Treat all exterior program elements (i.e., parking, service access, playground) similarly. It is often helpful to draw bubbles in relative scale to each other. Connect related bubbles with lines [use dotted or dashed lines to represent a particular type of relationship (i.e., public versus private)]; move them close together to show proximity; use heavy lines to show heavy or frequent

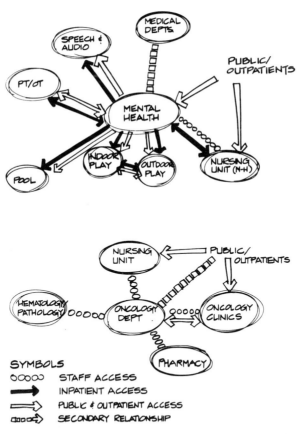

FIGURE 2-2 *This is an example of a typical bubble diagram. Note how the symbols connecting the bubbles indicate different types of circulation, or different types of relationships between program spaces. The diagram is from the Development Plan for the Children's Hospital of Denver by Kaplan/McLaughlin/Diaz Architects/Planners, San Francisco.*

traffic flow. If there are too many bubbles, collapse those which are closely associated. For example, bedroom, bathroom, and closets may comprise the single bubble representing a master bedroom. Moreover, you may want to annotate the diagrams to clarify or convey additional information.

There are a multitude of other diagrams that may help in study of the problem. Some demonstrate circulation, showing vehicular, pedestrian, and service movement; others, such as an "adjacency matrix," catalog all spaces and categorize the relationship between two spaces (i.e., direct, indirect, or unrelated). For complex programs there are more sophisticated bookkeeping methods for collecting and analyzing data, and these are beyond the scope of beginning- and intermediate-level studios.

Save all your diagrams. Sign and date them. They are an important part of the record of design decisions. You may want to refer to them when designing to test new strategies. They can also be incorporated in some form (i.e., reduced) in the final presentation (see Chapter 5 for more details). In any case, they help to demonstrate graphically to clients (or a jury) the logic behind key decisions and thus provide evidence of genuine accountability.

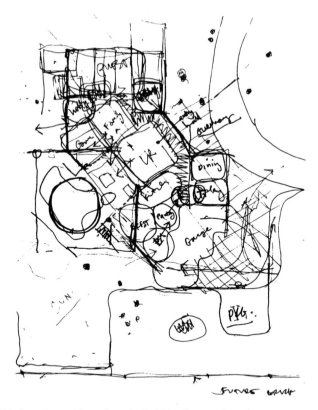

FIGURE 2-3   *In this "condensed" version of a bubble diagram for a large residence in Florida, the bubbles are drawn at relative scale and pushed together to emphasize the importance of spatial adjacencies. Design and drawing by the author.*

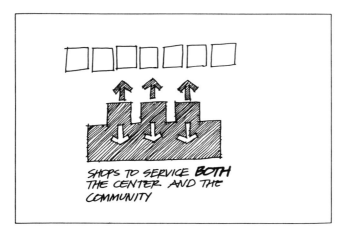

SHOPS TO SERVICE *BOTH* THE CENTER AND THE COMMUNITY

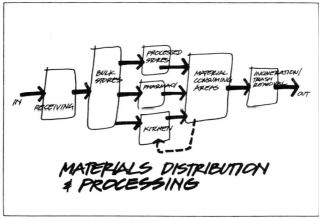

MATERIALS DISTRIBUTION & PROCESSING

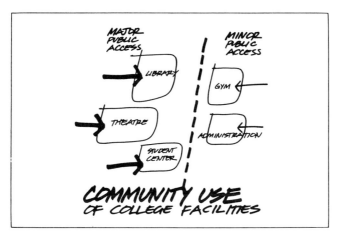

COMMUNITY USE OF COLLEGE FACILITIES

FIGURE 2-4 *More examples of programming graphics: Diagram of relationship of building and community, flowchart, and illustration of public access to private institution. These are from* Problem Seeking: An Architectural Programming Primer *by William Peña with Steven Parshall and Kevin Kelly, AIA Press, 1987.*

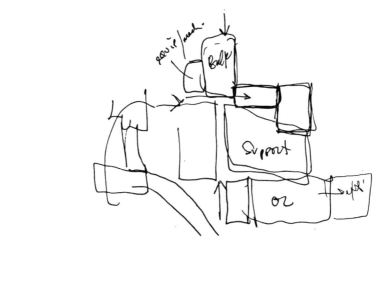

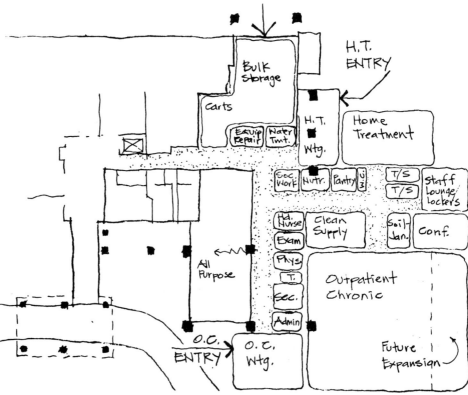

FIGURE 2-5 *These two diagrams illustrate the evolutionary sequence from the roughest initial concept sketch of large chunks of space ("collapsed" bubbles) to a more detailed clustering of common services and major components of a proposed new renal dialysis facility for a hospital. Drawings by the author for the New York City architectural firm of Norman Rosenfeld, A.I.A. Architects.*

CONCEPT DEVELOPMENT

As in "get a life," it's fairly important to "get a concept." It is surely an avenue to the project's soul. In a sense, design begins with how the program is framed or concept-ualized; I cannot overemphasize how enormously creative this process can be. A concept may be inspired by one or all of the objective program elements, the site, the community, or anything that may be associated with the project. A personal mandate from the client, a seemingly unimportant comment from a typical user, a particularly uplifting or depressing view, a relevant philosophical or political position—all these factors may contribute to the nascent concept.

A strong design concept facilitates decision making at all scales, from building footprint to door hardware. When decisions, then, are less arbitrary, the architecture truly becomes greater. Moreover, when changes are introduced by the client over the course of design development and construction documentation, or when changes occur during construction due to an unexpected field condition, the design intent is usually *not* diminished when there are powerful initial ideas. For example, on one of my projects, a continuous *recessed* perimeter lighting scheme was designed to illuminate a change in ceiling height—a functional and sculptural feature. Rather than using the recessed fixtures as designed, the contractor and owner opted for a less expensive alternative: A bare strip fluorescent with translucent lens *flush* with the ceiling. The original concept was sufficiently bold that this change, while not quite as interesting, retained the visual excitement I'd anticipated.

> *SUPPLEMENT 2-6:* Here is an example (from my practice) of creating a concept in a retail setting. (Reprinted from *Commercial Renovation*.)
>
> A concept can begin with the particular product. From psychological research, we know that the more a product is associated with meaning, the more readily it will be remembered. If a customer is interested in a product over and above his/her immediate need for that product, he/she is very likely to remember it and look for it again. Architecture can create a context or framework which reinforces themes that are both related to a product and that promote any intrinsic interest and meaning for the customer. For **PRIME TIME**, a store in Charleston, SC specializing in products for entertainment and leisure time, the concept developed was that of "stage sets." Each set corresponds to a different department. In contrast to the more conventional dedication of every square inch to product display, the use of some space for creating "context" yields returns in customer behavior. (See floor plan, Figure 2-6.)

Scheduling Note

As always, look at the big picture (i.e., the project schedule). Programming is an essential part of the design process, and some (or even much) of the work may well be done for you by the faculty (or the client). Nevertheless, take this phase seriously. Budget time for programming, but make sure that it is *appropriate* for the complexity and nature of the project. Build-in time for contingencies, and note there will be some overlapping tasks (refer to Figure 1-2).

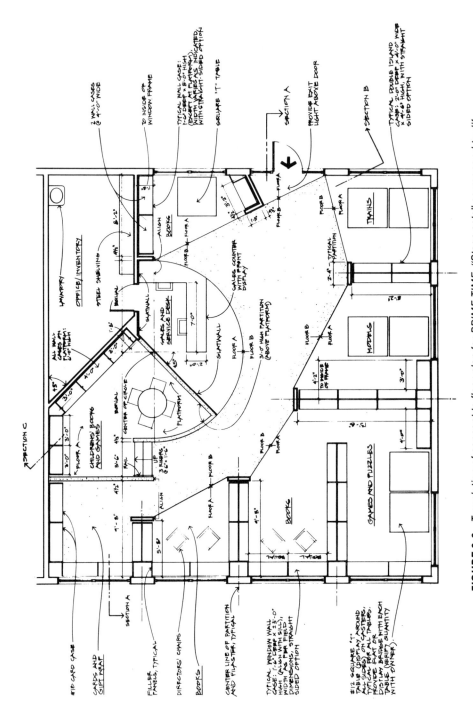

FIGURE 2-6 Translation of concept to floor plan for PRIME TIME: "Stage sets" correspond to different departments within the store. Design and drawing by the author.

SOCIAL RESPONSIBILITY

"Design excellence and social responsibility are inextricably connected." This quote by James Stewart Polshek, F.A.I.A., appeared in the *A.I.A. Memo*, February 1992, in response to winning A.I.A.'s 1992 Architecture Firm Award.

As design *professionals*, architects (including students) have an obligation to serve the personal interests of clients, and equally important, have a transcendent social responsibility. *Automatically* challenge what you judge as less than noble and ambitious programmatic goals. Do not necessarily accept a list of functions at face value; identify and exploit hidden opportunities to make more socially responsive buildings. Clients may be somewhat "nearsighted"; they may not be aware of greater possibilities. And this does not necessarily translate to inflation of the construction budget or increasing the scope of work. Be prepared to "sell" new ideas to the faculty; back them up with facts and observations from your research. Being persuasive often simply amounts to illuminating a well-studied idea.

> *SUPPLEMENT 2-7:* Let's examine the generic challenge to achieve a degree of social awareness and community responsibility among projects of modest scale. (Reprinted from *Commercial Renovation*.)
>
> A small-scale retail project might seem an improbable domain in which to apply socially responsible thinking. Cigar-smoking, greedy, environment-raping developers (please take no offense at this caricature; some of my best friends are developers) can sometimes be most successfully challenged to reach a more noble level. Witness the following case studies derived from my own practice.
>
> Educational and social activities not only constitute a direct community service but potentially give valuable exposure to businesses. For example, a computer store in a suburban setting now offers evening classes and demonstrations for beginning users. A specialty bookstore invites local authors to address small groups and book clubs. And a camera store offers instruction on basic photography and darkroom techniques. The attitude of service not only provides a public resource, but it intensifies product interest and broadens the potential market. While there may not be direct financial return on the time invested, real service is never wasted. These creative programming suggestions did not increase costs, but did have some design implications. Accommodation of small gatherings may be facilitated by using mobile fixtures and by oversizing circulation space that is normally occupied by lightweight seasonal displays. Flexibility or multiple use also is achieved with platforms; these can help zone a store and are ideal for casual seating. So, creative, after-hours use of retail space can expose and effectively promote goods while educating and enriching those present. Thus we can attempt to elevate retail settings as a positive cultural event, and design professionals should strive for that ideal wherever possible.

Environment/Behavior Factors

A significant body of modern architecture has been influenced by social and behavioral forces. Demands for better mass housing, a humane workplace, and a cry for quality across the entire spectrum of public spaces have catalyzed architects' awareness of contributions from the environment/behavior field. This broad field represented by environmental psychology, sociology, and cultural anthropology has in turn been stimulated to investigate current architectural problems. Especially challenging issues arise as designers struggle to assist the growing population of elderly, the homeless, and people with AIDS.

Gerald Weisman, Ph.D., an expert in environment/behavior research, points out that understanding something of the patterns of human use and need in general can be of central importance to all architectural design. My interview with Dr. Weisman follows.

> SUPPLEMENT 2-8: Gerald D. Weisman, Ph.D., Associate Professor, School of Architecture and Urban Planning, University of Wisconsin–Milwaukee, discusses the application of environment/behavior (E/B) principles to design.

AP: Do you think basic environment/behavior principles are relevant for use in beginning design studios?

GW: Well, sure! They're so fundamental that they shouldn't be presented as something separate from design. It is clear that throughout history, there have been efforts to deal with social issues, what's presumed to be the social good, issues of human use, and human beings. In the past, there often hasn't been sufficient information—research—available to implement or to help realize those efforts. That's what E/B studies tends to support.

"The question," then, is educational philosophy and design philosophy and the intertwining of those two. I think for designers who focus purely on formal issues, beginning design education is kind of like marine boot camp; the message is clear: "All preconceptions and whatever you have done prior to this is of no value, no relevance—we're going to teach you the one true way." If you take a more inclusive view of what architecture is, the challenge then is to build in a positive way on the experience that students bring, rather than being trapped by it. I think many students come with the assumption that design has something to do with people, and that you need to accommodate that. Common sense.

In terms of design, I believe that environmental experience is at the heart of things, and I think many architects would concur with that. We tend to focus, perhaps overly focus on aesthetic satisfaction as THE three-dimensional experience we worry about. But certainly there is a large group of architects who focus on facilitation of community life. Increasingly, architects have focused on attribution of meaning; however, this may translate only to lip service to issues such as comfort and security. I try to begin with the question, "What are the dimensions of experience that are relevant to this particular project? This particular building type? And how can we bring them into being?" For me, in terms of beginning design education, that is most important; whether students at this level are aware of the available research literature is less important than trying to frame the task of design in those terms.

AP: You're trying to instill an awareness of what's out there rather than trying to instruct on how to translate that information to physical design?

GW: More than awareness. That it is a fundamental approach to the doing of architecture in the same way some people say: "My approach to architecture is contextual, or rooted in structure and technology." My approach to architecture is rooted in patterns of human use and need. Not that the others aren't valid if one chooses to do that. But I think that the social/behavioral approach should be right up there as one of the choices. Ideally, there should be some integration. I view that as the central one, but it's not just some obscure thing that you plug in as needed.

AP: What about translating these ideas into physical design? Do you think this is the goal that's so difficult for students to try to accomplish?

GW: Yes, but you can make a lot of headway with that by sending students out to do careful observation and comparison across settings. One of the things I think is particularly important is that really satisfying places serve several functions or contribute to several dimensions of environmental experience simultaneously. I tell students to go to a supermarket and compare that experience to a farmers' market.

Or if they can find one of the few remaining corner stores in a small town and get some sense of how rich the life of places can be, but rarely is these days. Lots of people view E/B studies as kind of a functional approach to design. On one level that's true, but functions become so debased that it's just the manifest function: "A supermarket is where I go to buy food." *NO.* Now, supermarket is subdivided into a collection of shops; there's a place to sit and drink coffee. There's a recognition that experience can be more richly textured than that.

AP: So a student should seek special opportunities within a given program and not accept a program at face value?

GW: Oh yes. My supermarket example is to say, "What is the goal of architecture?" And the goal of architecture is to create wonderful places. Then for me the issue is: How does one define place? And for me place isn't limited to spatial configuration, proportions, and materials. Those are the setting and the stage for experience and use of that place.

AP: Some architects intuitively incorporate E/B principles into their projects. Is that a valid foundation for design decisions?

GW: That's a profound question. It's one that's puzzled me. I think that architects or clients or the architectural press have a debased conceptualization of creativity. It's as if the creative solution is one that has never been seen before. Architects whose work I value—who are responsive to issues of human use in a lot of ways— people like Sert and Esherick, their stuff isn't flashy, by and large.

AP: Could you give an example of how E/B issues are considered in design in, say, an office?

GW: There's a complicated set of issues. Certainly in an information age, the things that foster productivity are increasingly things we value. That there should be some sense of community among employees, that there should be free exchange of information, that people should feel some investment in the organization— it's kind of different from the assembly line model, where you try to reduce the person to the automaton and get that much more out of them per unit time.

AP: Do you think that when a student considers some of these factors, creativity is somewhat inhibited?

GW: It gets back to what constitutes creativity. I think people have a limited sense of the meaning of creativity. If you think of creativity as creative problem solving or as being best reflected not when you have a blank slate but when you have some set of goals that seem to be mutually contradictory—and you can find some reconciliation of them—to me, that's real creativity. Not just, "don't get in my way and I'll do anything I want." That's novelty. In that sense it shouldn't be inhibiting. For a lot of students, it provides a point of departure. Traditionally, design education has assumed the model where you sit there until you get the big idea, and it's easier to do that if nothing gets in your way—no program, no background, just do it. I think for lots of students, that doesn't work. They've got to fill their heads with a lot of information first. It's hard to think without information.

AP: What advice would you give to students in the studio?

GW: Try different approaches to design. Expand your repertoire of tools. Why is it so much more common and in many ways easier to focus on physical form than to focus on physical form that contributes to a wonderful set of experiences? How do you capture that? How do you communicate it?

AP: I'm trying to emphasize the program and the "predesign" tasks as much as "design" itself.

GW: This follows the CRS [now CRSS] tradition. The question is: "What is the problem that the designer is attempting to solve? And the conceptualization of the problem is, in many ways, at least as important as its resolution. For example, look at the way in which Peter Eisenman defines the problem as opposed to Joseph Esherick as opposed to whomever else.

AP: So really, creativity in design arises from the way the problem is framed.

GW: Absolutely. It's not just a matter of different styles, it's world view, and what's on the table and what isn't.

> *SUPPLEMENT 2-9:* Interview with Dr. Scott Gordon: A client's view of the design process . . . which ultimately rests on the personal relationship between architect and client.

AP: What do you really want from an architect?

SG: I want the architect to be able to read my mind—to get to know me so well that he/she could make consistent field decisions without consulting me, and try to keep personal taste to him or herself.

AP: How do you react when an architect suggests ideas that are contrary to your own?

SG: I'm open to suggestions, and similarly I would hope my architect is open to my ideas—be thoughtful, don't make snap judgments. Not all of us clients are air heads! I'm interested in seeing how my ideas could be made even better. . . . If there's no common ground, then you will have to end the relationship. The architect should get to know his clients very well; in-depth interviews to determine exactly what the needs are because sometimes clients don't even know what the needs are.

AP: Describe your image of the architect in general.

SG: The architect is like a private investigator: A fact-finder, and must be inspiring within constraints. I have an interesting story about my project. I went through design and construction documents (about twenty-five drawings!) for a larger building, and then determined it was going to be too expensive. For me, it wasn't too hard to let the initial design go, it was harder to break it to my architect that we couldn't get this built!

AP: That's amusing, but it is an interesting point. Perhaps it is a failing of the architect to keep the big picture in sight: If the design doesn't work for whatever reason, the architect has a responsibility to work with his client to realize a successful project—that's why he was hired.

SG: The client, too, has a responsibility to get personally involved through all phases of design and construction—so he's not just a name on a contract. Architecture is a team sport.

AP: Any advice for students about to enter the field?

SG: In college, you'll probably make friends you'll have for the rest of your life. Maintain those contacts—the person across the hall in the dorm may be a future CEO of a multimillion-dollar company and need an architect for the new corporate headquarters!

3

The Site

*Like voting in Chicago, go
"early and often."—William P. Miles*

Yokohama Beach on the island of Oahu, Hawaii. *A perfect site?*
Photo credit: Andy Pressman.

Palm trees swaying in cool breezes, powder blue skies, warm sunny days, white sand beaches, turquoise ocean water, dazzling orange sunsets, lush green foliage, fragrant flowers and berries, chirping exotic birds with big beaks . . . all just beyond the cabana . . . it's another day in paradise.

Barren desert, dry wind, and tumbleweed. Every few minutes a prairie dog's head pops up and then disappears. In the flat distance, a huge semitractor–trailer rumbles by at very high speed . . . only a few miles from the elite Southwest artist's colony: This has possibilities.

Steel, glass, and concrete, tall and angular. Shimmering surfaces, dark canyons, sidewalks teeming with pedestrians. . . . Amid all this urban density lies an asphalt oasis: "Quick-Park." The land of a developer's dream.

Location, location, and location: As the scenes above indicate, any given site and its surrounding context are comprised of very unique attributes and powerful environmental forces. The spectacular, the mundane, and the grim characteristics of a proposed site must be observed, inventoried, analyzed (much like program elements), and considered as factors that influence the architecture. This is where the "place" of "place making" originates. *A Take-Home Message: Integration, optimal fit, and harmony of building and site are extremely important in attaining design excellence.* Architect Cesar Pelli said it even better: "We should not judge a building by how beautiful it is in isolation, but instead by how much better or worse that particular place has become by its addition."

APPRECIATING THE ENVIRONMENT

In the Introduction to *Design with Nature*, the classic text by Ian McHarg, Lewis Mumford succinctly restates the wisdom of Hippocrates: "Man's life, in sickness and in health, is bound up with the forces of nature, and that nature, so far from being opposed and conquered, must rather be treated as an ally and friend, whose ways must be understood, and whose counsel must be respected." In light of the urgency associated with conservation and environmental protection, the application to architecture could not be more salient today *no matter what one's philosophical, moral, or cultural stance.* Thoughtful responses to the environment not only help tie the building to its site, but may have real impact in preservation of vital ecologies.

Landscape Architecture

Landscape design and our responses to the manipulation of land form, water, and vegetation constitute what may well be the least appreciated and most underrated architectural specialty. As the following contributions demonstrate, there is often a large measure of overlap between landscape design priorities and those of building design. Thus, it is critical that the student be conversant with the vocabulary and the values of this discipline.

SUPPLEMENT 3-1: Landscape architect Lawrence Halprin pens this overview. His writing, lectures, exhibits, and projects have been on the cutting edge of the discipline for over forty years. Halprin's brilliance lies in a vision that promotes global awareness while maintaining sensitivity to the micro-scale. Some of his best known projects include Sea Ranch Master Plan, Ghiradelli Square, and Seattle's Freeway Park.

LANDSCAPE ARCHITECTURE

Landscape architecture as a design profession deals with the total environment. It works, however, at many different scales from whole regions that cross political boundaries and ecological zones (like a national park) to small personal house and garden designs.

Some people think that landscape architecture deals only with open spaces left over after buildings are designed. In fact, the opposite is true. On a conceptual level, it is vital to think first about the whole configuration of human life on the planet and then develop an overview about how a particular composition will work at appropriate scale. This conception includes transportation networks, open space systems, and functional requirements for food-growing facilities, workplaces, recreational areas, and so on. Landscape architecture should focus attention on how the whole integrates.

The basic tool for landscape architecture is the land itself and its configuration. We need contour maps to establish grades, elevation changes, drainage, vegetative cover, soil types, and wind patterns. We need to understand where wetlands are located and what animals are present. This ecological background and knowledge preambles the beginning of design studies. This is our fundamental resource. After that comes knowledge and information about the human ecology—the demographics, archeology, and history of the area; the language and living patterns that currently exist; and the part that art plays in the value system of the community. Landscape design should be holistic in its approach!

After gathering all these factual resources as a foundation, the next part of the process is still conceptual. You ask yourself, on a design level, how to use the previous information to develop a sense of community. The word "community," in this case, refers back to its original Greek meaning of home and environment. In other words, how can a house, a garden, a street, a plaza, or a neighborhood fit together to form a living pattern that enhances life? At this stage you start to evolve a plan in space—a plan that locates things in relation to each other.

Then, you come to the specific design issue. At this point, design usually shifts into specialty areas, but with a full overview of how the whole project fits together. Architects, structural engineers, and civil engineers focus on their areas of expertise.

At this point, open space design becomes vital as the matrix of the living pattern. It details the way overall design links into and utilizes existing landscape configurations, the way existing land uses fit, the way grading works with existing contours. It takes care not to destroy existing vegetation, scar hillsides, or mangle existing drainage patterns in streams. Conservation of existing natural resources is a major concern and influences the amount and configuration of structures and the way they are sited on the land forms. Questions of density, height, skylines, and view corridors all need to be studied and protected on a macro-scale.

On the micro-scale, where people are walking, the choreography of human scale needs thoughtful study. How do we interact on streets and paths, in gardens and plazas? How do we interact in the life of the street, in sidewalk cafes, or in festivals?

Finally, the quality and character of the design is developed through sketches and three-dimensional models. Spaces must be designed not only through two-dimensional plans, but also with great emphasis on the sensory experience people will have there—the kinetic feel of movement, the mix of sound and smell, the variety of opportunities for creativity, enjoyment, and human interaction. Constantly remember that the purpose of these designs is to make places for the full range of human experiences.

How can you begin to operationalize the study methods referred to by Halprin? The act of spending a few hours at different intervals throughout the day, over a period of time, will expose you to the dynamic events occurring at the site—both natural and human-made. Ideally, one would camp out for a year to get a sense of the inherent rhythms, cycles, and patterns there. Alas, in traditional practice and studio, that is a bit impractical (though not for some designers). Antoine Predock, the Albuquerque-based architect, is a champion of this direct approach. He is quoted in *Architectural Record*, July 1991, as stressing the importance of understanding the natural context over time. He says architects *must* "sit on a site, put their butts on the ground, feeling and sensing the spirit of the place."

An intimate knowledge of the site can electrify design concepts. In the school setting, how does one become intimate with the site? Start with a simple walk-through. Initially, your class may schedule a group visit. However, you should plan on as many trips as possible during the course of the project, as your design develops: Go before breakfast, ask your instructor for a special trip during studio, have dinner at the coffee shop across the street. The goal is to log some quality time there and in the neighborhood, and constantly test design ideas.

> *SUPPLEMENT 3-2:* Award-winning and noted landscape architect, Paul Fried-berg, of M. Paul Friedberg & Partners Landscape Architecture & Urban Design, has offices in New York and Tel Aviv. He discusses a variety of topics, including achieving success in design, working with architects, and encountering the site.

How to Achieve Success?

There are no formulas. The design world is fluid. To use a platitude, change is a constant and we provide new ideas to respond. There is no way to teach anyone how to formulate an IDEA. We only speculate where ideas come from. What we can communicate is a way to think. To discriminate, so that ideas may have relevance.

It's also been curious to me that designers, who have an effect on the environment and people, are not exposed to philosophy and ethics in their curriculum. These disciplines provide us with values, an understanding of who we are, our aspirations, hopes, and capabilities. Armed with this knowledge, talented form makers can provide meanings to forms. That's success.

What's My Experience Working with Architects?

Ironically, some of my best work has been accomplished with the least talented architects. For they have given me free reign. I have always found it difficult to work with designers who do not feel, understand, or respect the nature of other sensibilities. The world is systemic. Integration and cooperation are essential to any successful enterprise. Recently, I have discovered that working with artists expands my perspective. The artist's sensibility tends to be complementary to that of the landscape architect. It's a mutually reinforcing relationship. One that could and should work with architects.

How to Encounter and Understand the Site

The site is an attitude as well as a physical presence. Most designers relate to the site from the property line in, and to the most immediate context. I see the site as a complex of interwoven observations and experiences. Any relationship to site starts from where

I come from, what I go through, and where and when I arrive. Once there, I asked whether I am to be confronted or presented. Is the site to be one or a sequence of experiences? Is the site volume or a space? Then there are questions that arise when a site has not been urbanized. When the transformation alters the larger context. This is an issue that relates back to one's own philosophy and ethics. I've always found it easier to confront transformation of a site that has already been urbanized.

How Should a Designer Deal with Environmental Conservation?

Conservation is a matter of personal values. My work is primarily urban. I endeavor to accommodate human conservation, biological rather than botanical. My work is focused on accommodating need, to provide an expanded vision, to broaden one's outlook. It's a triangulated relationship between you, me, and a place.

Who Are We and Should We Be Who We Are?

I've watched the times change from the 60s, 70s, and 80s, where we as professionals have developed oversized egos with misplaced values. We now seek meaning and pleasure in ourselves. The dialogue is intraprofessional, intellectual, and exclusive of people. It's always curious to me why people are not present in the articles in architectural magazines. Are they considered intrusive, irrelevant? Is this omission an indictment? We are not designing objects and environment. We are designing how people live—life styles. We can provide meaning or create obstacles. We have the option to ignore, follow, or the power to lead. The choice starts with social values, our perspective of society, and our relationship to it.

FIGURE 3-1 *The design is animated when people make themselves an integral part of the composition. The design challenge is to facilitate this possibility. Photo of Pershing Park, Washington, DC, courtesy of M. Paul Friedberg & Partners.*

EXAMPLES OF SITE INFLUENCES ON DESIGN

Vegetation. Proximity to a wooded area may suggest a particular architectural expression. Pinecote, the Crosby Arboretum Interpretive Center by Fay Jones, F.A.I.A., takes full advantage of the surrounding Mississippi pine savannah. Says Jones (*Architectural Lighting*, March 1988): "The time of day and the seasonal changes modify the shadows that frame the light. . . . The edges [of the roof] are not crisp at all. Like the pine straw and pine limbs, they progressively thin out from something that's close and dense to something open and fragile." *Take-Home Message: Design concepts can be derived from the natural qualities of the site. Pinecote Center is a fine example.*

Climate. Sun—orient building and outdoor spaces to coordinate heating/cooling characteristics with seasonal, regional, and programmatic factors—for example, design fenestration, overhangs, and other devices to allow penetration of low winter sun and block high summer sun; consider thermal characteristics when selecting cladding materials; promote and control the quality of daylighting; consider using deciduous trees that can help filter sun in summer and allow penetration of sunlight in winter. Evergreens, of course provide a year-round barrier. In tropical latitudes, tall palms provide shade without blocking cool breezes at window level.

Wind—protect/shelter entries from cold winter winds; capture summer breezes for good ventilation and outdoor areas. Moreover, the force of wind produces a variety of stresses and strains which can lift the roof off a house or cause skyscrapers to sway. These potential stresses should be considered for a particular location and factored into the design.

Rain—avoid siting the building in low areas subject to flooding (without some sort of control system); address water runoff from paved and built areas.

Arthur Erickson's 1977 Fire Island house is a good example of a building very much attuned to the exigencies of a climate influenced by salt air and intense beachfront light. The house is finished in cedar boards which resist corrosion, and two mechanical features control lighting and views. Hinged fences, which are attached to the deck, can be raised or lowered. When the beach is empty and the light low, the fences can be lowered. When they are upright, the bright reflected light is at least partially blocked, and a degree of privacy is insured. The living room roof is also mobile, with the capacity to slide open and reveal the summer night sky.

Slope. Steep—may suggest multilevel scheme and zoning of functions by level with interesting three-dimensional potential; accessibility issues; design slender forms that align with contours to minimize cutting and filling and disruption to site. Flat—maximum potential for plan based on regular arrays of identical units; construction is more economical than on steep sites.

A notable example of how a design responds to slope is The Portland [Maine] Museum of Art by architect Henry Cobb (of Pei Cobb Freed & Partners). Behind its oversized but thin front facade, the building visually steps down a long sloping site through a series of distinct masses. This scheme underscores the natural dynamics of the slope while helping the new building to relate more easily to the smaller scale of two historic museum buildings that sit at the base of the site. The discrete masses of the new museum serve to house a unique sequence of galleries designed from cubelike modules. The articulation of the roof and elevation as the museum drops down the slope seems to amplify the perception of natural light; a series of octagonal lantern skylights yield illumination likened by critics to that achieved in Kahn's late museums.

Actually *exploiting* a sloping site in direct support of programmatic objectives may also result in an effective design. The public library in Great Neck, NY, by architects Gibbons and Heidtmann (now Gibbons, Heidtmann, and Salvador) is just such a design. A basement level facing a large pond can be entered only from the lowest part of the site. This effectively separates the main public library (at the top of the slope) from the basement level that is used as a youth center. A special advantage of this scheme allows use of the youth center when the library is closed. Thus, the site is incorporated as a natural zoning device.

Noise, Smells, and Bad Views. (Oh well, sometimes it's not another day in paradise.) Provide buffer zones (and distance, if possible)—something to dissipate the problem; materials selections (i.e., a translucent material such as glass block, to let in daylight and blur the view); special construction detailing can help a lot toward acoustical separation.

Barker, Rinker, Seacat & Partners were commissioned to design a recreation center in Commerce City, on Denver's industrial fringe. While the region is known for its beauty, dominant local features such as a strip development, oil refinery, warehousing, and a dog track presented decidedly negative site characteristics. The architects responded by designing an inwardly focused building with exterior sweeps of translucent glass block. This "glass masonry" allows penetration of sunlight while effectively muting the frankly bad views. Interior window walls, skylights, and a hub atrium/lobby help make the recreation center an interior oasis.

Good Views. Consider sight lines both *to* and *from* the site; study what is appropriate relative to your concept. Frame views from the site to heighten drama, or configure building elements to mediate views to specific areas.

Josh Schweitzer's weekend retreat is sited in the dramatic (and sometimes seismic) landscape of Joshua Tree, California. It is a spare structure from which one can seemingly become immersed in the beauty and rawness of the desert. The essence of the retreat lies in its windows: Meticulously placed, eccentrically cut, and breathtakingly effective at framing views of mountains and desert *from* the site.

Shepley Bulfinch Richardson and Abbott's Center for African, Near Eastern and Asian Culture provides a good example of the control of views *to* a building. In response to pressures to conserve open space at the Smithsonian, 96 percent of the new cultural center was located underground. Three entry pavilions represent the only aboveground structure. The effect is not only to preserve an expansive quadrangle, but to maintain views to the very essence of the Smithsonian—the original "castle" designed by James Renwick in 1849.

Context. Acknowledgment or some kind of response to surroundings—obviously very circumstance specific—may include massing, materials, "picking up" regulating lines (i.e., fenestration, cornice), siting of the building, extension of existing circulation patterns into the site and building, and so on.

Kohn Pedersen Fox Associates' 125 Summer Street, a new 300-foot-tall office tower in Boston, is a fine example of contextual responsiveness. The new office building was set back on an irregularly shaped site, behind two nineteenth-century granite-clad five-story structures. The principal entrance was inserted in the gap that existed between the two older buildings, matching their height, maintaining the building line, and echoing the classically inspired facade elements.

Traffic. Locate access to parking away from busy streets and intersections. Minimize the number of curb cuts, and vehicular and pedestrian conflict (i.e., prevent people and automobile routes from crossing).

Thinking about traffic may seem mundane and self-evident, but this is decidedly not the case. The most celebrated and infamous example of how easy it is **not** to address pedestrian circulation is Tysons Corner, Virginia, near Washington, DC. A relatively recent and genuinely huge mosaic of commercial, retail, office, and residential space, Tysons Corner is an archetypal "Edge City": A high-density, mixed-use development that is not a municipality, although it is sufficiently large and populated to qualify as one.

A score of studies and journalistic accounts have documented that walking is virtually impossible. Tysons Corner sits in a network of two major expressways, two cross-county arteries, vast parking lots and garages, and innumerable on/off ramps. The speed and sound of the cars, trucks, buses, and tractor-trailers alone is intimidating to anyone even considering crossing the street from an office building to a shopping mall. The reality is that to cross the street, one has to have a car.

Sociocultural Context. This factor may have implications for modifying the building program to meet community need. Think about the conditions of a particular group in a particular place and time. Consider their resources, struggles, and future.

Charles Harrison Pawley's Caribbean Marketplace in Miami, Florida epitomizes response to sociocultural factors. Located in the Little Haiti section of the city, the Marketplace represents two events: The revival of a very poor neighborhood, and the new life being established in the United States by Haitian immigrants.

In a former warehouse, the Marketplace sports new gables, garden lattice, pretreated lumber, corrugated metal, and tropical colors. A system of booths offer a combination of everyday and exotic items and produce. The feeling of the place captures the unique tradition and flavor of the Caribbean Market with the fresh prospects of reestablishing that tradition in mainstream American society.

> *SUPPLEMENT 3-3:* William McDonough is a founding member of the A.I.A. Committee on the Environment and its Environmental Resource Guide. As the principal of his own firm in New York City, McDonough is a true leader in the movement toward environmentally conscious design. With one of his projects as an example, he discusses the goals and logic underlying major design decisions.
>
> It is difficult in this day and age to imagine that a building which might actually damage the health of its occupants or the environment could be considered beautiful. Yet, current understandings often do not take these concerns into either the practical or aesthetic design agenda. We have found that by adding both small- and large-scale ecological concerns, as a layer in the design process, the process itself becomes enriched, more ethically responsible, and a delightful ground for architectural design which goes beyond the issues of short-term stylistic exercise.

In 1991 we were invited to a competition for a new day-care center in Frankfurt, Germany. The program brief called not only for the requisite facilities, but also for a "low entropy" concept. The intention here was to create a building that would have minimal environmental impact and would have a primary focus on the amount of energy required to both construct and operate the building.

Our design concept included a series of conceptual underpinnings which informed both the design itself and the decision-making process. The goals we set for ourselves offered powerful guidance as we sifted through the vast number of design options leading to the completed design, and in a sense, removed some of the "arbitrariness" at critical junctures in the process.

We followed a design process similar to that used by Paul MacCready for the design of the gossamer condor (the first human-powered flight aircraft). We had a clear goal, imagined we had never seen a building before, and explored whatever technologies we could find that would assist us in achieving our goal.

The goals and their logic were as follows:

1. The building would not require fossil fuels to maintain comfortable survival temperatures and would rely on current solar income, perhaps even going so far as to become a net exporter of energy. Like a tree, it would be more productive than depletive over the long term. The solar collector pipes are integrated into the skylights and are served by photovoltaic pumps which provide fluid only when the sun is shining and avoid any possibility of freezing.

2. The building would have a long life. In order to amortize the capital resources embodied in the building, including the embodied energy, long-term utility is required. Durable and safe materials, as well as a design that could be converted to many human purposes in the future, such as housing, ensure long-term practical utility.

3. The concept of waste would be eliminated. In nature there is no waste, only constant cycles of conversion and production. We seek to integrate safe recycled material, build efficiently, and see that whatever comes from the construction and operation of the facility is appropriately returned to natural systems. For example, water conservation is designed into the building, and effluent streams are proposed to be treated ecologically and returned to the ground. Solar energy is stored for future use and produces no emissions.

4. Natural ventilation is abundant and encouraged. Cross-ventilation is designed into the rooms, electronic air monitoring systems are anticipated as ambient air pollution has become a problem in many cities, and air-to-air heat exchanges are utilized to minimize energy loss.

5. Daylighting is the principal form of lighting. The skylights and windows provide both south and north light to all rooms, and in conjunction with the passive solar heating component, the occupants of the building, even the children, can operate a shutter system to suit their desires for both heat and/or light.

6. The landscape concepts reflect naturalistic concerns. The existing trees have been saved, site disruption is minimized, solar access is assured, and the rooftop is used for planting a small, dense replica of the original climax forest. The children of Frankfurt are also to donate the trees for a park in Leipzig, Frankfurt's sister city in the former East Germany, to offset the carbon dioxide produced by the construction and operation of their center. This helps the children understand the value of having minimized the building's embodied energy in the first place, its solar operation, and their responsibility for thinking globally and acting locally.

FIGURE 3-2   *The Frankfurt, Germany, day-care center design keeps large broadleaf trees close to the building, enhancing the building's solar systems as well as the views to the site. The complex is connected to an existing playground to the north by way of a small train track that runs along tree-lined paths. A small, stony brook carries rainwater away from the buildings. The roof gardens strengthen the sense of a living building by covering the concrete roof decks of the main buildings. © 1991, William McDonough Architects. Caption reprinted by permission of the American Institute of Architects.*

THE INVENTORY

This section can be used as a guide and checklist for recording site data, and deriving the most from your frequent visits. In general, the mission is to identify the inherent makeup of the project area—both objectively and impressionistically (what are the possibilities and problems, and what is the "karma" of the site?). Use the following outline as appropriate; not all items may apply to a given case, and as with the programming information, understand that some of the material may be provided by your faculty.

Start with the Big Picture

1. Buy a good map at the local bookstore or check the library for maps, including the applicable U.S. Geological Survey or Sanborn maps for urban contexts (these may be available at the local city planner's or zoning office; make a telephone call to inquire). This is a way to begin assessing regional issues—land use (zoning, adjacent building types), access (the nature of traffic: Roads, highways, sidewalks), topography, open space, public transportation, and any other features that are important in the area. Attempt to gain a sense of the sociocultural context.

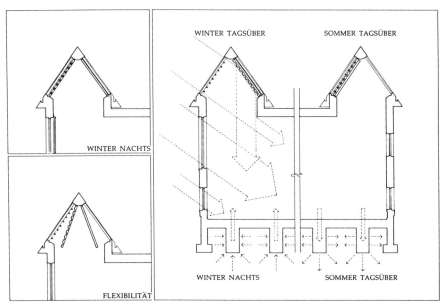

FIGURE 3-3 *With the day-care center, McDonough uses engineered glazing to achieve multipurpose integration by way of glazed roof ridges that provide shelter, warmth, hot water, insulation when needed, and light (warm south light in the winter and cool north light in the summer). Inside the peak joint of the parallel glazed roof ridges hang two shutters that building occupants can swing up to shade or fully cover the interior side of either the north-or south-facing sloped, superinsulated glazing. Solar collectors store heat in subfoundation heat sinks with photovoltaic-powered pumps. © 1991, William McDonough Architects. Caption reprinted by permission of the American Institute of Architects.*

2. Do some research about the history of the jurisdiction and the site (what are the building traditions, i.e., materials, typologies, etc., and *why* are they traditions?—what are they responding to?); all this may have an influence on design. The A.I.A.'s *The Architect's Handbook of Professional Practice* calls for a description of the community services (i.e., religious, shopping, health care). Good architecture is comprehensive and compulsive.

3. Pound the pavement; take photos and sketch typical scenes and details *after* you've walked through undistracted. Try to get an overall feeling—the "unique spirit of the place" (in Kevin Lynch's terms; his book, *Site Planning*, written with Gary Hack, is a fine resource). Make personal judgments as to the value of aesthetic, social, and other visible elements. Know where you are: Always be able to relate or "key" your position (and the photos) to the maps. If you're not comfortable making notes in the field, try talking into an inexpensive pocket tape recorder.

4. Be aware of anything close to your site that may strongly influence design decisions. Pay particular attention to the immediate context: Buildings and open space, views, smells, sounds, pedestrian traffic, vehicular traffic. (When is the area most congested? Which roads bounding the site have less traffic?) There is little question that these environmental factors are, collectively, all intrinsic to "the site." The gestalt also includes buildings in the neighborhood that can provide valuable cues for the architect in terms of massing, detailing, and material selections.

Zero-in on Your Site: Preparation

1. Obtain all available documentation about the site. A scaled site plan, survey, and/or aerial photographs showing boundaries, topography (if not flat), north (you may need to bring a compass), easements, and so on. This basic information is usually provided in class; if not, you may have to go to the local planning agency, or find some other means of obtaining it (i.e., contact the owner or people in local architectural or engineering firms who may have familiarity with the neighborhood).

2. Make multiple copies of the site plan in preparation for your visits. Observations and notes can then be recorded directly and accurately on the plans (see Figure 3-6).

3. Bring a camera (wide-angle lens is preferable), and sketching equipment. Bring a ruler or tape measure; you may want to take and/or confirm specific dimensions and relative locations of various site elements.

Zero-in on Your Site: Record Data

1. *Views.* Photograph the site. I would also suggest sketching. Awareness of detail is heightened when you actually draw it. In his wonderful book, *Landscape Architecture*, John Simonds instructs: "Get the feel of the land . . . look, listen, sense." Capture views approaching the site (by foot and/or car) and looking from the site. And study details (whatever may be useful, i.e., existing structures, rock formations). Remember (mentally or on paper) to key all snapshots and sketches to the site plan.

2. *Microclimate.* Investigate solar path; determine sun angles at various times of the day, and how they change throughout the year. There are many readily available resources, including *Architectural Graphic Standards*, that graphically depict how sun angles vary with time and geographical location (latitude). Get a sense for the altitude (angle above the horizon) and azimuth (surface angle measured from the south–north line; see Figure 3-4).

Observe shadows and shade patterns from nearby buildings, trees, and other features. Also note potential glare problems from reflections from nearby water or shiny facades of existing buildings.

Determine direction (and velocity) of prevailing summer and winter winds. Document any changes to typical wind patterns due to hills, buildings, or dense vegetation.

Note any other pertinent climatological and meteorological data, such as patterns of temperature variation, humidity, precipitation (including monsoons, snowfall, or drought), and hurricanes. The national A.I.A. is a good source if local references or the Weather Service are not accessible.

3. *Slopes.* Field verify that the topography indicated on the survey is accurate. Show where the land varies from steep to flat, and note the orientation of any slopes. (Contours are lines of equal elevation, and usually occur at intervals of 1 to 10 feet, depending on the scale of the plan; see "Understanding Contours" later in this chapter.)

Determine how water runoff relates to the slopes. Try to visit the site during a rainstorm. Document drainage features of all types.

Back in the studio, draw a few key cross sections through the site.

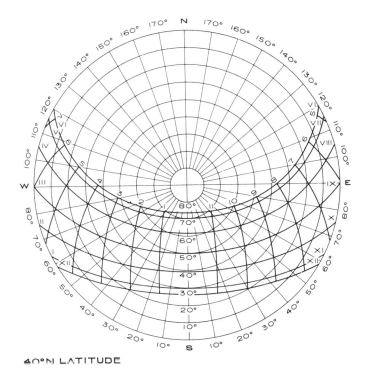

40°N LATITUDE

FIGURE 3-4 *Solar path diagrams depict the path of the sun within the sky vault as projected onto a horizontal plane. The horizon is represented as a circle with the observation point in the center. The altitude angles are represented at 10° intervals by equally spaced concentric circles; they range from 0° at the outer circle (horizon) to 90° at the center point. These intervals are graduated along the south meridian. Azimuth is represented at 10° intervals by equally spaced radii; they range from 0° at the south meridian to 180° at the north meridian. These intervals are graduated along the periphery. The solar bearing will be toward the east during morning hours, and to the west during afternoon hours. The declination of the sun's path changes in a cycle between the extremes of the summer solstice and winter solstice. Thus, the sun follows the same path on two corresponding dates each year. The elliptical curves in the diagram represent the horizontal projections of the sun's path. They are given on the twenty-first day of each month. Roman numerals designate the months. A cross grid of curves graduate the hours indicated in arabic numerals.*

EXAMPLE: Find the sun's position in Columbus, Ohio on February 21, 2 P.M.

STEP 1. *Locate Columbus on the map. The latitude is 40° N. Use the diagram.*

STEP 2. *In the sun path diagram select the February path (marked with II), and locate the 2-hour line. Where the two lines cross is the position of the sun.*

STEP 3. *Read the altitude on the concentric circles (32°) and the azimuth along the outer circle (35°30′W).*

From "Solar Angles" by Victor Olgay in Architectural Graphic Standards, *John R. Hoke, Jr., Editor. Copyright © 1988 John Wiley & Sons, Inc. Reprinted by permission of John Wiley & Sons, Inc.*

4. *Vegetation and Wildlife.* Trees—note species—evergreen or deciduous, density, height, and width of canopy.

Identify all types of ground cover.

Animals: Are there moose, koalas, spotted owls, or other creatures great and small living on the site? Describe their habitats.

5. *Existing Objects, Materials, and Public Works.* Inventory and describe condition, approximate sizes, and confirm on plan—much of this is usually indicated on the

survey. Include furniture (i.e., benches, picnic tables); lighting; retaining walls; paving; utilities (electricity, gas, water, sanitary sewers, storm drainage, phone lines); curbs, steps, ramps, handrails, fences; fire and police protection. If there are any structures on the site, they need to be evaluated carefully for possible relationship to proposed new project.

6. *Noise and Smells.* Listen for anything potentially disturbing (i.e., an interstate highway bisects your site, your neighbor is an international jetport).

Are there signs of pollution (i.e., is the site upwind from a baked bean factory or a paper mill)?

7. *Subsurface Conditions.* This is probably not too relevant for a school exercise (since it is assumed that your instructors will suggest a buildable site), but information on subsoil and groundwater conditions and data from percolation tests and borings (investigated and analyzed by geotechnical engineers) determine such things as bearing capacity, suitability for septic tank drainage systems, water runoff characteristics, permeability, and risk for erosion. Note the presence of topsoil and its influences on potential planting. Be aware that these studies are fairly routine in practice (and are usually commissioned by the client).

Depending on site location, seismic factors may be extremely relevant for design exercises. Check with faculty.

8. *Zoning.* Zoning is the legal process by which local government specifies and regulates land use and building type, size, and context (refer to Supplement 2-4). Some items you may need to consider include setbacks, yards, maximum lot coverage and building height, off-street parking, floor area ratio [FAR (ratio of total floor area to site area)], sky exposure plane, and of course, permitted uses. If in doubt, consult the instructor or the actual zoning ordinance, and as always, do not hesitate to call local officials—it can be a quick and efficient way of obtaining information you need.

There may be other restrictive covenants: for example, a homeowners' association requires a 60-foot setback, whereas zoning requires only 20 feet. *Diagram those regulations that have an effect on your site and design.*

9. *Renovation of an Existing Building.* This provides a somewhat different set of cataloging and documentation duties, although many of those mentioned above may still be applicable, especially if an addition or outdoor space is programmed.

If not available, scaled (and most important, dimensioned) "as-built" floor plans and elevations must be developed. This kind of survey work can be accomplished rapidly, with delegation of work spread around to all class members. Note floor-to-ceiling heights, fenestration dimensions, sill heights, door sizes, and so on. Getting on hands and knees to measure a building may be a dirty job but has its rewards: You are forced to really *see* detail, and in some cases uncover the building's "soul." Photography here is critical—missed dimensions (there always are a few) can usually be determined by counting bricks, planks, and the like, from a snapshot— any element with a known modular size can be used to achieve a close estimation of an overall dimension. Existing systems (and all associated components)— mechanical and structural—must be recorded. Check the roof and basement; these may be sites of future development. All this information might be available from the original architects or the building department.

Be aware of special architectural detailing—craftsmanship and design features worth preserving or responding to—both inside and out.

10. *Miscellaneous.* Anything else specific to your site and immediate vicinity not mentioned above (i.e., proximity to bodies of water, floodplains, mud slides, grazing cows, final approach to the airport, or how the garbage is removed). Attempt to determine if there are plans for future development in the area.

DIAGRAMMING THE DATA

With all the inventorying of site data complete, the implications can now be investigated in the studio. Use copies of the site plan, perhaps in a reduced form, to overlay information collected in the field. Try one diagram for each inventory category, or combine several categories. Employ symbols to convert the data graphically—to make it easy to understand at a glance (i.e., show steep grades in dark gray and flat areas white, with light gray for variations in between). Annotate where necessary. Another example is the figure-ground (plan) diagram: Looking at neighborhoods in urban districts, building masses are black and open spaces are white. As with the programmatic diagrams, *save all drawings (sign and date them).* They are an integral part of the design process, help to form a rationale for design decisions, and can be used artfully and persuasively in the final presentation.

The inventory and subsequent analysis gives coherence to development of the site. Start generally (with a small-scale site plan) by identifying and justifying logical areas to build and to circulate (with cars, people, service, and emergency vehicles). Begin to define areas that must be preserved in their natural state, and how the integrity of that state may be assured or accentuated by an architectural presence.

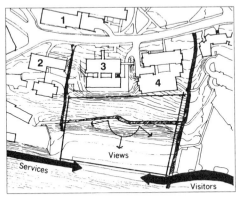
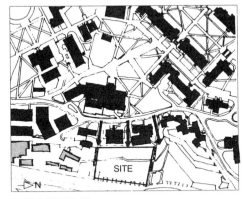

MICRO SITE PLAN

1   STUDENT UNION
2   FACILITIES PLANNING
3   FACULTY CLUB
4   HALL HEALTH CENTER

MACRO SITE PLAN

■ TRADITIONAL CAMPUS IMAGE (COLLEGIATE GOTHIC)
■ MIXED IMAGE (LATER ADDITIONS)
▨ INDUSTRIAL IMAGE (SERVICE BUILDINGS)
➡ VIEW CORRIDOR

FIGURE 3-5 *These diagrams, developed by NBBJ (of Seattle), were used to study some of the site influences on Fluke Hall, a technology center of offices and laboratories at the University of Washington. Site selection was part of the challenge for NBBJ. The "Macro-Site" is a variation of the figure-ground diagram, and the "Micro-Site" conveys access, slope, and view information. © Copyright NBBJ, David C. Hoedemaker, Rick Buckley, designers.*

Conversely, what areas scream (or whisper) for development? In other words, zone the site; judge how existing patterns (pedestrian, vehicular, open spaces, etc.) should be extended to and through the site. Is there a natural focus of some sort on the site? If so, should it be left alone, framed, or developed? Your observations from spending time at the site will almost automatically address these issues and raise others that are crucial. *Take-Home Message: It is the site elements that may give clues and have the greatest impact on shaping and orienting the building and supporting circulation.* John Simonds, in *Landscape Architecture*, makes the point eloquently: "To preserve or create a pleasing site or landscape character for an area . . . ranging from completely natural to completely man-made . . . a harmony of all the various elements or parts must be retained or developed."

Experiment with many alternatives in the *interpretation* of the data. Location and orientation have such an influence on the architecture that given the same program, a building on one side of a site would have a very different expression than if located on a different side. It is interesting and useful to predict the differences in design responses as a function of differences in siting.

As with the program analysis, site analysis varies greatly with the scope, substance, and context of the project. Above all, *use common sense* to weigh the importance of site factors.

MARRYING PROGRAM AND SITE

Determining how the program and site fit together might be likened to leading a talk show on dating and marriage. You, as the host will ask: "Do the program and site constantly fight?" and "Does one try to change the other to make the relationship work? Is there simply an initial infatuation stemming from a blind date, or are there long-term implications? Does a mutual support (of setting and function, as Kevin Lynch might say) bring out the best qualities in each? Can there be some sort of ongoing 'chemistry'?" Or, as *The Architect's Handbook of Professional Practice* asks, are site and program "right for each other"?

Gordon Cullen, in his book *Townscape*, suggests: "There is an *art of relationship* just as there is an art of architecture. Its purpose is to take all the elements that go to create the environment: Buildings, trees, nature, water, traffic, advertisements and so on, and weave them together in such a way that drama is released."

Now is the time to start testing the goodness of relationship: The fit of program requirements (as defined in bubble diagrams) and site potentials (as defined in site analysis diagrams). Begin to arrange the bubbles as an overlay on the site plan (Figure 3-7 is a model for this kind of diagramming). Consider the spatial needs together with the physical realities of the site. Also keep in mind your "concept" for the project. There will no doubt be some conflicts. The design process is getting more exciting and challenging! Attempt a rough blocking-out of *many* alternatives and possibilities. Even at this early stage this will help toward optimizing both program and site relationships. Keep these beginning explorations very loose—use soft pencils, thick markers, cheap trace.

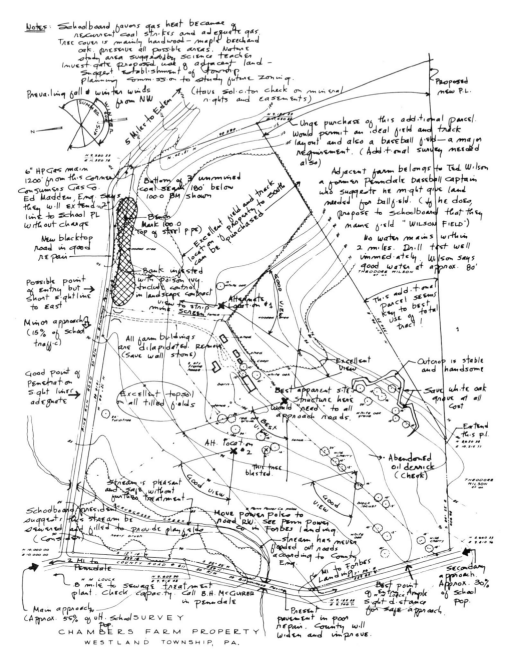

FIGURE 3-6 *This is a superb example of a site analysis diagram, including inventory information together with supporting commentary written in the field (on a copy of the site plan). Reproduced from J. Simonds,* Landscape Architecture, *McGraw-Hill, New York, 1961, with permission of McGraw-Hill, Inc.*

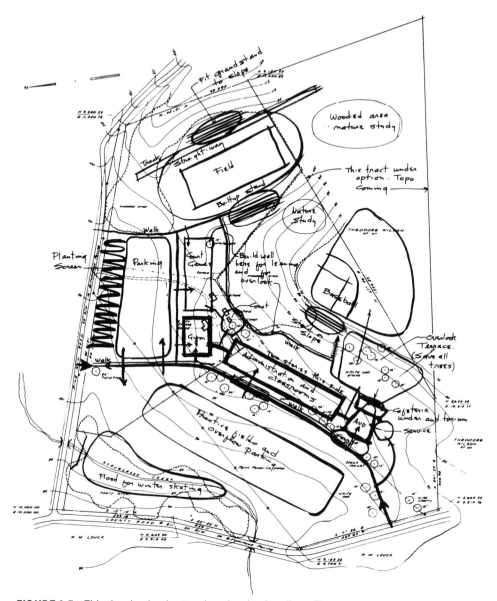

FIGURE 3-7 *This drawing begins to relate the site data (from Figure 3-6) to program elements—a logical next step in the design process. Reproduced from J. Simonds,* Landscape Architecture, *McGraw-Hill, New York, 1961, with permission of McGraw-Hill, Inc.*

ENTRY SEQUENCE

The idea of procession, designing the approach from entering the site via car (drive-in, drop-off, parking, walking from car to building) or via foot (pedestrian ways from sidewalk to building) can be a delightful extension of design themes of the building to the larger site context. Or the entry sequence can function as a contrast to, say, the building lobby, where experience is then heightened and accentuated. In any event, strive for control over the design of these outdoor areas, which can have lasting impact on the total architectural experience and have much to do with place making.

By itself, the entry sequence can be a rich, eventful experience. It doesn't necessarily have to be the shortest distance between site boundary and entry. There may be an intentionally circuitous path that allows for surprise and discovery. Or, one may catch a glimpse of building to come around one turn, and a panoramic vista may be revealed around another. I'll never forget the experience of traveling to Baxter State Park in north central Maine. After about 30 minutes on a seemingly unending monotonous, meandering dirt road surrounded on both sides by walls of pine and birch, the road curved sharply, the woods cleared, and the snow-covered peak of Mt. Katahdin loomed in our windshield, then suddenly, disappeared into a new stand of trees. What theater!

As effective as dramatic punch and soaring emotional response may be, I would like to reiterate Simond's notion of harmony. In particular, I want to stress the importance of harmonizing site elements that form an entry sequence. If the specific design approach engages or grows from the site, the architecture of building entries can be very intimate with the larger site issues. If the specific design approach is one of theater (to highlight the best features of both site and building), a more inwardly focused or object-oriented architectural response may be appropriate. *The Take-Home Message is that design decisions become less arbitrary when considering the significance of entering the proposed structure in a context beyond the boundaries of the building itself.*

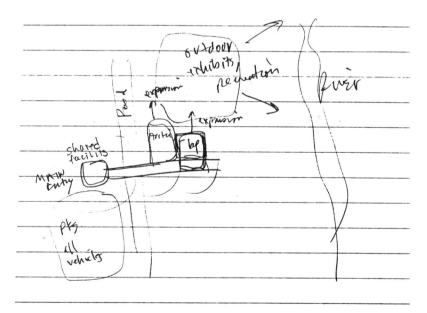

FIGURE 3-8 *An example of a primitive "napkin" sketch—diagrammatic layout for a museum complex in Finland informed by a few essential program and site factors. Design and drawing by the author.*

DAYLIGHTING

Use of natural light and views can be a major form determinant in making architecture. Caren M. Connolly, Visiting Professor at the University of Wisconsin-Milwaukee, talks about her personal approach regarding landscape architecture: "I consider daylighting part of landscape architecture and environmental concerns. The thing I try to use most often is not plant material, but light and shadows. When you have a window and at certain times of the day, the leaf pattern goes across your wall, I consider that a landscape element. I stole this idea from Lutyens! In my teaching, I try to reinforce a concept of borrowing a landscape. If you don't have a budget for landscape, but there's one in view, make sure the windows in your building look right out on it. There are often nice things on other parcels, or conversely, if something's really ugly, make sure you *don't* put a window there! I'd like to add that landscape architects traditionally have been collaborative and integrative, and the best landscape architecture programs really stress the word *multidisciplinary*. Architects, engineers, and landscape architects have to work together; mutual respect is critical. I would also like to recommend that architecture students study natural systems as electives—botany, biology, zoology—so that they understand that architecture isn't separate."

Jeff Harner, a Santa Fe architect profiled in the August 1991 issue of *Architecture*, comments on the special qualities of light in the southwestern desert. "Here, natural light is almost like a building material." This idea captures the important role that daylighting can play in designing buildings.

Daylight and outside views are precious resources. Every effort must be made to facilitate penetration of natural light (even to belowgrade spaces) and promote direct lines of sight to windows for areas inhabited for big blocks of time. A common mistake in student projects is the inclusion of fully sealed rooms or those that are far away from outside walls.

Two of my favorite master manipulators of light and shadow are Louis Kahn and Tadao Ando. Monographs of their work are filled with extraordinary demonstrations.

> *SUPPLEMENT 3-4:* Virginia Cartwright is a daylighting consultant and an Associate Professor in the School of Architecture at the University of Oregon. She sets forth a concise and informative summary of the nature and impact of daylighting in buildings. Her views are very much rooted in aspects of the site—climate, latitude, and local weather are seen as motivating a range of design decisions. Professor Cartwright's advice on model building will become a familiar but profound refrain. (The section on lighting in Chapter 4 provides additional perspectives on both daylighting and artificial lighting.)

Daylighting is the use of light from the sun and sky to provide illumination within buildings. Daylight enriches architecture with character: Changing from morning to evening, day to night, and summer to winter. Each day brings a different light. This light changes, subtly or dramatically, the nature of built form and space. To create architecture that enriches peoples' experiences and retains its meaning over time, architects must design with light.

The light from the sun has been the primary source of lighting buildings until fairly recently, and even now it is the most common source of light in many parts of the world. The sun's light comes directly from sunlight, and indirectly, through diffusion through the earth's atmosphere, from skylight. At night it reaches the earth indirectly by reflection from the moon.

FIGURE 3-9 *In this modestly scaled residential addition in Princeton, NJ, a trellis above a cantilevered deck allows sun to illuminate white clapboard siding and create a glow that can be seen from a distance. The shadow in the foreground neatly describes the configuration of wood trellis members. Design by the author with Raymond Novitske, A.I.A., Associated Architect. Photo © Norman McGrath.*

Climate and latitude affect the quantity and quality of daylight. The higher the sun is in the sky, the less atmosphere it has to pass through and so is much more intense. Moisture in the air, such as clouds or humidity, changes the light. In places with clear, cloudless skies, the light is intense and dynamic. There are both strong highlights and deep shadows. Forms are clearly articulated. The northern latitudes, characterized by overcast skies and rainy days, have a softer light. The overcast sky provides a lower level of light that is uniform in all directions. Forms have soft shadows, making it more difficult to understand their three-dimensional character.

Buildings that include daylighting as a design element use various windows, clerestories, and atria to bring the light into the interiors. Under clear skies, buildings incorporate shading devices on the south side and often have very small or no windows on the east and west sides, where it is very difficult to control glare from the low-angle sun. Buildings designed for cloudy climates often have larger windows and operable shading devices for the less frequent, sunny days.

In daylighting architecture, the design of the interiors is just as important as the design of the exterior. The size and proportion of rooms, and their relationship to the windows or skylights, are critical to good daylighting design. The best lighting scheme provides light from two sides, giving a more even distribution of light with little glare. Rooms with high windows and ceilings receive light far back into the space.

The organization of activities, furniture and its layout, and the color of the interior surfaces are another set of critical design decisions for daylighting buildings. It is important to design the appropriate lighting for each activity. The position of furnishings and their design enhances or obstructs the distribution of light within the building. The color and, most important, the reflectance (whether light in value or dark) affect the amount of light in the interior. Given the same-size window, highly reflective rooms will be much brighter than rooms with dark surfaces. In general, ceilings should be the lightest surface and floors the darkest.

The best means of designing with daylight is to use models. The more carefully made and more detailed the model, the closer it will represent the patterns of light within the building. Models can be taken outside to be studied and photographed under real sky and sunlight conditions. Not only are they very effective tools for making design decisions, but are also an excellent means of presenting design ideas to critics and clients. As the models become more accurate, it is important to make sure that surfaces are carefully represented and joints do not let any light "leaks" into the interior. More sophisticated analysis of daylighting can be done with models with light meters.

MISCELLANEOUS CONSIDERATIONS

As a function of the particular project assignment, the following topics may be relevant for site planning and design conceptualization. One thing that is relevant, though, for all projects (regardless of personal design philosophy) is that site evaluation and development are, respectively, part of the design process and the architecture.

Indoor/Outdoor Transitions

The quality of the relationship of building and site may have a lot to do with just how they are physically engaged. Blurring the distinction between these realms can elevate functioning over the entire site. Identify program spaces that would benefit from a flowing of activity or a special dialogue with the outside environment. Consider anything that filters or shelters, such as arcades, pergolas, overhangs, and exposed framing. Again, harmony of building design theme and site characteristics help in form development. Materials can be used to great advantage—for example, a lobby opens to a small courtyard; brick pavers used in the lobby extend through the court, serving to unify and reinforce the connection. Moreover, expression of access (physical or visual) to outside space can animate an elevation. For example, Frank Lloyd Wright's Taliesin West in Scottsdale, AZ, is frequently recognized as a building so resonant with its site that the two entities are almost as one. The apparent contradiction lies in Wright's selection of materials and forms, which remain distinct and assertive, yet are perfectly consistent with the desert landscape.

Alternatively, indoor/outdoor transition may be defined by a dramatic and abrupt difference between building and site. This approach may serve to focus attention on a particular attribute. Building form and/or materials can support this idea, which in turn should support programmatic goals. For example, Richard Meier's Giovannitti House in Pittsburgh, PA, with its white porcelain enamel panels and bold forms, contrasts sharply with its suburban setting and appears offset as a unique architectural jewel.

Understanding Contours

Some students find it difficult at first to understand the representation of land forms or topography by contour lines on site plans, surveys, or maps. It takes only a little experience to comfortably recognize a contour pattern (i.e., for valleys, ridges,

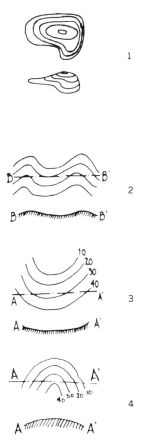

FIGURE 3-10 *These are graphic depictions of contours—in plan—which are then translated to elevation (1) and cross sections (2, 3, 4). From Kevin Lynch and Gary Hack,* Site Planning, *3rd Edition, MIT Press, Cambridge, MA, © 1984 by The Massachusetts Institute of Technology.*

uniform slopes, etc.) and relate it to actual field conditions. Contour lines trace points of equal elevation (usually measured as altitude above sea level) and represent a vertical separation or interval. Cultivate the habit of checking the scale relative to the contour interval shown on the site plan or survey; you may find that sketching cross sections through the site are very helpful and revealing. Contour lines do not cross (except at vertical planes); spaced evenly they signal a constant slope; close together, a steep slope; far apart, a flat or gentle slope. Visit the site and compare it with contours depicted on the site plan; there will be no ambiguity about understanding the shape of the land.

Parking

Like it or not, the automobile is a fact of American life, and parking it may not be pretty. View the accommodation of parking on your site as another design *opportunity*. [Always be on the lookout for any special design tasks that may seem ordinary or as adjuncts to the program (i.e., parking)—they can be turned into real

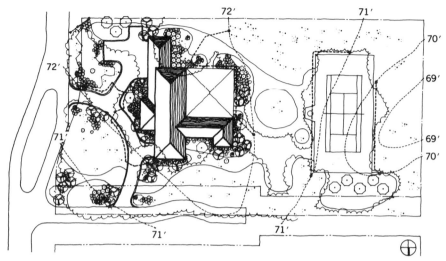

FIGURE 3-11 *Some amount of grading or modification to contours will probably be required around new structures. In a simple example, note how the contours (represented by dotted lines) were manipulated on this site plan around the tennis court, house, and driveway for a project in Kissimmee, FL. Design and drawing by the author.*

assets that add much to the architectural identity of the project.] Consider it part of the challenge to design an unforgettable or at least pleasant part of the entry sequence to the building.

In general, once an area has been identified as reasonable for parking, design goals include (1) reducing the visual impact from almost *everywhere*, (2) close proximity to building entries (this may be negotiable depending on the project and typical duration of parking), (3) keeping people traffic and car traffic separated, (4) providing barrier-free spaces very close to entries, and (5) simplicity of layout (minimize turns and number of entrances and exits; in small lots, one for both ingress and egress is sufficient). We've all found ourselves at one time or another trapped in some mazelike parking lot that should have been in a Hitchcock film— so, strive for simplicity! And avoid dead ends! Reference books such as *Architectural Graphic Standards* describe specific parking layouts, rules of thumb, dimensions, turning radii, number of spaces for a given use (usually included in your faculty-authored program and/or mandated by city ordinances), and drop-off design criteria. This is a good starting point from which to understand the basic functional and space requirements, but remember that these are strictly "cookbook" and imply no innovation.

To summarize and simplify the conventions: Allow about 400 square feet per car (includes stall and circulation); standard car stall—9 feet wide by 19 feet long (13 feet wide for wheelchair-accessible spaces); aisle or lane widths are a function of stall angle—the selection of which depends on total space allotted for parking, and design intent—angles vary from 90 degrees (perpendicular parking, which accommodates two-way lanes and is most space efficient) to 60 degrees [employed most often, promotes ease of maneuvering (with one- or two-way lanes) as well as efficient use of space], to 45 and 30 degrees (afford best maneuverability, but less efficient use of space; also suggest one-way lanes). Minimum lane widths are 20 feet for two-way, 12 feet for one-way. Parallel parking, the bane of novice drivers, may be another option in some instances.

Achieving a balance between packing in as many cars as possible (in terms of space efficiency) and creating a character and quality consistent with the overall design is vital. These are not necessarily mutually exclusive goals. Consider walkway design, orientation of traffic aisles in relation to the building (if pedestrians are indeed utilizing them, you don't want to force people to slalom between rows of parked cars), landscaping, space for plowed snow, and accommodation of service and/or emergency vehicles. Is there a way of breaking down the scale of the lot so that there's not just one big sea of asphalt? Are there logical separations in the program to accomplish this (i.e., staff, public, service)?

Some examples of reducing the unpleasant aesthetic impact of parking lots include designing earth berms around the periphery, lowering the lot level or proposing a terraced scheme (this strategy tends to preserve sight lines to the building and may depend on topography), constructing walls or other screening devices (which may further give unity to, or hide, the site and building), and by the shape of the lot itself. Choose appropriately durable materials of contrasting texture and color for walkways in the lot—relate these to materials of other pedestrian paths in the area.

The Site Context Model and Drawings

Sometimes a group or class project in the form of a model built at the beginning of the project showing immediate surroundings (buildings, open space, etc.) is very valuable. Space for the specific site is left neutral, with the capability for individual students to plug in their schemes. Caren Connolly emphasizes the importance: "I like to get students to work in model because I think they'll be willing to build an environment around their building, whereas they won't in drawings." *The Take-Home Message is always to be aware of and show the context in the medium in which you are working. Usually, if it is out of sight, it is out of mind.* If drawing, indicate at least edges of the surroundings in plan, elevation, and section (and, of course, in any three-dimensional representation). This includes such ordinary items as a north arrow (a constant reminder of solar path and the direction of those cold winter winds) and a graphic scale or, better yet, some scale elements, such as people and the ubiquitous car. (See Figure 3-12 for an example of a site/context massing model.)

GLOBALIZATION OF ARCHITECTURE

The practice of architecture often brings together a huge range of specialists, consultants, and personalities across professional, academic, business, political, and cultural domains. The convening power of architecture may be one of its great yet-to-be-exploited potentials.

Linkages between individuals, disciplines, corporations, even governments often arise through the collaboration required to produce buildings. The linkage effects that result from such collaboration can be considered globalization. The trend toward globalization demonstrates that site considerations are not limited only to the immediate plot of ground on which a building sits.

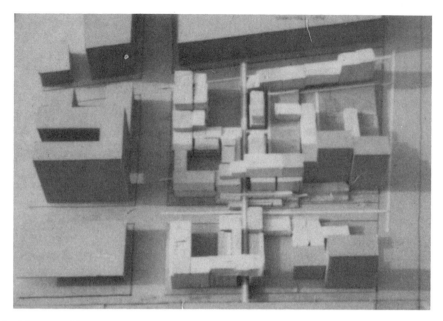

FIGURE 3-12   *This is an example of a small-scale site/context massing model of a mixed-use complex in Manhattan, where wood blocks represent the proposed scheme and chipboard represents existing buildings. (Take full advantage of the wood shop in your school.) Clay is another popular, easy-to-work-with material for these kinds of models, which are very useful tools early in the design process. The larger-scale, more detailed variety (showing elaborate elevations on existing buildings) become salient at later stages when designs are more resolved. Design and model by the author.*

As more firms market their services (or follow their American clients) abroad, there is the increasing probability that young architects will find themselves spending a significant portion of their time working on projects in other sociocultural settings. It becomes especially important then that the architect not only appreciate what other disciplines may contribute to a project, but also what impact indigenous conditions are likely to have on the design.

For the student, preparation for globalization translates to getting the most out of a liberal arts education. A particular emphasis on sociology and anthropology can offer all kinds of insights and be of terrific practical value in understanding and responding to the sociocultural context of proposed architectural projects. As you listen to lectures in these classes, make an effort to imagine them as briefings for your next international endeavor. Ask questions, phrasing them so as to test the validity of the way you are applying the social science. Make your professors speak to the realm of "applications."

Metrication

Students (and faculty) should begin to think about doing a project using the metric system. Both a symptom and requirement of globalization, metric conversion is upon us. The Omnibus Trade and Competitiveness Act mandates metrication in response to European moves requiring all imported products, beginning in 1992, to be of metric standards. And beginning in October 1992, metric measurements will be required in many U.S. federal agency projects. The A.I.A. Board of Directors has updated and clearly articulated a policy embracing metric conversion.

Although it will clearly take some time to implement the metric system throughout the entire U.S. construction industry, more frequent use on projects of all types will undoubtedly begin to replace our imperial system of measure. My experience in designing a project in metric suggests that it is analogous to learning a very simple foreign language. Once initial hesitation and the reflex to translate constantly from one system to the other is overcome, one actually approaches *thinking* in the new metric "language." After a brief orientation time (and buying a new scale), it's easy to become facile—you'll start dreaming about designing buildings dimensioned in millimeters, and picturing sites in meters instead of feet and inches. No worries about working with the change, it's no big deal. (However, it *is* a big deal for some U.S. manufacturers who must retool. It is also a big deal to impose metrication upon the increasing number of existing buildings to be renovated or restored, building codes and standards, and other building industry and political interests—that is why it is difficult to make predictions about how long the process of metric conversion will take.)

> *SUPPLEMENT 3-5:* Perhaps more than anyone else in architecture today, Eugene Kohn appreciates the growing impact of the remarkable developments in communication and transportation which have so effectively shrunk the planet. Shepherding the international activities of Kohn Pedersen Fox Associates PC, he is also sensitive to the complexities of conducting global business as it is so intimately fused with social, cultural, and political forces. While Kohn's message has particular relevance for the future of architecture, it is grounded in the time-honored discipline of the contextual ideal.

GLOBAL ARCHITECTURE IN A FRACTURED WORLD

The challenge we all face today is to promote political autonomy without inviting fragmentation and to encourage globalization without excessive cultural homogenization.

Striking this delicate balance is a critical task for architects operating in the world today. As builders bridging cultures, architects can, on occasion, be a positive force countering the forces pulling the world apart. Enhancing the position of architects and their buildings is the growing importance of cities. As national borders lose importance in light of the multinational corporate activities, cities and their global citizens take on greater meaning and prominence in the world. In the process, an archipelago of global cities such as Tokyo, New York, London, and Hong Kong is gaining more importance.

For architects, globalization must be more than just the internationalization of their products and services. Now more than ever, it is imperative for those involved in the development of large urban projects to "think globally but act locally."

Until recently most architects did not need to practice globally. Architects tended to work outside their own countries by invitation only, as when Frank Lloyd Wright came to Japan to design the Imperial Hotel; Le Corbusier went to Harvard University to design the Carpenter Center for the Visual Arts; and Jorn Utzon went to Sydney to design its Opera House, now a national symbol. In each case the designer brought his particular aesthetic to the site and created a spectacular building.

During the 1980s, several forces combined to change the practice of architecture dramatically. As businesses globalized and expanded operations internationally, particularly financial institutions, more and more white collar jobs were created and the demand for "The American Office Building" grew, changing the face of cities throughout the world. To satisfy this need, some multinational companies asked their American architects to follow them abroad.

In the 1980s real estate matured into an international business. Buildings were developed and traded as objects and these objects became major assets in the ever-increasing real estate portfolios of the international companies. Some buildings were bought and sold like stocks and bonds with little concern for their functional and architectural qualities. In the 1990s, I believe, buildings will be viewed no longer as assets specifically for trading but be designed as assets for the users leading to a more productive working environment.

In working abroad, architects have generally favored one of two approaches. The first method can be traced back to the 1920s when the International Style was born. This style celebrated the triumph of technology and delighted in the newfound ability to place the same objectlike structure anywhere in the world, regardless of local conditions. One of the principal players in the International Style, Mies van der Rohe, recast glass and steel high rises in various cities around the world: As residential towers on Lake Shore Drive in Chicago, as the corporate Seagram's Building in New York, and as an unbuilt proposal for an investment office building right in the middle of the City of London. The International Style represented a dramatic breakthrough against the backdrop of strong regional differences, but over time as their numbers increased their deleterious effect caused some cities to lose their individual character, particularly in America.

Today, a number of architects still adopt a similar philosophy and export signature formal solutions. For some clients this is the ideal approach. For them, because commissioning a building is akin to collecting the work of well-known artists, their goal is an objectlike building unaffected by local character. Selectively, this approach is not unsuccessful and can provide inspiration both aesthetic and intellectual.

Object building succeeds more if sites are less urban and when they are accomplished works of architecture—well executed and when they do not proliferate the urban environment, eroding the qualities of the positive aspects of that city.

The second approach blends the architect's aesthetic and formal sensibilities with consideration for the local conditions, local procedures, planning parameters, culture, and the spirit of place. While the first approach remains valid, we believe that success anywhere requires an architect to be locally in tune adapting his or her architectural language to the place. This philosophy is not unique to our practice. In his design for the Team Disney Building in Orlando, Florida, Arata Isozaki brought his Japanese aesthetic together with the whimsical spirit of the Walt Disney Company to create an outstanding building abroad.

Both of these approaches are obviously enhanced by the work of talented and sensitive architects. Stylistic and philosophical considerations are not exclusive to either approach. In fact, a modern building can relate by contrast to a traditional context through its massing—relation to heights of adjoining buildings, materials, color, and details.

Our contextual approach begins at home. Even among American cities, there exists a tremendous diversity of site conditions, historical background, and regional culture, as the following examples of our work illustrate.

- The Procter & Gamble General Offices Complex in Cincinnati sits as a gateway to this very traditional city while revealing the company's conservative and community-oriented corporate culture. The design of the new building is tied to the original Headquarters building through its placement on the site, its massing, choice of materials, and by the larger garden space to which both buildings share.

- The confident elegant curved green-glass prismatic office tower at 333 Wacker Drive in Chicago reflects its unique site condition. This only triangular site in the loop, strategically important, is formed by the juxtaposition of the city grid and the bend of the Chicago River.

- In Montreal, Canada we designed an office tower for IBM that relates to Mont Royal, the highest topographic feature of the city, as well as a low-scale cathedral adjacent to the site. The building has a strong sense of presence on the skyline and an appropriate pedestrian scale at the street.

By engaging in a dialogue with our clients and colleagues around the globe and by tackling the challenges of varying and unique building types, we have become better architects. Our experience in Japan, in particular, is a paradigm for striking the delicate balance between globalization and promotion of local culture.

We are presently collaborating on the design of the Nagoya Station Building, which will be one of Japan's tallest and largest buildings when completed in 1999. This mixed-use complex contains 4.8 million square feet of transportation, cultural, retail, hotel, and office facilities and is an example of the forward-looking urban models being developed in Japan.

Relating to the entire country and beyond as well as locally to the city, the complex literally and metaphorically will be a twenty-first-century gateway of the city. In addition to bringing our creativity and technical knowledge of tall buildings to Nagoya, we brought our recent experience designing vertically stacked, mixed-use buildings in the United States. Collaborating with master architect Mr. Seizo Sakata and the architects of Taisei Corporation and JR-Tokai, the end result will be a building that not only enriches Nagoya but also one that is the result of two cultures working together.

At the moment the world seems to be at a very important juncture which may establish trends either toward a hostile alienation or harmonious globalization. While differences among the peoples of the world will always exist, as they should, it is up to us to work together for mutual understanding. Just last week, I met with Mr. Henry Drzewiocki, the Architect of Warsaw, with whom we are working on the design of the new National Bank of Poland. He told me: "It is important that the building you are designing be a Kohn Pedersen Fox work of architecture that is unique because it draws its inspiration from the context of Warsaw and not a predetermined design parachuted in." Therefore, what is important and special is a building that blends our creativity, talent, and skill of execution with the local influences.

The citizens of the world have the chance now not just to avert crisis, but to elevate the world to a new level of international discourse. As architects we are sensitive builders and creators not politicians or soldiers. We are a force for harmony and beauty, aiming to improve through the built environment the quality of life for all people. So, in these unsettled times architects can still be a positive, sensitive, and unifying force spanning a more intimate but fractured world.

4

The Design

How to avoid having your work seen as "artificially inseminated rather than passionately conceived."—Coy Howard*

*Coy Howard, a jury member for the P/A Second Annual Conceptual Furniture Competition, is quoted from the May 1982 issue of *Progressive Architecture*, p. 163. P/A's International Furniture Competition was last held in 1987.
Photo credit: UP AND DOWN © 1947 M. C. Escher/Cordon Art-Baarn-Holland.

*"Well, well, I . . . to me–I . . . I mean, it's–it's–it's all instinctive, you know. I mean, I just
try to uh, feel it, you know? I try to get a sense of it and not think about it so much."*
—Annie Hall (from the screenplay by Woody Allen and Marshall Brickman)

For most students and practitioners, there is indeed an "instinctive" element to
design. That instinct or talent, informed by the program, site, and concept, will
surely lead to the creation of excellent architecture. Design is not something that is
tacked-on after analysis, or after solving the space-planning puzzle, nor is it purely
aesthetic. Rather, it is a way of looking at and addressing problems that starts from
day one of the project and extends into the final stages of building. Don't get the
wrong idea: Intuition or instinct alone is no substitute for rigorous research,
analysis, and sweat.

THE MAGICAL SYNTHESIS MYTH

This chapter might be entitled, "Design *Development.*" It should be obvious by now
that the so-called "predesign" program and site analysis tasks discussed in previous
chapters comprise *far more* than mere analysis and logical diagramming. Design
starts with the way in which you read the program; how the problem is interpreted,
how you engage the [simulated] client, and even how you conduct research and
collect information. Assessing a site, visualizing possibilities, arranging bubbles of
spaces on the site, conceiving of concepts . . . this is all very creative stuff that comprises the first stages of design—synthesis, yes; magical, no. *Take-Home Message:
Design is not necessarily a neat, clean, linear process. If there is "magic," it is the spirit and
the soul that arise from a passionate, perhaps instinctive, and an almost systematic involvement, and excitement with the project at every phase.*

FACILITATING DESIGN

There is no conscious intent in this book to advocate any one theoretical approach
to architectural design. As a primer, the issues raised here (and in all other chapters)
are meant to introduce and demonstrate some generally applicable principles for
both studio and actual projects in the search for creating built form and establishing
an inherent order.

Aspects of designing are individual and often very personal. The process and
results can be as varied as the projects undertaken. James Stewart Polshek, whose
firm is the recipient of the 1992 A.I.A. Firm Award, believes that the approach to
and style of his projects are a function of the particular circumstance. What unifies
the work of his office is an "openness to many different forms—contemporary and
traditional, Western and non-Western—and a willingness to assimilate and incorporate those forms when appropriate." (The quote, by Helen Searing, is from *James
Stewart Polshek: Context and Responsibility*, published by Rizzoli International
in 1988.)

Standardized methods for designing, blanketly applied across all projects, are
not recommended. They may be effective at demonstrating minimal competence
(i.e., at protecting the safety and welfare of occupants, and will help to pass the state
licensing exam), but they also may limit possibilities, or worse, rigid methodology

may inhibit brilliance. *The Take-Home Message is that all factors affecting design (programmatic, site, technical, and aesthetic, and all that these imply) must be weighed and brought together in a mutually reinforcing poetic balance.* Therefore, the following sections continue to lay out key ingredients for *facilitating* design rather than prescribing a specific formula.

Examples of Organizing Elements

Development of a *circulation system*, that is, moving through the building, is a powerful means of ordering and linking the programmed spaces on the site. *The program and site analyses will give strong clues about the formal nature of the circulation patterns.* For example, a linear scheme (a path to which spaces, including open spaces, are connected) may offer a real richness for serial development, clarity, and hierarchy in accessing spaces, and allow for easy future expansion. There are many ways of conceptualizing the linear idea, including the spine, axis, indoor street, and sequential path (i.e., one that is curved or angled)—with alternatives and permutations (i.e., parallel, perpendicular, and secondary routes). All of the aforementioned may accommodate a number of special events and contribute quite a bit of variation along the way. Relating functions to the path can establish focal points, or areas of real importance. An axis terminating in a distinctive way can have tremendous impact. An example is the stair in the Sainsbury Wing, the new addition to London's National Gallery (by Venturi, Scott Brown & Associates). Paul Goldberger (*The New York Times*, May 17, 1992) describes its function beyond just circulation: "The stair widens as it rises, as if opening up to the art to be found at its top, and as we climb there is a real sense of mounting toward a goal, of aspiring . . . the stair [is] not merely a part of the mechanical process of circulation but a potent symbol of pilgrimage toward art."

In any case, easily perceived circulation is essential to orient the user (especially for very large scale projects such as hospitals or shopping malls) and provide information about how the building functions. There should be natural cues built in to the architecture; a good test I invoke is whether lots of signage is required to identify the building from the outside and to know how to proceed on the inside. If the answer is, "Yes, I need all sorts of arrows and direction," there may be a fundamental problem with the essential images and the order of the building. One additional note: The most efficient buildings are those with the minimum amount of area dedicated to circulation (this of course depends on the building type)—be judicious in optimizing area and concept.

Integration of all building systems should be a logical outgrowth and reinforcement of the basic concept and organizing elements. This adds real power, meaning, and effectiveness to the architectural concept. Returning to our linear circulation example, the structural system could align on both sides of the circulation, and mechanical and electrical systems could have major distribution trunks following the circulation as well. These strategies are potentially very buildable and efficient. Further, as a high-use and high-visibility element, circulation would be an ideal place to focus design attention and budget, a place to revel in the purpose of the project. Be creative here! Use all site factors to full advantage (i.e., daylighting, views); be opportunistic about programming issues (i.e., what functions can spill, mix, or take advantage in some way of this amenity?). Some of the early work of Kallmann and

McKinnell (now Kallmann, McKinnell & Wood), specifically the Physical Education Facilities at Phillips Exeter Academy, highlights movement systems as the essence of building organization.

Another form of linear circulation, *the grid*, can also be a helpful planning and organizing element. The time-honored basis for the layout of numerous cities and villages, there is much precedent for its use. The work of Mies van der Rohe is infused with reverence for the grid in three dimensions. See Supplement 4-11 for a view of the grid as a basis for structural planning.

The tradition of utilizing *a major central space*, the core around which other spaces are organized, is another long-standing approach to ordering the program. When surrounded by functions or circulation on all sides, obviously it becomes an inwardly focused element (an oasis in a tough context?). Natural light and air can pour into the space, greatly affecting those around it. Examples include atria, lobbies, and courtyards. Application of the central space idea along with other forms of circulation are common. Some contemporary examples include the Ford Foundation in New York by Kevin Roche John Dinkeloo & Associates, and many of the Hyatt hotels by John Portman and Associates.

Other common organizational devices include *radial patterns, dispersion schemes* (where program elements are separated across a site), *doughnut- or racetrack-shaped schemes*, and the idea of *hierarchy* (where most spaces are assigned a hierarchical priority or weight, i.e., convenient location and/or special form for heavy public use, and higher floor and/or more regular pattern for private use).

Experiment with refinement of bubble diagrams on the site plan. Joining spaces of comparable scale and like function may present a most efficient and buildable scheme. At the very least, structural and mechanical system integration would be greatly facilitated. In some instances the fact that massing reflects this special pattern of internal functions or systems may result in an interesting visual representation of the program. This fact may be used to spur full investigation of three-dimensional potential.

These may be helpful *starting points only* for initial planning, again perhaps to be mixed, matched, and otherwise messed with. The key is to be in constant touch with the collection of program and site data as identified in Chapters 2 and 3. As Jerry Weisman alluded to in Supplement 2-8, design is not necessarily simply a question of finding the one big formal idea (although *sometimes* it might be), superimposing it on the site, and squeezing-in the functions. Creating order, delight, and a sense of place out of a great deal of important information and resolving a myriad of conflicts is the big challenge.

Three-Dimensional Considerations

Architecture (like dreaming) is experienced in full color and in all three dimensions. As a result, from the first doodles on napkins (or yellow trace), there should be a keen awareness of three-dimensional qualities related to general space organization. Dynamic three-dimensional sculptural spaces (consistent, of course, with project mandates) are part of what makes the whole of architecture something greater than the sum of its parts. There is a magnetism, a unique force of attraction to engage buildings with this kind of inherent volumetric spatial interest. Often, these spaces serve as the focus for the project. Moreover, three-dimensional solutions may be the optimal means of achieving certain functional relationships.

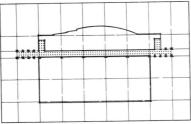

Circulation

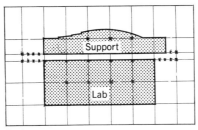

Enclosure

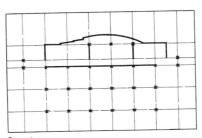

Structure

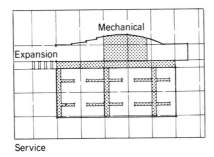

Service

FIGURE 4-1 *This series of diagrams (coupled with those in Figure 3-5) forms a study of basic issues of site, circulation, enclosure, structure, and mechanical systems of Fluke Hall at the University of Washington. Integration of these issues is resolved to form a basis of functional integrity. © Copyright NBBJ, David C. Hoedemaker, Rick Buckley, designers.*

FIGURE 4-2   *Pennzoil Place in Houston, Texas, by Johnson/Burgee Architects elevates the simple grid to dynamic sheets of sculptural mosaics. Photo by the author.*

In considering the program and site, always look for occasions to develop three-dimensional relationships. Examples include lobbies with visual access to mezzanine functions; light scoops for bringing daylight deep into interiors; monumental spaces for *really special* civic impact; and bridges and overlooks traversing double-height (or greater) volumes. At the larger "room" scale, the same thinking applies: Should there be differences in ceiling heights (perhaps reinforced by artificial lighting, i.e., lower over workstations for more direct light and intimacy, and higher over circulation for diffuse light and more public scale), or floor-height changes (i.e., raised or sunken levels to help zone activities, etc.)? All the answers to these questions regarding interior volumes and exterior massing are very likely to give further direction and meaning to the appearance of elevations.

Take-Home Message: In developing designs, it is necessary to think in cross section as well as in plan. It is worth reiterating the value of amplifying the experience of soaring space, with the qualification that this tactic is relevant to the project aims. For example, an intentionally constricting, dim corridor leading to an airy open space will generate more emotion than a progression with less contrast.

The idea of *enclosure* to capture space is relevant here. It serves to define an area—both outdoors and indoors, up and down. It can be achieved by a minimum of means; from a simple beam to a solid wall . . . degrees of openness, flowing space, or tight, confined space are all within control of the designer.

A typical beginning-student mistake is to address successfully the space planning/functional aspects, neatly laid out on the site. The two-dimensional scheme is then simply lifted up, with varied roof heights as a function of internal space requirements (recall that Charles Linn alluded to this common error in Supplement 1-2). This might get you a comfortable "pass" on the licensing exam design problem, but cannot be considered an elegant *architectural* solution; it's your basic three-dimensional *diagram*. The flaw is in thinking in plan only.

History

In a column on an exhibit of the work of McKim, Mead & White, the famed and prolific turn-of-the-century New York architectural firm, Paul Goldberger (*The New*

FIGURE 4-3 *Here is an example of a great central space (the family room) which serves as the focal point of the design for this 6500-square-foot house. The skylit, double-height volume is ringed by a second-story bridge connecting master bedroom suite in one wing to the childrens' bedrooms in another. Design by the author with Raymond Novitske, Associated Architect; photo © Dan Forer.*

York Times, August 18, 1991) wrote: "These architects looked to history not for something to copy, but for inspiration; . . . [to] spark creativity." Analyzing, understanding, interpreting, and finally invoking ideas from the past can facilitate arriving at design solutions in the present. For example, as Roger Kimball illustrates in the October 1991 *Architectural Record*, Louis Kahn mapped history to contemporary needs. The galleries of the Kimbell Art Museum are traditional in concept but contemporary in execution and feeling. Kahn's design of the Yale Center for British Art is arrayed about "courtyards with commercial rental space on the ground floor, and is reminiscent of traditional Italian Renaissance townhouses." Kimball goes on to proclaim that "nothing could be more contemporary in its use of materials, disposition of light, and ambiance than that elegant urban museum."

FIGURE 4-4 *This is an example of a low-budget, small-scale project where some three-dimensional quality was sought out and developed. The lobby and mezzanine/conference core of this factory for a sailmaker in Falmouth, ME, bisects large work bays and received the most design attention. The mass of a scissors truss was expressed above the mezzanine, where the conference area was set back to create a deck overlooking the lobby below. The concept was to create a focus for the lobby and to enhance perception of a discrete volume and special place above the first floor. Design and drawing by the author.*

SUPPLEMENT 4-1: "Why is it important to 'know history' in the design studio," I asked Lydia M. Soo, an Assistant Professor at The Ohio State University. Professor Soo received her Ph.D. in History and Theory of Architecture from Princeton University and an M.Arch. from the University of Illinois at Urbana–Champaign.

Since the end of Modernism, with the renewed recognition of the evolutionary and self-referential nature of the discipline, schools no longer deny the importance of the history of architecture in the design studio. What continues to elude teachers and students, however, is how a knowledge of history can be applied directly to design. The traditional survey of the history of architecture from ancient to recent times, presenting buildings in relationship to the cultures that made them, does have value for students by contributing to their liberal education and by developing their sensibility for what quality is and how it is created. The "historian's approach," however, is in itself insufficient for providing tools of design. Following an introductory survey, the student, whether or not within the context of a course, must approach past buildings in a highly focused analytical and conceptual manner, that is, using the "architect's approach" found in the kind of "history" books written by Robert Venturi and others. By understanding past buildings in terms of typological lessons of form, space, light, circulation, structure, material, technology, and so forth, the student can create a repertory of ideas that he or she can draw from during design. When understood as a lesson in design, the most bygone and dusty building, barely noticed by the student in history class, can have immediate relevance.

After receiving a design problem, a simple way for a student to incorporate history into his or her work is to collect and analyze past examples of the same building type. During the design process how the student chooses to apply conceptual ideas from these works or any others, whether consciously as a theoretical argument or subconsciously as a source of inspiration, depends on his or her own personal values. Many students, however, in the tradition of Gropius and the other Modernists, prefer not to know history, arguing that preconceptions will form in their minds that will inhibit the creation of a pure and original solution. Modernism, with its classical compositional techniques, has proven that this attempt to deny our past is hopeless and meaningless. Instead of understanding the history of architecture less, students should understand it more, gain control over its inevitable influence, and use it. The same can be said for other aspects of architecture and even disciplines that exist completely outside it which excite the student. Whether or not they can be applied directly to design, wide-ranging interests and experiences ultimately are valuable in the design studio. They, along with a knowledge of the history of architecture, promote the kind of broadmindedness and sensitivity essential to the creation of buildings that end up in history books.

Aesthetic Issues

"I believe in an 'emotional architecture.' It is very important for human kind that architecture should move by its beauty; if there are many equally valid technical solutions to a problem, the one which offers the user a message of beauty and emotion, that one is architecture."
—Luis Barragan

"Architects need to see the building as part of a complex society. But a building is not socially responsible unless it is very beautiful."—James Stewart Polshek

In a discussion of aesthetics, Strunk and White, in the famous little book *The Elements of Style*, describe some universals applicable to visual qualities of buildings: "Here we leave solid ground. Who can confidently say what ignites a certain combination of [forms], causing them to explode in the mind? Who knows why certain notes in music are capable of stirring the listener deeply, though the same notes slightly rearranged are impotent? These are high mysteries. . . ." *The Take-Home Message: Indeed, there are no rules for creating beauty (and be wary of those who compulsively claim otherwise).*

Understand that much of the aesthetic expression, including massing and basic form making, materials selection, and elevation development cannot be thought about independently; it may result from a wide range of issues, already integrated into the design process from the program and site analyses. For example, adjacent buildings may have a huge impact in an urban context on specific elevation detailing. A concept related to technological or structural systems may dictate an aesthetic direction. Or if there is rationale for historical allusion, certainly aesthetic criteria will be derived from that viewpoint. And obviously, basic form has (at least) something to do with the programmed activity within.

Following is an elementary/partial list of factors (in no particular order) that can be considered and manipulated in support of design concepts. Note also that the way in which they are manipulated (as Strunk and White point out) reveal something of the spirit, the expression of the self.

To introduce the list, let me restate that *facts of site and program will suggest design features*. Some clarifying examples: Overhangs, light shelves, or other shading devices to control the sun are very visible parts of the design that can impart richness and beauty to an elevation while simultaneously solving a problem. A projecting bay window might be selected to provide views up and down a street in order to maximize observation of children at play; hence, a potentially dynamic three-dimensional *aesthetic* feature results from a programmatic requirement.

• Scale is an important factor in imagining and designing interior space and exterior massing. It is generally defined as size in relationship to human proportion. Scale can be controlled to reinforce concepts (i.e., grand—to express power or monumentality, or small—to encourage intimacy).

There are various techniques to break down the scale of huge spaces which may be dictated by the program. Articulation of building components or materials, even changes in color for example, can give human scale to a big blank wall. Conversely, overscaling may be a desirable tactic: Larger-than-ordinary windows for a fire station in a residential neighborhood can serve to reduce perception of overall building size, and thus relate better to adjacent housing.

A subcategory of scale may be considered as anthropometrics/ergonomics, or the relationship of human body measurements and performance capabilities to the environments in which specific tasks must be accomplished. This field documents norms or the typical case but becomes crucial when studying how well varied groups or individuals with exceptional characteristics function in a particular space. Young children, the elderly, those who use wheelchairs, even persons of different ethnic origin may exhibit anthropometric/ergonomic variations that will have an impact on configuration and sizing of architectural elements.

• Proportion is an index of the concordance of various parts to each other. Leonardo da Vinci, Vitruvius, and Le Corbusier, among others, have devised theories of proportions based on the human form that could be applied to buildings to create beauty. And there are other mathematical approaches, including the "golden section." Be sure to consider beauty and harmony of the building components as a *part* of the greater surroundings.

I think it is quite salient to quote from John Dixon's July 1976 Editorial in *Progressive Architecture* on the work of the brilliant Finnish architect Alvar Aalto: "Above all, Aalto demonstrated . . . in all of his buildings—***design determined by human experience rather than mere abstraction***: the changes in ceiling height that signaled degrees of privacy, the windows placed for the view rather than the formal pattern . . . the handrail shaped for a satisfying grip." [Italics/emphasis by the author.]

• Light and shadow can be used to articulate or amplify forms (i.e., projecting window jambs on elevations produce shadows, creating a sense of depth and emphasis on verticality).

• Perspective conveys depth and distance [i.e., angled walls (in two and/or three dimensions) can seemingly elongate or foreshorten distances].

• Ornament suggests a beautifying accessory that can also be part of an intentionally expressed building system (celebrating the inherent aesthetic of a construction technology), or perhaps some applied decoration (i.e., a stage set to evoke whimsical imagery).

• Focus is a quality that is important in virtually all design disciplines: It crystallizes and draws attention to the most important aspect(s) of a scheme. The focus of a building could be a major public entry, or a main central space—your concept will clarify its application and expression. Special massing, scale, materials, lighting, orientation, and so on, might be used by the designer to reinforce the focus as an important node in the building.

• Visual coherence of all building forms or materials has to do with achieving the sense of harmony. Some unifying thread weaving together disparate parts (if indeed there are disparate parts) should be sought. A frequent occurrence in student projects is a form that appears tacked-on, almost as an afterthought, a three-dimensionally unresolved, discordant piece of the program. Be careful, try to avoid this; usually it is a symptom of too much plan emphasis.

• Symmetry/asymmetry are terms that describe arrangements on either side of an axis or center. Symmetry implies a very formal order, whereas asymmetry is less formal and potentially more dynamic. Subtle manipulations in an asymmetrical framework can produce interesting results. For example, the Barcelona Pavilion, designed by Mies van der Rohe, epitomizes the beauty of an asymmetric balance in forms and materials. Look to your program and concept for applicability. (The investigation of symmetry/asymmetry from several viewpoints—perception/physiological psychology, cultural anthropology and semiology, and traditional analysis of visual art—can be a fascinating and worthwhile study.)

• Contrast/blending are ideas that have been discussed in Chapter 3 in relation to italicizing the best characteristics of both the site and the structure. The principles apply at the building scale as well. For example, consider *blending* in a dense urban site where buildings are tight on either side; the front faces a major street, the back is open to a court. One response might be to pick up the hard edges and solid forms along the street, while the back facade loosens up with softer and more open forms. H. H. Richardson's Glessner House in Chicago exemplifies this strategy, at least in the sense that a fortresslike front facade gives way to an open, almost delicately articulated rear courtyard. In *contrast*, the new I. M. Pei–designed entry pyramid at the Louvre in Paris employs the converse strategy with its glazed skin in sharp opposition to surrounding classical forms and textures.

• Rhythm is the cadence of some kind of design theme at a building or detail scale (i.e., fenestration, exposed structure, or material) in some kind of regular pattern or modulation. Varying the pattern of a particular rhythmic scheme may reinforce a concept or highlight a feature. Expanding or contracting the space between recurring elements can add novelty while preserving the rhythmic scheme.

• Variety is the "spice of life"; avoid boring, arbitrary themes. This is not to say that more neutral or "background" buildings do not represent good architecture given certain conditions. But even if this type of building is appropriate, there must be *something* very special about it: Perhaps in its craft or detailing, or in some aspect that imbues it with the forces of magic and spirit.

Brainstorming Tips

• Assume that your project *will be built*. This kind of a mind game will ensure your personal investment that is so important in designing. You should get a great big kick out of your own work!

In his seminal text on environmental planning, John Simonds implores us to bring drawings alive—imagine yourself as not just one typical building user, but *each type*—from a maintenance person, to a manager, to a CEO, to the public—imagine how each actor would specifically do his/her job or experience the project. In this fashion, your sketches and design do come to life.

• Remain open to new ideas [i.e., sketch freely and copiously (in the words of Graham Williams, A.I.A., one of my mentors, SKETCH, SKETCH, SKETCH!)]. Generate as many rough, unbridled, unconventional (*and* conventional) ideas as possible. Fight against the natural tendency to erase—use overlays—you may want to retrieve an idea later. I always encourage students to draw through at least half a roll of 12-inch yellow trace for each class period in the first stages of a project. Extra credit for using an entire roll!

• Trial, error, and refinement is an old dictum that constitutes a fine strategy for stimulating creativity. Sometimes, design decisions end up as arbitrary, and you need a starting point from which to jump in. (Remember: For the most part, all design decisions should be accountable.) So just put marker on trace and record **all** ideas. They're a basis for further exploration and discussion.

• Resolve conflicts in *all* dimensions. In a July 21, 1991 article in *The New York Times*, Wendy Steiner wrote: "The essence of the architectural task [is] switching back and forth between two- and three-dimensional conception." Modify an element in plan, then see what happens in section and model (or perspective), and vice versa.

• Embrace failure and mistakes! Ideas that don't work can provide some of the most useful information and motivation to innovate.

• Frugality can come at later stages of design. It is not necessary to employ every design feature ever learned simultaneously—but now is the time to try something if the urge is upon you. Edit *after* desk critiques.

• View specific problems as unique assets. For example, in a renovation there is an existing structural column in the middle of an important space that seemingly disrupts the space. Attempt to *highlight* it—put glow-in-the-dark pink tiles on it; add another (nonstructural) matching column to create a gateway, or set up a circulation path, or create a focus or support core.

• There are always going to be conflicting needs; it takes time and experimentation to test possible outcomes for spatial relationships to evolve in accordance with the design concept or theme. If, however, it appears that too much revision is required, be prepared (and willing) to start anew. *The time has not been wasted*; the exercise usually results in a deeper knowledge and understanding of the project.

• If frozen, work on an unrelated task; come back to the problem at a later time from a different perspective. Isolate the problem; do more research, become more informed about it; return to the site; visit or read about a related and architecturally significant work. Try changing drawing scales or media (if drawing, build a quick-and-dirty model, and vice versa). As always, talk to colleagues and instructors.

• Most important, *develop the habit of being confident, assume success, and enjoy the process.*

Common Mistakes

• Many times a student believes that he/she has such an incredibly good singular idea that it must be carried through to the final design. Infatuation should not get in the way of the larger goals, and openness to alternatives (perhaps equally infatuating but very different) is the mark of experience. EXPLORE ALTERNATIVES! REVISE! Clients often change their minds midway through a project, or have different design ideas, or simply might not like what you've done for no apparent or logical reason. You must learn to be enthusiastic about developing other schemes and responding to new input.

• Avoid the "tail wagging the dog" syndrome. No one feature should be that precious; do not let an impressive detail dominate decision making.

• I've seen student projects where there are *lots* of terrific ideas and concepts. This can be problematic: When too many things are happening simultaneously, there is no one strong point of view. Do not *dilute* a good, solid concept.

• Obscure references and concepts that are so personal or that can only be perceived by an elite few are not in the public interest and bring into question the role of the professional. But this must be qualified: Sometimes, depending on the circumstances, there may be a good reason for being less than totally clear or explicit. One cannot script or predict personal reactions to art—this certainly encompasses the artful aspects of any architectural work. Do make sure that any intentional allusions in the architecture have *significant objective meaning*. Moreover, ideas must be understood in three-dimensional reality—buildings are not experienced in eighth scale, in plan, on the drawing board.

• Some students feel that whatever is drawn must be perfect—this couldn't be a more inhibiting and destructive belief at the first stages of design. LOOSEN UP!

• Many experienced designers, not to mention students, feel insecure during the creative process. This is natural, there is always the question of whether you'll come through with the brilliant final product as expected. If you're one of the many who share these feelings, acknowledge and accept that this is the way you operate, and with a systematic approach, perseverance, and experience you will gradually learn that there is really little question about the outcome.

• Remind yourself that architecture supports or ideally facilitates activity; it is not the end in itself. With a focus on building form rather than the bigger picture of place making, it is easy to lose sight of the goal; for example, a museum's exhibition space may be such spectacular sculpture itself that it overpowers the artwork it is designed to display. At the same time, do not be too timid or weak; I know this sounds contradictory, but I'm just laying out the issues you must learn to balance!

• At reviews, critics ask students, "Why did you make that particular design move?" And I cringe when I hear the response, "Because I like it." I cannot overemphasize the value of a thoughtful reason behind important design decisions, even those involving more subjective issues of "taste."

• Outdoor spaces that are "left over" from the building mass are another common occurrence. See Lawrence Halprin's Supplement 3-1.

TOOLS

The following discussion of tools (drawings, models, and computers) identifies some options for facilitating the design process. Presentation tools are discussed in Chapter 5. Like the process itself, the choice of what to use is quite personal. There are advantages and disadvantages of each tool, and usually students play with a combination of all three at different stages of design, or simultaneously—as in going back and forth from two to three dimensions. Architect Steven Canter, quoted in the August 1991 issue of *Architecture*, says, "The best approach is to use whatever tool is best suited for each part of the job."

Again there are no rules; initially, use what's comfortable. It is also important to experiment and develop expertise in a variety of modes. As language is central to thinking and communicating verbally, so too are graphic and visual tools central to thinking and communicating three-dimensional form. If you can't dream it and communicate it, it can't happen.

Select the appropriate scale in which to work. This is really a critically important decision (and depends on the specific project)—too large a scale can make early conceptualizing extraordinarily difficult. Start with the site plan scale (typically, 1 inch = 40 feet or 1 inch = 20 feet) for diagrammatic layouts, sections, context/massing relationships. Work up to $\frac{1}{16}$ inch = 1 foot, and as the project becomes more resolved, use $\frac{1}{8}$ inch = 1 foot for buildings in the range 10,000 to 15,000 square feet. Scales of $\frac{1}{4}$ or $\frac{1}{2}$ inch are required to study interiors with any detail in models and drawings. Consider looking at important pieces of the building at the larger scales. The bigger the scale (and size of drawing or model), the more detail needs to be shown and, of course, the more time it takes.

Whatever tools you may be using, and this applies to presentation graphics as well, should communicate expeditiously, that is, *not waste valuable design time.* For example, a student used four hours to meticulously crosshatch walls in a plan and section to make them read easily at a distance. The same task could have been accomplished in a fraction of the time with, say, a few strokes of thick, dark marker. Remember the importance of time management and the priority of maximizing design time. (Refer to Ernest Burden's valuable Supplement 5-1 for timesaving tips and for advice on producing professional-quality graphics.)

Take-Home Message: Use the tool in the beginning stages of a design project that helps you focus best on three-dimensional imagination and abstract thinking.

Drawings

Just in the way that the smell of sawdust from freshly cut wood and exposed steel, conduit, and ducts at a construction site holds a raw sensual appeal, the feeling of soft pencil (or fat markers) on canary trace is *almost* an end in itself. There should be an inherent pleasure—a melange of tactile, visual, and auditory stimuli that invite you to continue drawing or pursuing your medium of choice.

The instruments are simple and inexpensive: Pens, markers, pencils (with or without color), and paper—from sketchbooks to trace, and of course napkins on airplanes (for architects such as I. M. Pei) or napkins on Greyhound buses (for students and sole proprietors), where some of the best ideas are drawn.

Freehand versus hard-line (use of parallel rule and triangles) is another choice. The mechanical drawing wizards in high school will be inclined to rely on the hard-line approach; that's okay, but as I mentioned, learn to be proficient with all techniques. To me, there's a certain consistency to freehand sketches in early designs—there's an appropriate ambiguity to the lines; things aren't resolved to a high degree conceptually, so why should they be graphically? Hard-line drawings imply a precision that may not be intended by the designer. However, some students find the use of straight edges liberating, and that kind of assertion cannot be disputed. Choice may even be a function of the design concept (see Figure 4-7).

William Kirby Lockard, in his exceptional book, *Drawing as a Means to Architecture*, states: "Perspective is the most natural way of drawing space, since it is how we see space; . . . . . The experience of a building is an infinite number of perspectives." Lockard believes that designs should be *studied* in perspective, not just in plan, section, and elevation.

Axonometrics or isometrics produce distorted three-dimensional images of space and are therefore limited in *conveying a feeling of reality*. They are simple to draw, and as aerial views, may be useful for assessing and developing massing potentials. In general, their application may best be suited to studying construction details at a large scale, for example, wall sections.

> *SUPPLEMENT 4-2:* In this Supplement, William Kirby Lockard, F.A.I.A., captures the essence of drawing as a potent, yet accessible tool in the design studio. His books, including *Design Drawing*, have helped and will continue to assist thousands of architecture students in developing and enjoying this fundamental skill. In addition to teaching at the University of Arizona, Professor Lockard has his own practice in Tucson.
>
> The design studio experience is arguably the finest form of education. To be asked for your individual response to a complex human problem, to have an opportunity to test and improve your ideas in open discussion, to bring them to a final synthesis and defend them intellectually, knowing there are no absolute solutions, is one of the highest uses of human intelligence. You can get a Ph.D. in many disciplines without being expected to be similarly creative or responsible.

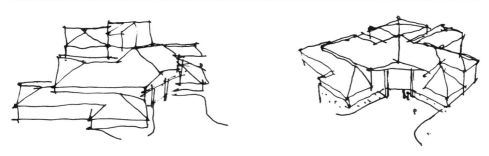

FIGURE 4-5 *Two sketches of the exterior of a house help to gain a sense of its massing. The views are looking down to help visualize the entire form at a glance. Design and drawings by the author.*

FIGURE 4-6 *This is a very precise interior perspective, used to both analyze the appearance of the "floating" ceiling and convey the feeling of experiencing the space for the client. The drawing attempts to approximate a photographic view, although the emphasis is on forms rather than detail. Design and drawing by the author.*

FIGURE 4-7 *The style of this rendering of a museum complex in Finland was chosen to relate to the arctic circle site. Etched into the snowy expanse, the complex is intended to resonate with the environment as much as it exemplifies the Finn's capacity for assertiveness in the face of natural extremes. Design and drawing by the author.*

One source of frustration and humiliation in beginning design studios, however, is the tacit assumption that students have had an equal opportunity to develop all the abilities needed to generate and communicate their design ideas. Students are usually asked to present their ideas for discussion and evaluation in what may be for them a foreign language—*drawing*. Students may have had twelve years of instruction in English, math, science, and social studies, but to assume they have had anything like an adequate or equal background in visual or graphic abilities is nonsense. Even if students have had a background in drawing, it probably will have been as either art or drafting, neither of which teaches using drawing as a tool for creating and testing design ideas. Beginning students may mistakenly believe that drawing is a matter of talent, and that its primary purpose is to present or "sell" whatever they design. Design students need to learn early how closely and beneficially drawing can be related to the design process, and that it is absolutely learnable.

Drawing is for the environmental designer what a piano is for a composer; not primarily for performance, for the composition may be for other instruments, but for composers to play and hear their musical ideas and improve them. Until designers can represent or "play" the ideas they are developing for themselves and for their teachers with all the tonal dimensions music involves, they will be limited to single-finger melodies and single-dimension responses from their teachers, but that mustn't keep them from undertaking the learning of the playback instrument.

Unfortunately, students' ideas are inevitably judged from their drawings, and while it is impossible not to be influenced by the eloquence of the drawings, most design teachers try to look through the drawings to the ideas they represent. It is most important that students learn to look through their own drawings in a similar way, accepting their drawing ability for the moment and never letting the fact that others in the studio draw better than they, keep them from drawing. Early design studios should help students learn to accept, like, and believe their own drawings.

If you are fortunate, your school still teaches drawing. If not, you will have to undertake the learning on your own, but there are many good books on drawing, and if asked, most of your design teachers will be glad to constructively criticize your drawings in the studio. You also have quite a while to learn, something like eight years, because it can continue through your apprenticeship, and should continue as long as you are an architect. Remember that drawing ability is not a genetic accident or providential gift but, in every case I know of, a clearly learned behavior.

In addition to confirming that drawing is learnable, early design studios should lead you to experience the power of drawing as a creative tool. You should learn to draw expectantly, showing your mind the problems, relationships, and opportunities in your drawings. The best proof of this role for drawing in the design process is that as you draw up your very first studio presentation—making some of those drawings for the first time—you will see, in your drawings, many opportunities you literally hadn't seen before—and will probably actually solve some of your problems in the process of drawing. How much better your solution could have been if you had shown your design mind those problems earlier. The best drawings are never those final presentation masterpieces hanging on the wall, but the ones that showed you the opportunities for improving your ideas, and are now crumpled in the wastebasket.

Models

Study models, those that are quick, dirty, and can be ripped apart with ease, are invaluable aids in developing and testing three-dimensional ideas. In fact, the models I admire the most look like they've been targeted by smart bombs, they have so many rips, tears, and changes. William Lam, the award-winning and much publicized lighting designer who has taught at M.I.T. and Harvard, offers some common sense advice to students: "Build a model, hold it up to the window, then the faculty doesn't have to speculate about the lighting effects for 20 minutes!" (See his Supplement 4-13.)

My preference is chipboard, Elmer's glue, and Spray Mount. Chipboard or illustration board can be cut easily with a mat knife or scissors, and the white glue sets very quickly. A useful technique that I use follows: (1) Trace the preliminary design—floor plans and elevations. (2) Roughly cut out the tracings with a scissors. (3) Purchase a can of Spray Mount—spray the adhesive on the back of the tracings, and set them on the chipboard. (4) Cut the chipboard following the lines on the tracings, and *voilà*, you have the major pieces of the model.

Now the real fun begins. After assembling the parts or some of the parts—you may want to leave one side open or have the capability to lift off roof or floors to see what's happening inside on larger-scale models—experimenting is unbelievably easy. Use scraps of cardboard to test, develop, and manipulate new forms and sculpt three-dimensional space; cut away part of a floor, and perhaps glue only a small piece of it back. Get some pieces of balsa wood or cut cardboard strips to simulate beams or columns, or build structural components (i.e., trusses). Buy empty plastic bottles from a drugstore in cylindrical or square shapes—cut them in half to create a vaulted skylight or bay window; do the same with a table tennis ball and you have a small dome—there are many ways to create your own rough model kit of parts!

Return to the floor plan or section, make an adjustment, and see what the implications are in the model (and vice versa). Cut and paste freely—the glue (or tape) makes it simple and quick. Remember to keep the context in mind, even at the large building scale.

Clay is another effective model material. Its application, though, is limited to studying exterior massing in small scale. The material is so plastic that the advantages in molding things are obvious. Lego or any modular childrens' building blocks are also good for the study of massing and give you an excuse to regress in service of the ego (i.e., have fun). (Refer to Supplement 5-4 on supplies.)

There are always stories about architectural firms that don't build models, that it just takes too long, that they don't want to waste precious billable time, and so on. These are the firms you don't want to work for! It's nonsense (although some projects don't lend themselves to models, i.e., purely interior space planning). Study models can be built very quickly, are great props for clients who can use them to demystify two-dimensional drawings (they can be touched and are interactive), and most important, help the architect visualize and maximize three-dimensional potential during the design process.

Another added benefit to building a model is to generate many perspectives through photography. Slides of study models can be projected to block out an infinite number of views (at any size), from flybys to worm's-eye, to the most important: Eye level. Detail can then be added efficiently by drawing rather than building this into the model. *Tip 1*: Add some scaled grid lines on/in the model prior to photographing; this will aid in sketching more accurately. *Tip 2*: Place the model on the site plan (at the same scale, of course); this helps to draw-in part of the context (i.e., roads, sidewalks, curbs, etc.).

Use a fast film for the smallest-aperture setting to maximize depth of field (so that most of the model is in focus). If photographing a model interior, minimum scale is about $\frac{1}{4}$ inch; $\frac{1}{2}$ inch is best—so you can fit the lens inside. Exterior views can be shot easily at smaller scales as well. (See photographer Norman McGrath's Supplement 5-5 on photographing presentation models.)

You may want to attempt to utilize a slide of the context superimposed on a slide of the model (taken from roughly the same point of view), as a base for blocking out a quick and accurate rendering of the building *and* its surroundings.

FIGURE 4-8 *Here are two examples of exterior massing models. They have been pulled apart and put back together on numerous occasions during design, and still functioned as essential parts of client presentations. Designs and models by the author.*

FIGURE 4-9 *These quick study models of interior spaces, even though quite crude (with a few light leaks), are very effective at simulating the impact of daylighting. The scale was $\frac{1}{2}$ inch = 1 foot for each model. The use of scale elements (such as people and furniture) adds considerably to the overall perception, particularly by nonarchitects. Designs and models by the author.*

Computers

Steven Canter, again quoted from *Architecture*, states: "It's inappropriate to be a slave to the computer's absolute precision. You don't need it to the same degree at every stage in a project . . . you need to know when and where [computers] are appropriate." In an article in the September 1991 issue of *Progressive Architecture*, Dennis Neeley feels that "advancements are coming faster than the schools are reacting. Every student should have a computer: It is the parallel bar of the future." This may be an extreme view at this time, but there is no arguing about the potential power of the computer for the beginning student.

Mark Roth, Information Center Manager and Introduction to Computers in Architecture course instructor at the University of Wisconsin–Milwaukee, cautions that with current software, much of a student's attention is focused on how to manipulate objects in three dimensions rather than on designing. Moreover, with a computer, it is difficult to be conceptual with the loose forms that are so easily and quickly sketched on trace. He recommends course work in Autocad or other drafting software, not only as an adjunct to design studios but simply to increase marketability upon graduation.

SUPPLEMENT 4-3: Kent Larson is a partner with Peter L. Gluck and Partners, Architects in New York City. He uses the computer as a design and presentation tool and has written frequently on the subject for *Progressive Architecture* and *Architectural Record*. Mr. Larson adapted this Supplement from an article that appeared in the October 1991 issue of *Progressive Architecture*.

COMPUTER MODELING AS A DESIGN TOOL

Why has computer graphics become such an essential tool for scientists, film animators, and even graphic artists, while architects still find it controversial—and very few use it for design?

There are many reasons: Senior architects and design faculty are often uncomfortable with the technology (most used slide rules in college), access is limited (computers are locked in labs just as books were chained to desks in the Middle Ages), other media are available (drawings and models have served architects well for thousands of years), images are crude (few architects have produced compelling computer images), and fees are low (George Lucas's animators work on systems costing in the six digits, whereas architects settle for relatively primitive Macs and PCs).

But the main reason may be that we have not decided how to use the technology. Is it for developing design?, visualizing design?, documenting ideas?, presenting to clients?, presenting to the architectural community?, simulating lighting and materials?, simulating movement through space?, or simply to replace the pencil in the contract document process? The techniques and tools required for each task may be very different.

Conceptual Design

It is unlikely that computers will soon replace the pencil as a tool to rough out conceptual design ideas. Freehand sketches are very efficient—a few simple lines can imply much more than is actually on the paper. A powerful modeling program is often more of a barrier than a help in the process of trying out ideas. Computers require precision and coordinates, and an inexperienced designer using a computer is tempted to incorporate an inappropriate level of detail to what should be a schematic study of major concepts. As systems become more intuitive, however, they will be useful earlier and earlier in the process.

Resolving Design Ideas

A computer model can be used much like a chipboard or clay model—but with several important differences. A physical model is a true three-dimensional representation of a building that exists in "real time" and space, allowing for a fairly accurate perception of form and relative scale. An image of a computer model is a two-dimensional abstraction that must be seen one view at a time, imposing a certain barrier to the perception of form. Most architects will agree that a physical model is easier to study than a computer model built to the same level of detail.

On the other hand, the computer model can be more easily revised, allowing for the generation of many alternatives. Changes or additions can be made quickly while viewing the model in plan, elevation, perspective, or isometric. It can also evolve as the design develops with an increasing level of detail, whereas a physical model must be reconstructed each time there are major changes. Pieces can be repeated, rotated, stretched, or compressed, and elements added or deleted instantly. This allows for the kind of careful fine tuning of detail and proportion that is not possible with a physical model. Which is better for developing design ideas? Experience will make it clear which media are best for which design problem. Often, both should be used simultaneously.

Visualization and Evaluation

Computer models are much better than hand drawings for the visualization of a developed design. Multiple perspectives, isometrics, and elevation views with a great deal of detail—can be produced more quickly and accurately. Although detailed physical models may be ideal for this purpose, rarely does an office or design student build a detailed scale model until the design is fairly set, and usually it is to present the scheme, not to understand it better. In most cases, computer models provide the designer with the ability to evaluate a design with greater accuracy and a higher degree of detail much earlier in the process.

Presentation: Artful Images

There is a long tradition of hand-crafted architectural drawings as art. Few architects or students have had access to the expensive and complex animation systems that are capable of producing beautiful and subtle (or photorealistic) images. Design faculty are understandably unimpressed by the crude and lifeless images produced by the CAD systems used by most schools and offices. As with any other media, it takes skill, experience, and access to the proper tools to produce good-quality work. Increasingly, pieces of the high-end technology used in the film industry will spin off into the hands of architects and students.

Simulation

Design students spend most of their time exploring basic issues of form, scale, adjacencies, and so on—traditional media are fine for this and computers will simply make it more efficient. Most students deal only superficially with the more subtle issues of how a space would be experienced. As sophisticated three-dimensional computer graphics systems become accessible, the complex play of light and materials in a space, and the experience of moving through it can be studied realistically, permitting a more profound evaluation of the proposal. This is perhaps the most exciting potential of the new technology.

Will this fundamentally change how design is studied and presented in schools? Eventually, this has to be the case, but only when schools find a way to give talented students unlimited access to state-of-the-art technology, with the support of interested and involved faculty.

CONSTRUCTION TECHNOLOGY

Since school projects focus on schematic design and rarely get built, there is a tendency among students to lose sight of the ostensible *raison d'être* of design: Getting work constructed. Knowledge of how buildings are assembled is obviously and critically important, but often overlooked in the most important beginning phases of the process.

FIGURE 4-10 *An example of a conceptual computer image of a religious school in Brooklyn. Courtesy of Peter L. Gluck & Partners Architects and Editel Graphics, New York.*

Designing in the studio removes the student (and architect) physically from the action of construction. Therefore, it is easy for the products of design—drawings and models—to become too much of an abstraction of reality; too much as ends in themselves. This situation is a problem; the *architectural design* process is meaningless and myopic without being truly and completely informed by the *construction* process. And as with all the other myriad of influences impacting design, awareness of the building industry and its practices can support and define design excellence. Always keep in mind what the piece of cardboard or the crosshatched wall really represents, how it is going to get to the site, who is going to put it in place, and how it will be joined to the adjacent component.

> *SUPPLEMENT 4-4*: I am especially pleased to introduce this next Supplement by Raymond A. Worley, Executive Vice President of Morse Diesel International. Morse Diesel International, founded in 1936, ranks among the largest U.S. construction firms. Raymond Worley, a forty-year industry veteran, oversaw construction of Chicago's Sears Tower, the world's tallest building.

BUILDING A FOUNDATION OF TEAMWORK

Every building project has three common elements: Goals, time, and money. Meeting the owner's programmatic objectives within the established schedule and budget

FIGURE 4-11 *There is real beauty to a construction work-in-progress. No wonder there are stylistic movements in the profession that promote and celebrate the expression and articulation of building components. Photo by the author.*

requires an understanding of the construction process as well as teamwork between the architect and the constructor.*

A successful project depends on the efficient utilization of materials, methods, and manpower to transform design into reality. The more thought the architect gives to this process, the more smoothly it will run.

In designing a project, the architect should examine the most challenging aspects first, allowing time to solve problems, order special materials, and assemble equipment and personnel. Consider how structural elements will meet. Two walls join—how? The flooring joists come together—where? The reality of construction will inevitably affect the aesthetics of design; plan accordingly.

Cost factors, too, have an impact on the realization of design. Achieving design intent within budget constraints takes pragmatic creativity. Currently, the catch phrase in cost management is "value engineering"—which is *not* synonymous with "cutting corners." Rather, it means determining what systems and materials will prove most cost-effective over the life, and for the purpose, of the project. For example, a bargain-priced HVAC system may need frequent, costly repairs, while a more expensive alternative may pay for itself in fuel efficiency. Spectacular illumination may play a critical role in establishing a building's identity, but expensive lighting fixtures in stairwells and machine rooms only burn money that could be used to better effect in public areas.

*Because so many terms describe contractual arrangements with the builder—general contractor, construction manager, and so on—we have elected to use the word *constructor* throughout this discussion.

The project construction team can offer valuable assistance in identifying opportunities for value engineering and other cost savings. Because constructors have daily, hands-on experience with purchasing, they know the latest materials and prices. Constructors can also help hold down the bottom line through scheduling techniques. A large part of any project budget lies in personnel requirements. By developing strategies to use time and personnel efficiently, the constructor can achieve significant savings.

Clearly, to make the most of these opportunities, the architect should involve the constructor early in the project. Teamwork is critical. All too often, the relationship between architect and constructor takes an adversarial tone. Yet the two are mutually dependent: The builder on the designer for concept, and the designer on the builder for execution. To work effectively together, both must recognize that expertise is found throughout the construction field, from heavy hitters in the architectural arena to heavy-equipment operators on the job site.

Only by working in concert can the team achieve the highest benefit for the project and the client. Only with teamwork can the architect and constructor manage the project's schedule and budget to reach the owner's goals.

Detailing

There is nothing like construction experience (for both students and architects), picking up a hammer, nails, working directly with materials, and attempting to follow details on the architect's plans to acquire a real sensitivity to the building trades. At least taking every opportunity to visit construction sites (and not just looking through the little holes cut in plywood barricades) is a step toward recognition of the complexities and fascination of building something.

The art of construction detailing (the way in which materials or components come together) is an important *design* task, but it is also the subject of another book. Development of details should be resonant with the initial concept, and informed by construction methods.

There are always going to be changes in the field, initiated either by contractors or clients. Therefore, details in general should be developed with a degree of tolerance so that inevitable minor changes will not diminish the architect's vision of the project. Selected details, however, will be so important in terms of the tasks performed or by virtue of aesthetic impact that they should not be compromised.

I believe that construction technology and detailing, to a large extent, is a subspecialty within the field of architecture. In the September 1991 issue of *Architecture*, George Heery states: "The construction technology frontier—where practical, cost-effective construction methodologies are to be found—lies with specialty subcontractors and building-product manufacturers, not with the architect, engineer, or even general contractor." It is the role of the architect to know where and how to get appropriate information, how to process and communicate it, and finally, to coordinate it with other construction trades. In other words, he/she must be an educated consumer. To accomplish this, the designer must possess a fundamental vocabulary in the language of building.

Bob Singleton, President of R.W. Singleton, Inc., builders in central Florida, believes that architects must somehow acquire field experience; a thorough appreciation of construction techniques, which have regional variations, is essential to the success of a project. He continues: "An architect *has* to be flexible. The changes I propose to architects [all modesty and thirty-five years of experience

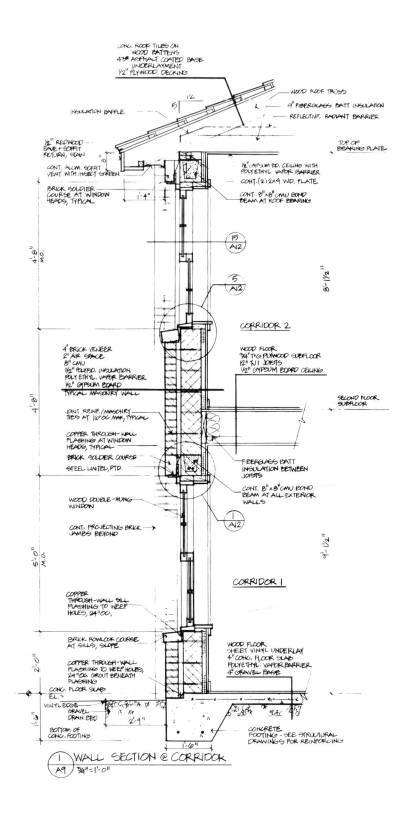

CONC. ROOF TILES ON
WOOD BATTENS
43# ASPHALT COATED BASE
UNDERLAYMENT
1/2" PLYWOOD DECKING

INSULATION BAFFLE

5 | 12

WOOD ROOF TRUSS

9" FIBERGLASS BATT INSULATION

REFLECTIVE RADIANT BARRIER

1/2" REDWOOD
EAVE + SOFFIT
RETURN, STAIN

CONT. ALUM. SOFFIT
VENT WITH INSECT SCREEN

BRICK SOLDIER
COURSE AT WINDOW
HEADS, TYPICAL

TOP OF
BEARING PLATE

1/2" GYPSUM BD. CEILING WITH
POLYETHYL. VAPOR BARRIER

CONT. (2) 2x4 WD. PLATE

CONT. 8"x8" CMU BOND
BEAM AT ROOF BEARING

1'-4"

4'-8" M.O.

8'-1 1/2"

15
A12

5
A12

CORRIDOR 2

4' BRICK VENEER
2" AIR SPACE
8" CMU
1 1/2" POLYSO. INSULATION
POLYETHYL. VAPOR BARRIER
1/2" GYPSUM BOARD
TYPICAL MASONRY WALL

WOOD FLOOR
3/4" T+G PLYWOOD SUBFLOOR
12" TJI JOISTS
1/2" GYPSUM BOARD CEILING

4'-8"

SECOND FLOOR
SUBFLOOR

JOINT REINF./MASONRY
TIES AT 16"OC MAX, TYPICAL

COPPER THROUGH-WALL
FLASHING AT WINDOW
HEADS, TYPICAL

BRICK SOLDIER COURSE

STEEL LINTEL, PTD.

FIBERGLASS BATT
INSULATION BETWEEN
JOISTS

CONT. 8"x8" CMU BOND
BEAM AT ALL EXTERIOR
WALLS

WOOD DOUBLE-HUNG
WINDOW

CONT. PROJECTING BRICK
JAMBS BEYOND

1
A12

CORRIDOR 1

5'-0" M.O.

9'-1 1/2"

COPPER
THROUGH-WALL SILL
FLASHING TO WEEP
HOLES, 24"OC.

BRICK ROWLOCK COURSE
AT SILLS, SLOPE

WOOD FLOOR
SHEET VINYL UNDERLAY
4" CONC. FLOOR SLAB
POLYETHYL. VAPOR BARRIER
4" GRAVEL BASE

COPPER THROUGH-WALL
FLASHING TO WEEP HOLES,
24"OC, GROUT BENEATH
FLASHING

CONC. FLOOR SLAB
EL. =

VINYL LOOSE
GRAVEL
DRAIN BED

2'-0"

1'-0"

BOTTOM OF
CONC. FOOTING

2'-4"

1'-6"

CONCRETE
FOOTING - SEE STRUCTURAL
DRAWINGS FOR REINFORCING

1   WALL SECTION @ CORRIDOR
A9   3/4" = 1'-0"

96

aside] produce a better and more economical building. Take advantage of your builder's knowledge and insight!

"I sure try to be diplomatic, though sometimes I don't come across that way. I have no problem with architects if they're willing to work *with* me. Young architects should know that there are plenty of people out there that have been around, maybe they don't have advanced degrees, but they have had a lot of building experience. So you've got to respect and listen to their special point of view."

The visual power of detailing can be demonstrated in the simplest elements (i.e., a handrail, a stair). When there is special attention to craft, consistent with that of the schematic building design itself, and when detailing reinforces concept, there is a greater likelihood of aesthetic impact. Indeed, a simple box can be a work of visual art with exquisite detailing.

Nagle, Hartray & Associates, Ltd. in Chicago maintain that the best decorative and cost-effective details are derived from construction technology. Of course, there are other views. Those held by some post modernists, for example, call for the development of ornamental details to convey or recall a particular image that may mask actual construction details.

SUPPLEMENT 4-5: Raymond Novitske, A.I.A., practices architecture in Alexandria, Virginia and has fifteen years of design and construction documentation experience. He addresses my question: Consider the impact of construction technology and detailing on schematic design. What should a student be aware of during concept development?

For architecture to be successful, construction technologies must be considered early in the development of schematic design. When construction materials, structure, and systems are studied early in the design stage, they can be used by the skillful designer to reinforce his/her goals and concepts in the final solution. This imparts substance and rationale to the final solution. The Gothic cathedral designers and builders selected technologies that helped strengthen their concept of church as interface between God and Earth. Technologies affecting height, construction, volume, acoustics, and light were chosen which worked together with siting, plan, and ornament to reinforce the cathedral's lofty purpose.

Technologies can also form the basis for design. Designing for energy efficiency may include using solar energy, earth shelter, or natural ventilation. Structural systems are the foundation for design of clear-span areas as well as light, lacy, invisible buildings. These technologies greatly affect form, materials, and plan of the final outcome. The world exposition crystal palaces and even Jefferson's Monticello are examples of technology forming the basis of the end result.

FIGURE 4-12 *Although there is no substitute for field experience to understand and conceive of effective construction details, it is important for beginning students to be aware of the issues concerned with their development and impact on preliminary designs. Sizes and types of joints and connections for structural and nonstructural materials, keeping out water, insulation, durability, expansion and contraction properties, and of course visual objectives are among these issues. This is an example of an architectural construction detail for a house. Floor-to-ceiling heights, wall thicknesses, overhangs, and so on, are all influenced by this detail.*

An example of an acceptable change is the substitution of wood frame construction for the concrete block shown behind the brick in the drawing. A detail that could not be compromised is represented by the continuous projecting brick jambs depicted to the left of the section through the wall. Project by the author; detail and drawing by Raymond Novitske, A.I.A.

As a student in college, I recall a design sketch problem given to us. We were asked to develop a design for a small overnight lodge and ranger tower along a mountaintop trail. All construction materials had to be carried to the site on foot. No utilities existed. We were forced to think about technology as a basis for a creative solution. The most successful projects incorporated technologies that expressed the designer's beliefs on what a mountaintop rest for hikers should be.

Since college studio promotes exploration of issues, construction technologies should be explored along with design. I do not advocate the simple application and consideration of existing technologies, but rather the development and investigation of concepts and systems that may give extra credence and clarity to a student's endeavor. Although general knowledge of the maximum size for a glass window or the maximum height of a masonry wall help the student design with reality, these limits may be extended by the kind of creative investigation college studio promotes. I recall a student's design proposal to use supporting structure for plumbing; steel tube pipe columns would perform double duty as plumbing lines. This proposal may sound laughable, but represents the kind of early investigation of technological concepts that develops understanding of building systems and creative problem solving.

The degree to which construction technology should influence student design depends on the type of project and level of student proficiency in handling numerous components affecting design. Construction technology is just another factor in design, and therefore becomes another tool the student can use to strengthen and support his/her overall design convictions.

Some examples of construction technology considered early in schematic design: Johnson's Crystal Cathedral [Garden Grove Community Church], Foster's Hong-kongBank, and Pei's New York City Javits Convention Center.

Working with Constructors

While it is improbable that students will be involved with constructors during school studio, I think it is very timely and enlightening to be exposed to their particular point of view regarding project delivery. Constructors' participation in design decisions is illuminated quite clearly in Supplements 4-4 and 4-6, and we learn how they define themselves as partners in the building process. An ability to relate to the problems and issues of those who erect our work will help to ensure a successful collaboration, good service to the client, and the best possible product.

In addition, in line with the aim of this book to titrate the insulated world of the studio with views of practice, a brief consideration of financial survival in the building industry is important. In the next Supplement, contractor William Keeley talks "bottom line."

> *SUPPLEMENT 4-6:* Making money is an important and often neglected issue for architects. Idealism and values notwithstanding, profit is a necessary fact of life, and survival depends upon it.
>
> William B. Keeley, President of Keeley Construction in Chicago, is a very successful general contractor specializing in renovations and tenant buildouts. The *Chicago Tribune* attributes Keeley's success and growth despite the slowdown in the construction industry nationwide in large part to understanding and responding to his clients' diverse needs. The firm's current projects include constructing new overseas plants for Fortune 100 companies.
>
> In perhaps the most candid Supplement in the book, Mr. Keeley shares some of the "trade secrets" of general contracting, and the way in which project delivery is

facilitated to the advantage of all participants. Moreover, although Keeley underscores the importance of design excellence, it is business acumen, establishing relationships, and aggressively pursuing new and challenging leads that will assure success in the 1990s. Architects must develop these abilities in school as part of an arsenal of skills to be prepared to engage real projects.

AP: Bill, give me some "trade secrets," things that a young architect needs to know about contractors when doing field observations.

WK: Contractors by nature have a dictionary full of excuses. We really do! "Hey, I can't run this ductwork, the electrician isn't done," or, "We can't paint—the sanding isn't finished, or the carpet's coming." With as many different components as there are in a project, guys just push the blame on somebody else. It's something I see even in a 70-year-old electrician with his own company—he goes, "The #&*!'n plumber is not outta here; the ceiling's not in. . . ." Architects need to know about construction to deal with this. A common problem with a deadline for a move-in date occurs when the negotiations between developer and tenant take longer than originally anticipated. The time window for construction remains the same when it now may be unrealistic. If we cannot get more time in the project schedule, we will have to say we *can* do it in order to close the deal. My point is, move-in dates need to be considered when negotiations are protracted.

I'll also say that people in different businesses have their own jargon—to communicate efficiently . . . and to prevent people from getting in their way and knowing what's really going on . . . it's contractor-speak or it's architect-speak . . . same thing.

As a contractor, and as I was coming up in the trades and learning from other tradesmen, it was very clear that the best architects had basic knowledge of construction. I would recommend hands-on building experience for any architect. There is the opportunity to see how a different technique can be used to reach the same goal perhaps in a more cost- and time-effective manner. We just finished one job, a high-end retail showroom on Michigan Avenue where we built some incredible radius light pockets. The architect's details showed where to put every last screw. The carpenter looked at it and said, "This is like a Swiss watch, not a soffit out of dry wall!" The architect should give the contractor some latitude—but don't misinterpret—we don't second-guess architects, it's just that we may be able to create the same detail with less labor and material, and minimize dollars.

Subcontractors in the field can have great ideas. I have a great subcontractor I like to bring on up to a job. He can make wonderful cost-effective suggestions that can be easily implemented. I don't know if the education process overburdens, or ignores, or demands a certain way of looking at problems. But I do know that when Joe looks at a plumbing problem—water comes in or it goes out—he makes it seem that simple. We along with the Turner's, the Schal's, the Pepper's, and the Morse Diesel's of the world—we all know the value of the knowledge that these subs have. If practical expertise can translate to a better price for the ownership or more profit, then we should contribute, and we're not shy about communicating.

AP: I like the idea of keeping profit in mind as part of the equation of becoming an architect. How do you do it?

WK: Being able to do a lot of things well is important. Learn as much as you can. Learn the finest, the most innovative and creative ways of doing things—then forget them—on occasion, depending on your project. I've made a lot of money doing big, ugly buildings but they were right for our particular client, and the building type. Be careful about coming out of school as the artist who has to express him/herself. And has to express the wealth of knowledge he/she has taken in all at once on this particular job. Providing design bang-for-the-buck, that is, value and responsiveness, defines design excellence for us. Our key is listening and trying to understand and interpret our clients' limits and goals. Providing total *service*—that's the best sales tool, the best marketing you can do. It's easy to be victimized by the desire to do big, beautiful magazine-cover projects. This isn't necessarily where you want to be, especially if you want to make money and solve real problems.

Diversification and response to market conditions are other factors that account for our success. Through the 1980s we were a developer's contractor. There was a ton of speculative money out there from the banks. Now with the disappearance of speculative developers, we have changed our focus and have gone more to end users. The developers we did millions of dollars worth of business with are just not around any more. In the 1980s we expanded companies; now we're downsizing them. We're only as good and as profitable as what we understand of our client's needs. Diversity is the thing that keeps us thriving—our willingness and ability to change—and these are characteristics students should keep in mind to be successful. At the same time we were doing this $125/SF jewelry store on Michigan Avenue, we were doing a plastics recycling facility for Du Pont on the South side. We had garbage on one end of the city, and we're bouncing diamonds off the walls on the other end!

AP: Talk a little about the importance of establishing relationships with everyone— clients, competitors, friends, and enemies.

WK: I don't think I was a terrific carpenter when I first got started on my own; there were a million guys better than me. But through relationships and being personable, people started to notice and respond—*it's so elementary.*

You have to make the transition from someone who is competent to someone who is competent *and* has business acumen. You can't be narrowly focused, do your thing in a vacuum—and survive, or be very successful. Business is such a strong element in the whole picture. It's a cliché, but you have to work hard (that's essential) and work smart.

AP: What else is important in a project's success?

WK: Collaborative effort; not this adversarial thing. The architect has to be the leader on the project; however, that leader, as any good leader, must listen to good advice from specialists. I've been on jobs (and architects have similarly) where it's easy to get in the position where via the plans or via the field conditions, one or the other plays "stump the architect" or "stump the contractor." The contractor says, "It's not on the plans or specs—extra!" or conversely, the architect draws something or has a general note such as, "Check all field dimensions," or "By submitting your bid you will do everything possible to make this job look like this plan." This basically says that if there's a field condition or something that was missed, the contractor is responsible—it's a confession of guilt (no matter who's at fault) on the part of the contractor to accept this!

It becomes a personality thing where either party can undermine the other in the owner's eyes—to get the owner's confidence in order to make the other guy look like a jerk. I have competitors who do this: They come in with a low bid, get the project, and then every step of the way they work at figuring out ways to challenge the architect or building condition to make it the owner's responsibility. They act like lawyers instead of construction managers! Green architects can get taken advantage of.

AP: What attitude should "green" architects have?

WK: First, the team approach is the key to a successful venture. You've also got to cover everything in a contractual and a competent manner. Leave less for interpretation, and therefore avoid arguments and violence!

Also, clearly define how changes are handled during construction. The change order system can be an imperfect one, especially on fast track jobs where the contractor may threaten to walk if approval from the architect is not forthcoming. The owner will say "Go ahead and do it" rather than risking the contractor pulling fifteen guys off the job and not meeting the owner's move-in date. Contractors can take advantage of this system. Owners don't want to hear about change orders—they'd rather you charge them a little bit more, build it in, do it that way. It's a valid approach, but it's not necessarily one you talk about.

Architects should be realistic about costs and fees upfront. Build in a contingency of a few percent. Something unexpected always comes up. Drawings and specs can't possibly be perfect or 100 percent complete. Is it really the contractor's fault that he ran into old concrete foundations when he's digging a new hole? I've been very successful in taking the job and making it more cost-effective either through choice of methods or sometimes redesign. If we can give some technical direction to the architect early on, we can save money for the owner and in the process, make a genuine contribution.

The art of being a good project manager in contracting, and I'm sure it applies to architecture as well, is in the ability to orchestrate a project: Crack the whip in one hand, conduct with a baton in the other—half lion-tamer, half Leonard Bernstein!

In terms of making money and marketing or selling, the same sort of skills apply. You have to know how to "move," to vacillate appropriately, you have to develop a chameleon-like ability, that is, change with the circumstance and with whom you are dealing to get things done and be effective. This is not to say that you compromise your integrity or goals; it's simply all part of working smart.

MATERIALS

Selection and application of materials should be considered as an important part of the design process. Look at materials in relation to typology (research what is typically used and why) and locality (use of readily available, indigenous materials can be economical and tie the building to its site, and local climatic factors may play a major role in material selection to enhance weathering properties and energy conservation). The design concept itself has a bearing on materials—much innovation is possible in specification and use; for example, take a precast concrete "T" and turn it sideways to form a sculptural parking screen, or a bench.

Note also that materials include interior finishes. To reiterate an idea from Chapter 3, indoor/outdoor transitions can be controlled—blurred or contrasted by extending or changing materials from inside to outside. Use more durable and easy-to-maintain materials in areas of frequent use (i.e., circulation paths). Also, areas can be zoned by using similar finishes. Other selection criteria range from the obvious to the subtle and include acoustical characteristics (see Supplement 4-15), and such factors as the presence of older and sensitive computer equipment which may require finishes that dissipate static electricity. Interior finishes can end up inflating construction budgets perhaps more than any other single factor, so be judicious in the use of extravagant and expensive materials!

SUPPLEMENT 4-7: Terry L. Patterson, A.I.A., Professor of Architecture at the University of Oklahoma, is an expert on the use of materials in architecture. Refer to his recent and important book, *Construction Materials for Architects and Designers* where reasoning and conclusions regarding the nature of wood, masonry, steel, and concrete are explored in detail.

THE NATURE OF MATERIALS

Building materials have properties that manifest themselves visually. Consequently, they project a discrete image that may be compatible or incompatible with other visual goals of architectural design. Building character derived from functional demands, geometrical relationships, site characteristics, environmental concerns, artistic concepts, or other influences will be embellished or diluted by the separate message from the building's materials. For example, if general harmony is promoted, the materials may reflect discord. If chaos is desired, the materials may embody order. If clarity and sureness of purpose are intended, the materials might declare uncertainty and ambivalence. Understanding the relationship between material properties and their visual impact lets the designer manipulate their contribution to the architectural goals with certainty. Regardless of one's theoretical persuasion, control of all visual aspects is imperative for a predictable cause/effect relationship in the design.

To maintain control of material expression, one must understand a material's spirit. Only then may building form and detailing purposefully express or violate the nature of the materials. Sensitivity to materials in the broadest sense does not require designing within their nature. This is only one philosophical attitude which, like any stylistic approach to design, does not have inherent correctness or incorrectness but only cyclical popularity. It is haphazard and accidental relationships between material expression and the larger aesthetic order that demonstrate insensitivity to materials and, consequently, a loss of control over part of the design.

Material nature is defined by four categories of properties: Form, strength, durability, and workability. A material's form is linear, planar, or blocklike. Its section is simple or complex. Form is precise or imprecise. Architecture that expresses the essence of material form will express these characteristics in its structure, connections, surfaces, and edges. Expressing strength involves a demonstration of the stress-resisting ability (tension, compression, or bending) most representative of each material's limitations or potential. Consequently, a building's sedate or heroic expressions of strength can match or oppose the natural tendency of its materials to be structurally sedate or heroic. The expression of a material's durability requires its weathering ability to be clearly challenged or accommodated. Expressing the protective systems for the less durable materials is a positive demonstration of low durability. Workability, being the ease of reshaping a material, tends to oppose the expression of a material's basic form. When the expression of properties are in conflict (which they are in several circumstances), another level of judgment is required of the designer. The appropriate degree of balance between the expressions of opposing properties must be determined and justified given the material context.

Frank Lloyd Wright is known for his sensitivity to building materials, through both his claims and his architecture. For the most part, his material use verifies a respect for their basic forms, strength potentials, and even durability limitations, his leaky roofs notwithstanding. His rejection of workability as a property suitable for expression in both words and practice was an attitude compatible with his focus on basic material form.

His brick, stone, and concrete block, for example, tended to express the blockiness of masonry in massing and detail. Brick thickness and rectangularity are often emphasized (Robie House pilasters, Morris Gift Shop detailing). Stone's compact shape and roughness is typically featured by projected units (Fallingwater, Jacobs II House). Concrete block's mass and rectangularity are often demonstrated in stepped forms and projecting units (Ennis and other block houses). His masonry typically demonstrated its affinity for compression in deep arches (Dana House, Heurtley House), in extensive direct compressive contact with the earth (Fallingwater, Taliesin North), in the stability of massing (Jacobs II House, Winslow House), and in its setting on lintels (or apparent lintels) at openings instead of setting on "air" (Robie House, Martin House).

Laying brick on a broad stone base and capping it with thick overhanging stone copings (Robie House, Martin House) framed the units in a protective sandwich. Philosophically at least, the walls are therefore safe from the deleterious effects of moisture from above and below. Thus a limitation of masonry durability (the vulnerability of the joints) is visually expressed regardless of the actual inspiration for the detailing. As is typical for all of his materials, the basic forms of his masonry are not extensively worked (reshaped), which goes mostly unnoticed until an obtuse-angled corner causes the right-angled brick to yield up a texture of partially lapped units (Hanna House). His occasional violations of material compatibilities remind us that Wright was always sympathetic to the visual needs of the circumstances even if they forced a material to do something that it did not want to do. Hidden steel, for example, sometimes helps his masonry and wood achieve remarkable spans that they could never attempt on their own.

Whether or not a designer believes that building materials are central to design, he or she must control their visual impact so as to avoid compromising other visual goals. This requires consideration of the materials' expressive ramifications in all phases of design from schematics through detailing.

COLOR

The wonderful world of color and texture is at the architect's disposal, another potentially powerful (and relatively inexpensive) factor to plug into the design equation, once again in support of project goals. Sometimes (but not always) there is more to life than gray and white! This can be tied-in with a materials selection; certainly the two should not be considered independently. Alas, as with aesthetic criteria, there are no rules for developing a successful color scheme. And try not to consider it only as decoration or something to apply after the design is developed. Color, as any other element, should be part of an integrated and multidisciplinary approach to the design process.

> *SUPPLEMENT 4-8:* Well-known graphic designer and color consultant Deborah Sussman of Sussman/Prejza & Company, Inc., Culver City, CA, writes this essay on the use of color in architecture. (I'm grateful to Teri Appel, Director of Marketing for the firm, for her valuable assistance.)
>
> I especially appreciated Ms. Sussman's quotes in *Architecture*, January 1992, wherein she comments on collaboration with architects: "The architect . . . may want to separate one form from another or to have the envelope read differently from the structure." The sources of her color schemes, as in one of her projects described in the same article, are quite fascinating. Chicago Place on North Michigan Avenue, for example, was based on the "cultural heritage of Chicago," including a "color palette from the works of Louis Sullivan."
>
> Color in the built environment plays a powerful—if often unrecognized—role. Color is always there, even when it seems to be absent. Color can evoke memory; it can be a metaphor; it is able to arouse the emotions, stimulating pleasure, comfort, curiosity, confusion, and even anger.

Color is a companion to structure, and it is always affected by and in turn, affecting light. It can express the dynamics of a building's structure. It can also perform a provocative and challenging role when interacting with structure, massing, and volume. There can be irony in the use of color in architecture. In practical terms color often plays a role by identifying architectural components as well as by helping users find their way around. Manipulation of color in the practical manner can be studied and learned.

However, the experience of color (reactions to and selection of it) is very personal. Almost everyone seems to dislike certain colors and love others—unanimity is out of the question.

As Josef Albers taught, color is relative: Relative to what is around it, how big it is, how much of it is used (a question of scale), what material it is put on. Also, one's memory of color while moving through an environment affects the perception of color. In other words, time plays as much a role as space, light, volume, quantity, and all the other factors that influence perception of color.

To be able to manipulate color as fully as possible as a mature architect, the student should feel free and adventurous when experimenting. Applied colors are infinite in number, whereas colors of natural building materials—stone, metal, wood, brick, and so on—are limited. The juxtaposition of both "manufactured" and "available" colors can yield the joy of discovery forever. It is interesting to consider the use of color throughout history and observe how radically it can differ in different hands at various times, and how valid such radically different approaches can be. Consider the "absence" of color in the work of Mies van der Rohe and in the "International Style" he pioneered, versus the personal, cultural, and emotive-colored statements of the Mexicans, Barragan and Legorreta. In each case, color is part of what the architecture is about. In simplified terms, Mies is about clarity of structure and abstract universal form. Color is a by-product of structure and is handled similarly anywhere in the world. By contrast, the Mexican architects use color to speak about their particular culture and their personal statements as architects and as artists. In each of these cases, the palette is fairly consistent over time.

In working with many architects for several decades I have dealt with an interesting and provocative range of attitudes. Some deal with color largely as an adjunct to structure, avoiding any references to history, building type, or "story." Others embrace the emotive, graphic, or evocative qualities of color. Many look to cultures where color plays a major role in the urban fabric. Color can be so integral to a city that its very name is inseparable from its origin, as in "Siena."

Finally, what matters when working with color is conviction, the knowledge that one has engaged with it as fully as possible, that one has emerged from the creative struggle with a feeling of "rightness." Then one's choices have the power to move others.

WHO 'YA GONNA CALL?

The creation of architecture is a multidisciplinary endeavor and a *collaborative* effort on anything but a tiny scale. The ancient "Master Builder" definition of the architect no longer applies, due to the complexities of design and construction and to constantly evolving new technologies. This is not to say that it's okay for students to be poorly versed in the more technical aspects of design and building. Quite the contrary: Students must be able to conceptualize, fully appreciate, and effectively communicate and coordinate with structural, mechanical, electrical, and geotechnical engineers; lighting, acoustical, curtain wall, security, food service, graphics, and cost consultants; landscape architects, interior designers, and other specialists depending on the project. Like the good family physician, you need to know when to ask for specialized consultation.

The analogy of architect as "captain" of the design team is a good one; he/she must possess a balanced view and have a broad knowledge base in order to derive the most from consultants, make informed decisions about building systems that strengthen design concepts, *and* lay the foundation for continuing, lifelong learning.

William J. Conklin, F.A.I.A. of Conklin & Rossant Architects, participating in an *Architectural Record* Round Table discussion on the engineering education of an architect (Mid-August 1981), argued that there are design theories where architects "don't see as the goal the integration of architecture and engineering, but the communication of design ideas and images . . . with architecture as art, with elements of historic recall, with expressing very different ideas than those of the Modern Movement." Mr. Conklin's view, though, is that engineering be emphasized "as part of the beauty of building design." *Whatever* philosophy is invoked, collaboration, coordination, and understanding of engineering aspects of architecture are required by the architect.

Do not fall asleep in your other classes! Architect Yann Weymouth, in the same *Record* Round Table, summarizes eloquently: "Any architect is trying to make a beautiful building, a wonderful place. To do that you need technology—you need to understand the materials, the structure, the air conditioning, the solar load, the seismic problems. You can't have design without the engineering. It's a whole thing." *The Take-Home Message: Apply what you learn in other classes to the design studio; make the engineering subject matter relevant to your own design project—it will become easier and even enjoyable to synthesize.*

The following (as well as some of the preceding) topics include a series of Supplements that are conceived as mini-consultations modeled on what sometimes occurs in practice, which affects schematic design. During the course of design projects, seek out those faculty members who are specialists and can provide you with useful critiques in the various disciplines. If your university has an engineering school, why not build some bridges and see an engineering professor? (or perhaps someone in psychology or sociology?)—bring your project and take an adventure into a new land.

Structures

Herman Spiegel, structural engineer and former dean of the Yale School of Architecture, is quoted in the Mid-August 1981 *Architectural Record*: "[Students should strive for] as much technical backup to their architectural studies as they can possibly get. . . . If the structural engineering accounts for 20 to 30 percent of a building, it will have profound influences on the design, the esthetics, the manipulation of all the resources to make the most beautiful project."

Obviously, the use of structure is a key factor in the successful completion of projects. The following three very diverse Supplements on structural engineering (as with the other engineering disciplines) suggest that there is a genuine art in its integration with the overall architectural intent and project development.

SUPPLEMENT 4-9: Chris Jofeh is a principal with Ove Arup & Partners. In charge of structural engineering for several years in the firm's Los Angeles office, he is now based in Cardiff, Wales. Arup's interdisciplinary teams have collaborated to produce some of the most spectacular engineering projects worldwide, including Centre Pompidou in Paris (with Renzo Piano and Richard Rogers), the Staatsgalerie in Stuttgart (with James Stirling and Michael Wilford), and the Hongkong and Shanghai Banking Corporation's Headquarters in Hong Kong (with Norman Foster).

Structural engineering of buildings exists to support architecture. On the way it must deal with the effects of gravity, vibration, wind, water, temperature, and earthquakes. It must be integrated with the building's services, cladding, and finishes. It must respect the fabrication and erection techniques available in the industry. It is limited by the assumptions built into the analytical tools used and by the narrow range of materials available. It must reflect societal concerns about good practice, robustness, ductility, durability, stability, strength, and stiffness (or flexibility).

It must do all that for about $1.00 per pound. In comparison, a car, with a design lifetime of one-tenth of that of a building, and with prototype testing and regular maintenance, costs about $5.00 per pound. A hand-held calculator costs between $50 and $1000 per pound. We expect a lot of our buildings and their structures, and we expect them to be built by the lowest bidder.

Structural engineering is a form-finding exercise.

Sometimes the form is generated by the need for slim floors, few columns, and reduced floor-to-floor heights; most conventional structures are like this.

Sometimes the form is generated by the techniques available: Gaudi's Sagrada Familia and other of his structures were generated by hanging chain models in which tensions in the chains represent thrusts in the masonry.

Sometimes the form is a result of limitations in the analytical techniques used by the designers. Before the introduction of computers into structural engineering, some designers of concrete shell roofs were obliged to prestress into the boundary members of the shells the assumptions about boundary conditions they had made to solve the equations describing the behavior of the shells. The shapes of the shells had to be mathematically describable.

There are buildings whose structures are the result of an investigation by their designers into the nature of materials: The roof of the Menil Museum in Houston, Texas, is a diagram of an exploration into the properties and fabrication of cast iron and ferrocement. The granite arches of the Pavilion of the Future at Seville's Expo '92 are another example.

Much structural work is anonymous, but the 1980s produced many buildings in which the structure was used by the architect, either as decoration or as the architecture. The steel roof structure of the new Terminal Building at London's third airport at Stansted, Essex, is an expression of the architect's perception not only of how the structure resists gravity, but also of how the kit of parts was assembled on site. The form was developed to satisfy the building's servicing needs and to permit long lines of people at check-in desks. The members were shaped and sized and the connections detailed to satisfy aesthetic criteria and the effects of asymmetrical loads.

What of the future? As the cost of computing continues to drop, nonlinear time-history dynamic analyses and other gigabit-hungry analytical techniques will probably become commonplace. Analysis is always necessary, but analysis alone is not enough. Design is what matters. Design is what provides the firmness and the commodity and the delight. Design comes from people working together to produce buildings that lift the spirit. Structural engineering is an essential part of that process.

SUPPLEMENT 4-10: McMullan & Associates, Inc. is a leading consulting structural engineering firm in the Washington, DC, area (Vienna, Virginia). President

Denis J. McMullan, P.E., assisted by colleague David Linton, P.E., provide some inspirational words to help young architects see what it may be like to develop future relationships with structural engineers.

Skill and art in structural engineering stems from the conceptual design which complements the architecture and brings it to completeness. In working with structural engineers, be positive, think creatively, and listen carefully. There is nothing more discouraging to an engineer than to work with an architect who has either adopted a very conservative structural approach requiring the engineer to do nothing more than size the beams and columns, or who has no idea how to make the structural system work and hopes that the engineer will magically solve the problem. Better to have early mini-workshops with the engineer. This usually takes very little time and can provide valuable insight and a guide to how the architect can proceed without falling into any of the traps noted above.

The most useful topics that should be discussed early in the design fall into two categories, lateral stiffening elements and gravity load systems. At the initial meeting, the structural engineer will be looking for ways to incorporate lateral bracing such as plywood shear walls, masonry walls, steel cross bracing or rigid structural steel, or reinforced concrete beam and column connections. An architectural layout that can naturally accommodate such items, especially the more efficient structural walls, will provide a cost-effective and efficient structural system. The more symmetrical the arrangement of these elements, the better. If the architect has plans for extensive door openings, large floor openings, two-story spaces, or extraordinarily large open rooms, this is the time to share these ideas with the structural engineer, even though they may not be reflected on the current concept plans. Glass walls will require a more rigid lateral bracing system since they are more sensitive to displacement. Large floor openings cause problems in transferring lateral loads to the resisting elements.

Gravity load systems are easier for most architects and engineers to visualize. To avoid expensive and perhaps unacceptably heavy structural solutions later in the design process, the design team should be trying to line up load-bearing elements from one floor to the next. Vertical supporting members such as columns and walls are generally less expensive than trying to span floor systems excessive distances. Although contractors naturally build from the ground up, engineers design from the roof down. It is a very useful exercise to have the structural engineer explain the load path from the snow load down through rafters, beams, columns, walls, and eventually, to the foundations. This will give the architect a feel for the structural design and will guide the decision-making process as the design unfolds.

Meaningful challenges need to be presented to achieve the best team performance. Mundane solutions should be rejected in favor of innovative thinking—lean on the engineer for original solutions; even the most stubbornly conservative engineer can be persuaded to meet one more challenge.

Be aware when the design changes from concepts and schematics to real working drawings that cannot be changed easily without extra effort and additional expense. Remember—everyone wants to benefit financially from the project!

Throughout my career, I have encountered many different types of architects. There is the architect who believes that if he/she just had my computer, he/she would not have need of my services! There is also the architect who really wishes that sky hooks existed so that he/she would not have to compromise his/her dream in order to make it stand up. Meetings with a structural engineer should not be like going to the dentist. My favorite type of architect can share in the challenge of excellence in engineering blended with wonderful architectural design.

It is invigorating to work with an architect who challenges my skill in engineering and diplomacy. This architect may design pyramid roof structures that have no bottom chord tie and which may need to be supported on hip rafters that come down over little more than very large glass windows or glass doors at the corner. A structural engineer's basic instincts scream for a post at this corner, but if a post would compromise the design, another solution must be found.

Usually, in this instance, I end up cantilevering a beam over glass doors or windows to pick up the gravity load supported on very small columns. A tension ring is used to resist the outward thrust of the hip rafters. An architect once asked me if I could keep the columns to less than 2 inches in size! I think he was joking. For the most part, nothing is impossible. The solutions just become prohibitively expensive. In some cases, the addition of a column could save thousands of dollars in engineering cost and materials. It is the architect's and engineer's responsibility to balance the client's budget with the aesthetics of design.

The challenge before any architect in this relationship with his/her structural engineering consultant is to achieve the design solution within the bounds of physical possibilities, yet stretch those boundaries when necessary.

SUPPLEMENT 4-11: Douglas C. Ryhn, Professor at the University of Wisconsin–Milwaukee, provides an interesting introduction to and discussion of the grid as one type of structural planning tool. As Professor Ryhn elaborates, the idea of using a grid can arise from the building program (i.e., for a library, bay size can relate to the size of a shelving unit); or it can arise from the site (i.e., a sloping site can suggest long bays); or it can arise from a materials selection (i.e., the modular size of a brick, tile, or porcelain panel). Drawings for this Supplement by Douglas C. Ryhn.

TURNING THE TABLES ON STRUCTURAL PLANNING

The principal role of structural systems in architecture is to supply the spanning functions of beams, trusses, joists, and slabs, all of which assure the integrity of the spaces we need in buildings. The criteria for designing these spaces is determined by programmatic issues, site conditions, and other planning considerations. However, actual sizes and shapes of built space is governed to a large degree by (1) the length and distance between the horizontal spanning components and (2) the location and height of vertical support members such as columns. The combination of these horizontal and vertical components form what is referred to as structural bays, and they in turn define the coarse grain, structural planning grid. This grid is further subdivided to create the human scale or fine grain, space planning grid. These grids may become a mechanism that contributes to establishing order in building design.

If one imagines structural building blocks as having the configuration of ordinary tables, it becomes relatively easy to further visualize an actual building taking shape as these tables are nested side by side or, as in the case of a multistory building, stacked vertically one atop another. If all the tables are exactly the same size and shape, square for instance, this nesting and stacking is accomplished with ease, and the resultant massing has a recognizable orderliness. If, on the other hand, the tables are of differing sizes and shapes, the configuration becomes disorderly if not downright chaotic. And since the structure usually "shows through" the building skin, the final building appearance could also be one of chaos.

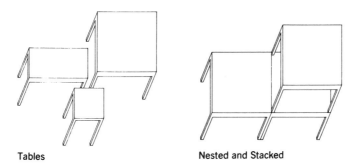

Tables   Nested and Stacked

All of this is not to say that buildings must be designed with square structural bays, for one soon learns that various other table combinations of differing sizes and shapes will also produce results of equal orderliness and beauty. A case in point would be the situation in which small tables are arranged to form a grid or "waffle" pattern, and spaces within the grid are filled with larger tables. This geometry is often referred to as a "tartan" grid, since it resembles a simple woven plaid design. Another equally interesting and useful grid arrangement employs tables of a rectangular shape, with sides twice the length of the ends, allowing them to nest into bricklike patterns of woven or herringbone design.

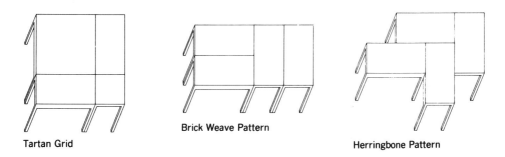

Tartan Grid   Brick Weave Pattern   Herringbone Pattern

Occasionally, square or rectangular grids are not adequate to describe all building conditions. For example, it may be desirable for part of a building to break away and develop an angular relationship to the rest of the building. In these cases, a rotated grid of orthogonal and diagonal patterns (developed as "field theory" by architect Walter Netsch) may be applied. Although there is reasonable freedom in the selection of the angle of departure, the most successful rotated schemes are those that preserve a geometric and dimensional relationship between grids.

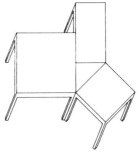

Rotated Grid

The choice of square, "tartan," rectangular, or rotated pattern to create a structural planning grid is one the architect should make early in design. The use of such a grid suggests one distinctive point of view on structural considerations. The larger point illustrated here is that a structural system can be a vital part of the original design process and the building can therefore reflect and magnify the importance of the structural system.

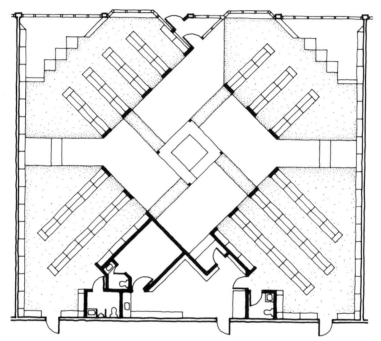

FIGURE 4-13   *The plan layout in this bookstore in Illinois is based on a grid rotated 45 degrees. This scheme has the effect of drawing customers into the store and encourages exploration. (Further, movement is implied by an exposed ceiling grid with lay-in acoustical panels that maintain the original orthogonal frame of reference.) Design and drawing by the author.*

Mechanical Systems

Environmental controls, including heating, ventilating, and air conditioning (HVAC), should be thought of as integral to the early stages of design. Donald Watson, F.A.I.A., has pointed out that buildings consume about 40 percent of the national energy budget for heating, cooling, and illumination. In view of this fact, Watson observes how surprising and disturbing it is that many recently designed buildings are *not* maximizing energy efficiency and environment-conserving potentials. One broad explanation for this may lie in our failure, in the studio, to stress sufficiently early integration of environmental systems with design concepts. In the following Supplement, Norbert Lechner demonstrates why he is a champion in helping students to design more-energy-efficient buildings.

SUPPLEMENT 4-12: Professor Norbert M. Lechner, of the Building Science Department at Auburn University, contributes this lucid "three-tier approach" to designing mechanical systems in buildings. Professor Lechner believes that such a method is being used implicitly on most good buildings and suggests that it be used explicitly. Refer to his excellent book, *Heating, Cooling, Lighting: Design Methods for Architects,* for more information—it is especially salient for the schematic design phase, that which is most appropriate for design studio projects.

MECHANICAL SYSTEMS/EQUIPMENT

Is the architect or the engineer the primary designer of the heating, cooling, and lighting systems? The surprising answer is *the architect* and for two different reasons. First the size of the heating, cooling, and lighting systems is determined almost completely by the architect's design of the building. A well-designed building will have less than half the heating, cooling, and lighting loads of a conventional building. Energy-efficient buildings using only 10 percent as much energy as a conventional building are technically and economically feasible—they have been built.

Second, the architect is the primary designer of the type and layout of the mechanical systems. The building design determines the number of zones, the location of mechanical equipment rooms, duct runs, location of the cooling tower, and so on. Although the engineer makes the actual specifications, his options are greatly limited by the architect's design. The best approach is for the engineer to have input at the early stage when the architect is making all the important decisions that impact the design of the mechanical equipment.

The Three-Tier Approach

It is useful to see the design of the heating, cooling, and lighting systems as a three-tier approach (Figure 4-14). The first tier, "Basic Design," includes such considerations as building form (degree of compactness), orientation, interior and exterior colors, size and location of glazing areas, window shading systems, envelope construction (thermal resistance), massiveness of construction (thermal mass), and so on. These are all major factors in sizing and selecting mechanical systems, and they are all the primary responsibility of the architect. The proper design of the tier one considerations will greatly reduce but not eliminate the size of the mechanical equipment. Thus the strategies of tier two, "Passive Systems," are used to further reduce the size of the mechanical systems.

FIGURE 4-14 *The three-tier approach to designing the heating, cooling, and lighting systems of a building.*

In tier two, "Passive Systems," natural energy sources are used for passive heating, passive cooling, and daylighting. Passive heating strategies use south-facing windows and clerestories along with thermal mass to collect and store up excess solar heat collected during the winter day for nighttime use. Passive cooling strategies include the use of wind for comfort ventilation or convective cooling, the use of water for evaporative cooling, and the use of radiators for nighttime radiant cooling. Daylighting strategies bring good-quality daylight into the building to make it possible to turn off the electric lights during most of the daytime hours. The energy-saving potential is tremendous when you consider that there are about 4400 hours of daylight per year, and that most working hours—about 2000—are daylight hours.

Even well-designed buildings fully utilizing the strategies of tiers one and two will in most cases still require some mechanical equipment, but the size, cost, and energy demands of this equipment will then be quite small. Thus, the third tier, "Mechanical Equipment," consists of designing the small amount of equipment still required. Although this tier is mainly the responsibility of the engineer, the architect must still be involved in many important considerations: Sizing and locating of mechanical equipment rooms; exposing or hiding the ductwork; establishing floor-to-floor heights and clearances with the structure for the ductwork; locating intake and exhaust louvers on exterior walls; locating the condenser unit (cooling tower) on the roof or on grade next to the building; deciding whether to use active solar, photovoltaics, windpower, and so on; and selecting the type of ceiling diffuser with its strong aesthetic implications indoors.

Because the heating, cooling, and lighting of buildings is largely determined by the architect, it is very important that he or she understand the basic concepts involved. For example, cooling is the pumping of heat from a building into a natural heat sink (Figure 4-15). In large buildings this is accomplished with cooling towers (Figure 4-16), and in small buildings with just a condenser unit (Figure 4-17).

A more thorough discussion of all of the above can be found in *Heating, Cooling, Lighting: Design Methods for Architects,* by Lechner, John Wiley & Sons, 1991.

The plumbing and electrical systems were not discussed here because they have little impact on the schematic or conceptual design stages. These systems have minimal space needs and are quite flexible in layout. Consequently, there is usually little problem in designing them at the working drawing stage. The main exception is the need for some small electrical and telephone closets in larger buildings.

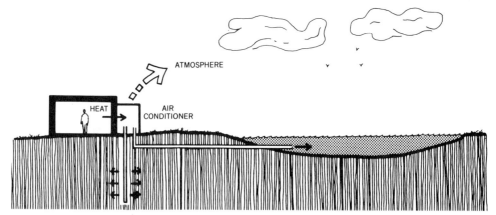

FIGURE 4-15   *Air, water, or the ground can act as the heat sink for a building's cooling system. [From Heating, Cooling, Lighting: Design Methods for Architects by Norbert Lechner, copyright © 1991 John Wiley & Sons, Inc. Reprinted by permission of John Wiley & Sons, Inc.]*

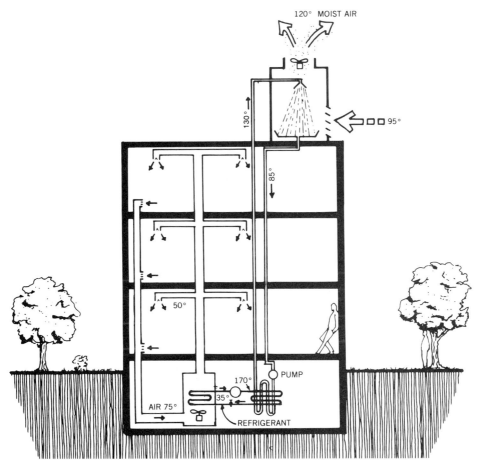

FIGURE 4-16   *A cooling tower cools water by evaporation. This "cooling" water is then used to cool the condenser coil located elsewhere. [From* Heating, Cooling, Lighting: Design Methods for Architects *by Norbert Lechner, copyright © 1991 John Wiley & Sons, Inc. Reprinted by permission of John Wiley & Sons, Inc.]*

Lighting

"There is no end to the possibilities of light—for it is the source of magic in architecture. I believe that light is the ultimate determinant of design. I am convinced that how we see things as a consequence of light is fundamental to the formation of human perception and imagination."—*Arthur Erickson**

In addition to Erickson's words, which capture some of the more intangible and even biological correlates of lighting, there are a host of technical and economic aspects addressed in the following two Supplements. Lighting is truly a multidimensional field which legitimately contains as much metaphysics as it does physics.

*Quoted in the *AIA Journal*, October 1977.

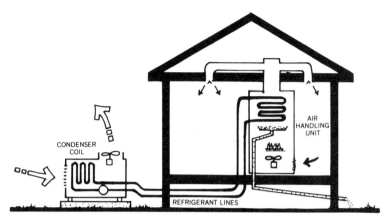

FIGURE 4-17   *A schematic diagram of a split system. [From* Heating, Cooling, Lighting: Design Methods for Architects *by Norbert Lechner, copyright © 1991 John Wiley & Sons, Inc. Reprinted by permission of John Wiley & Sons, Inc.]*

SUPPLEMENT 4-13:   Pioneering lighting designer, William M.C. Lam, President of Lam Partners Inc of Cambridge, Massachusetts, has taught at the Harvard Graduate School of Design and MIT. His classic books, *Perception and Lighting as Formgivers for Architecture and Sunlighting as Formgiver for Architecture*, emphasize the importance of the design process, elaborate theoretical concepts, and illustrate practical design methods and their application to projects.

It has always struck me that William Lam's work represented architectural wisdom in general as much as it does fine lighting design in particular. His interview for *Architecture 101: A Guide to the Design Studio* can be described in much the same fashion . . . so heed his words!

I asked Lam what he finds most frustrating about the way in which projects are developed in the design studio. He spoke of a natural but dangerous sort of near-sightedness from which many students seem to suffer. Lam observed, "Students often start by focusing only upon some parts of the problem." While he admitted that a certain amount of this compartmentalizing is necessary, the point to be constantly aware of is "translating the overall objectives into a building . . . an integrated form." The problem, Lam believes, is compounded by the order in which lighting is considered. He says: "There is the tendency to design the structure in relation to the plan, and then the mechanical systems, *and then* lighting—in that sequence. They're add-ons rather than part of the first concept."

The fact that the student is essentially operating alone (rather than as a member of a team as one might in practice) makes it all more difficult to consider a range of factors from the beginning. Nevertheless, Lam urges that the student try to at least conceive of *all* the issues from the first efforts to develop a design solution. Imagination then is not limited and the process becomes an "integrative" one rather than one of "erosion."

Lam was quick to point out that the design process can actually become easier in practice; a multidisciplinary *team* is less likely to get stuck in one approach or precon-ception: "Even when there are structural and plan concepts before a team is brought aboard, there is something to react to—other people are in the position to remind the architect that if you do 'X', it has certain implications for daylight or mechanical systems, for example, that he may not have considered."

Most preferable, however, even in a team effort, is the condition in which there are no preconceptions. Lam described the ideal stage in which, "Nobody has anything except a bubble diagram of where things want to be—you have the site, and if everyone's open to ideas—you get a kind of synergism. You don't know who the ideas came from, it's a little bit of everybody."

For the student working in studio, the ideal is necessarily somewhat different, focused more on specific learning issues than on a perfect simulation of practice. Lam is careful to acknowledge that projects in basic studio may often intentionally focus on one aspect of the design process. Even so, he says, "You do need to be thinking of the *whole* problem, and try to be at least conceptually aware of all the issues simultaneously."

I asked Lam to comment on the value of building rough chipboard study models. He responded emphatically: "Rough models are valuable not only for students but for practicing architects. To me, a good model is one that's done crudely enough that *it's a tool for study rather than a tool for documentation*. In this way, you don't mind knocking it apart and what you can't avoid is learning something from it—you build a model, you see what's wrong with it, and try to fix it. But if you build it too carefully, you've got this beautiful thing, and of course you don't want to destroy it. Eventually, you get to a more finished model, but the first model should be very conceptual. If you're afraid to destroy the model, cut a hole in it, move something, then why build it? If you want to explore or test something, and you find it's perfect to start with, then fine. I find that a lot of times, between students and faculty, building models is a marvelous way to get around misconceptions.

"To both students and architects I suggest that the best thing is build a model, photograph it, put some scale furniture or people in it, and photograph it as realistically as you can. If you have the actual model and come to present it, you may not have the time or the desired lighting conditions—for example, it might be at night and you may be trying to demonstrate a sunny condition. So you better have photographed the model with the sun; actually take it outside, see it, and take the photographs. In fact, if you photograph the model and project it large, it begins to look like the real building. This is as close as one can get to actually being in the space that you're thinking about."

While Lam insists that we must always try to appreciate the subtleties and complexity of human perception, he returns to the value of the relatively simple exercise of model building. He summarized, "If you do a physical model, you're actually looking at the thing; it's a genuine visual experience. You can put it under all the different conditions and actually *see it* inside and outside—it's not really a simulation at all! Also, when you have the model, the 'real thing' before you, it is more likely that something novel and useful will occur to you."

Finally, I asked Lam to be a bit more specific about lighting, to go back even before one thinks about making a model. He replied by asking that we first should recall the potential impact of good lighting, "to facilitate orientation, to provide focus, sparkle, even essential character of a space, and to satisfy fundamental biological needs for view and for sun as well as for the activity needs." Keeping all this in mind, Lam implores that we "ask the right questions about the spaces to be designed—just what are the qualities you want?" Lam mandates that we think about lighting early and start with diagramming early. He explained: "Freehand schematic diagrams and diagrammatic sections especially can be readily used to explore design concepts and develop designs in advance of model building. . . . Sketch lines of illumination and probable reflection and glare. Evaluate possible lighting designs according to advantages and problems of each solution. It's amazing how well the diagrams can help catalog real conditions and in turn, lead one to good *concepts* for lighting . . . which can then be tested in the model.

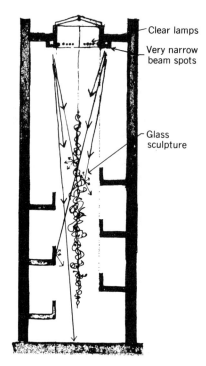

Clear lamps

Very narrow beam spots

Glass sculpture

FIGURE 4-18   *Concept diagram by William Lam for stairs illuminated entirely by light reflected from a central light-reflecting sculpture and spill lighting off solid balcony rails with all light sources at roof level.*

To execute this concept, scissor-type stair towers were redesigned to hexagonal, and glass sculpture commissioned accordingly. [From Canadian Center for the Performing Arts, Case study H1, William M.C. Lam, Perception and Lighting as Formgivers for Architecture, *1977, with permission of Van Nostrand Reinhold, New York.]*

"Most important is to recognize that lighting design is not a technical engineering-based discipline; it is applied perception psychology. A designer needs to know why things are perceived the way they are. If you know what a good environment is, you can design one. Think concept first, hardware last. Think about what wants to be lit, why, and how it should appear. Think and diagram in three dimensions. Diagram light in relation to architectural features, to artwork, to the furnishings and the projected activities in the space, and then where the light may come from. The reflected ceiling plan comes last. I am amazed how many architects, engineers, and not surprisingly their students start and end their lighting design with a reflected ceiling plan."

Our time was up and I invited Lam to add anything else he believed appropriate. With characteristic wisdom and I'm certain a wry smile, he said, "I would always emphasize the application of common sense . . . an underrated commodity."

SUPPLEMENT 4-14: Charles D. Linn, A.I.A., Editor at Large of *Architectural Record,* writes about lighting and the work of lighting designers. As an introduction to Mr. Linn's Supplement, I'd like to quote from his May 1991 editorial in *Architectural Record Lighting*: "To the inexperienced, design is independent of lighting . . . .

Lighting is meaningless until students learn how to make brightness interact with surfaces. It is in the design studios that students must learn to apply lighting technology, to weave light into buildings, to understand that fenestration transforms buildings into luminaires."

Lighting designers are people who are usually not architects but independent designers who have been hired just to design the lighting for their buildings. This is a curious practice—one might even say a disturbing one. Light is the most important stimulant to the human's sensory receptors—more information is conveyed by the lighting that reflects off surfaces into our eyes than by the stimuli to any of the other senses.

Yet architects usually leave the important activity of designing it to somebody else, neglecting it until after their buildings have been more or less completely designed. Often ellipses or vague grid markings are added to the ceilings of interior perspectives at the eleventh hour to give them a more realistic appearance, but seldom is much thought given to what the light in the room will really be like if downlights or troffers are actually installed there. These renderings make no attempt to show this.

So, the ways in which the lighting will affect the mood and feel of interior spaces is something that architecture students must learn to be aware of as they learn to design, just as they become aware of building materials, texture, color, and other design elements. Facade lighting also offers many options for distinguishing the appearance of a building. But whether the lighting is interior or exterior, the student should begin by understanding what light fixtures are capable of doing, so that their renderings do not illustrate the improbable or unfeasible!

For example, nighttime renderings of a highrise office building show sixty stories evenly illuminated from top to bottom. Where would the spotlights be located? Evenly spaced up a sixty-story light tower across the street? Improbable. Renderings of interiors are often illustrated using inappropriate light fixtures—or worse—none at all. For example, row upon row of track lighting is shown in a retail shop design, with no fluorescent troffers or downlights shown for general illumination. Although track lights are good for accenting merchandise, they are inefficient for general space illumination, and if incandescent, not energy efficient. Yet the renderer will show the room bathed in an even pool of light—that is visually dishonest.

In both examples, the students may simply be imitating something they have seen over and over, in books, on the desks of other students, or even in real life. I suggest two ways that a student can become more aware of light in buildings. The first is the easiest: Make a point to look at lighting. Go into stores, churches, office buildings, museums, or out on the street and observe the lighting. Look at what fixtures are like and what they do. What color is the light? What are the shadow patterns like? Does the light make harsh shadows, or is it diffuse? What is the light source? What is the color rendering of the light? Does it make the skin look rosy or pale or green?

It really isn't difficult to distinguish pleasant lighting from unpleasant. All that remains is understanding the lighting systems that create each kind. For this, advanced study of lighting systems is required, and that is beyond the scope of this Supplement.

The emergence of more complex energy-efficiency codes and regulations, coupled with an ever-more bewildering array of lighting equipment choices, makes it critical that students make an effort to learn to design lighting systems to accompany their design projects. Some say "How will I light it?" should be asked even before "How will I keep it from falling down?" With at least twenty different types of light sources commonly available today, informed architects can illuminate beautifully, while inexperienced ones may create caverns of misery for their clients.

Acoustics

"By intention or default, designers engender their buildings with acoustical environments. When the acoustic characteristics are appropriate for a given interior, they tend to go unnoticed. When room acoustics are unsatisfactory, however, owners and users suffer, and the architect is held responsible."—Darl Rastorfer*

Sound represents a design opportunity that should be consciously exploited. To achieve this goal, the student must learn something about the basic principles as deftly outlined by Gary Siebein in the next Supplement.

> SUPPLEMENT 4-15: Gary W. Siebein is Director, Architecture Technology Research Center, University of Florida, Gainesville, and has his own consulting practice in architectural acoustics. Professor Siebein writes on the "poetry" of acoustics and the importance of considering the impact of sound early in the design process. This essay is copyright © 1992 Gary W. Siebein.

SOUNDS

"From the back porch I cannot see the barn. Then the sound of Cash's sawing comes in from that way. It's like a dog outside the house, going back and forth around the house to whatever door you come to, waiting to come in. . . . I cannot see the barn. . . . After a while the sound of the saw comes around, coming dark along the ground in the dusk dark."—William Faulkner, *As I Lay Dying*, Vintage Books, New York, 1957, pp. 57–58.

Faulkner is describing what a physicist would refer to as the diffraction or bending of sound waves around corners. Dewey Dell is describing how she can hear the sound of the saw her brother Cash is using to make a coffin for their dying mother without being able to see Cash saw. This description of the behavior of sound is woven through the text as an essential part of the narrative. It is told in the everyday language of the characters, from rural Mississippi. The scientific concept has become transformed into literature.

The task of the architect regarding the behavior of sound is similar. One must be familiar with the scientific principles of the behavior of sound; the way sound resonates in buildings; and the way people react to sound. Yet this is not enough! The architect must weave these understandings among the basic elements of her architecture in a way that everyone can appreciate. The sounds of the building must come naturally from the shape, volume, materials, textures, and proportions of the design as well as from the activities that occur within the building. A room can enhance sounds within it the same way that the wooden body of an acoustic guitar or violin enhances the vibrations of the strings. Rooms can make sounds poetic. The architect must become so facile with sound that people are unaware of the technology he uses. People only experience the totality of buildings! Sound is among the most dramatic tools in the palette of the architect. It cannot be added to the space afterward. It must be considered during the initial conception of a space. It must reverberate with the most essential elements of architecture: Beams, walls, ceilings, floors, people, and furniture. The sounds and silence of architecture are created just as the building is created. Sounds bring architecture to life.

There are several ways that these ideas can be explored in a beginning design studio. Think consciously about the site and about each activity in the building. What type of

*Quoted in *Architectural Record*, August 1988.

acoustical environment is required for each activity? Are some activities noisy? Do some activities require quiet? What types of special acoustical effects are desirable? For example, a library reading room should be a quiet room to allow concentration. One way to achieve this quality is to have a room with a low ceiling and to line the room with absorbent materials. Another way to achieve the same result would be to give a high ceiling to the room and line the room with hard materials. Any sounds made in this room would be heard loudly throughout the room. This would make people more conscious of the noise they make and would also result in a quiet room.

The Site: Organization and Zoning

First is a common sense approach to locating activities on a site. Activities that require quiet should be located away from activities that are noisy. Quiet and noisy areas of the site can be determined from listening at different times of the day on the site. Acoustical amenities such as flowing water, bird or insect nesting areas, and other sources of pleasant sounds should also be identified and enhanced.

The Building: Organization and Zoning

A similar approach can be taken while locating activities inside a building. Zone noisy activities away from activities that require quiet.

Noisy activities that will disturb other activities in the building must be contained by sound isolating walls, floors, and ceilings. Windows must be limited in these areas. Vestibules with two sets of doors should also be used in these cases. Public lobbies that are adjacent to private areas, adjacent apartments, copy and print rooms in offices, and mechanical equipment rooms fall into this category.

Spaces that require extreme quiet should be contained in a similar manner. This would include bedrooms in residences or hotels, lecture rooms, theaters, music rooms, conference and telecommunication rooms, and so on.

Locate acoustically neutral buffer spaces between the rooms that generate disturbing noises and the quiet spaces. The buffer spaces can include corridors, storage, closets, and so on.

Provide acoustical transitions between spaces. Sounds from a pleasant activity can be allowed to spill out of the room to give one an indication of that which is to come. The transition can also be one of masking or obscuring ambient sounds to create a new acoustical environment. For example, a fountain in a city park or plaza creates its own environment of sound so that one does not hear the hustle and bustle of traffic on the adjacent streets.

Shape, Volume, and Materials of Rooms

The shape of sound-reflecting surfaces affects the way that sounds will project in a room. Flat, hard surfaces will reflect sound with a specular reflection. In this case the angle of incidence equals the angle of reflection. Zigzag or convex-curved surfaces will diffuse or scatter sounds.

Concave-curved surfaces such as domes will focus sound reflections in small areas of a room. This will create areas of the room that are very loud and others that are fairly quiet. Parallel sound-reflecting surfaces build up flutter echoes between them. This also creates annoying persistence of sounds in rooms.

The volume of a room should be limited. Sounds persist longer in rooms that have larger volumes than in rooms that have smaller volumes. The persistence of sound in a room after the source has stopped is called *reverberation*. In many rooms with high, sloping ceilings it is difficult to understand what people are saying while they are speaking because of excessive reverberation. This occurs in atria in office buildings, church halls, restaurants, classrooms, and great rooms in residences.

Room finish materials should be selected carefully. Hard, massive materials such as concrete, brick, concrete block, gypsum board, and plaster reflect sound. These materials should be used carefully in rooms where one wants to project sounds from one location to another, such as churches, lecture rooms, theaters, and concert halls.

Soft, porous materials such as carpet, acoustical ceiling tile, and fabrics absorb sound. These materials will help keep rooms relatively quiet. They should be used in restaurants, offices, corridors, lounges, lobbies, and living areas.

Details

Special details are often required to provide sound isolation in buildings and to control noise from mechanical and building equipment. Detailed development of the acoustical requirements for building systems and subsystems is beyond the scope of the beginning studio.

ORCHESTRATING DESIGN

One aim of this chapter has been to elaborate the multidisciplinary nature of designing buildings, especially large buildings. While expertise from other disciplines is required on *all* projects, executing smaller-scale work is likely to be well within the province of most architects.

Designing buildings involves consideration of a potentially enormous number of factors, each weighted differently, and of course *artfully* integrated, according to the project. Those factors deemed relevant (and described throughout the book) must be explicitly determined and addressed from project inception.

While teamwork and collaborative effort have been stressed, the architect is still THE CAPTAIN. The architect's conceptions must remain true, without undue compromising. It is in the development of those conceptions where input from, and management of consultants reinforce, inform, or in some cases establishes the means for implementation. That is why it is so important for architects to have a broad knowledge base. The architect is the direct liaison to the client; in most situations, he/she alone has the opportunity and privilege of learning about the client's issues often in an intimate manner, and has the ultimate responsibility for translating them to an architectural solution.

All architects view collaboration as an essential part of the design process; some regard *concept development* as collaborative, while others see collective effort as diluting the strength of a solution in some instances. The way in which consultants (and colleagues, for that matter) are worked into the design process is part of the architect's personal philosophy. Just as there is no single "right way" to create a concept, it must be clearly and absolutely stated that there is no disputing the value and importance of consultants' participation during the design process.

The Symphony

In terms of the five senses, nothing compares to the feeling of standing in the center of a building-in-progress, particularly if you've had anything to do with creating the project. For some, even the triumph of the completed work stands as a lesser thrill.

Perhaps, the open framing, the columns and beams, pipes and wiring, the shapes, textures, voids, and smells work together and suggest motion and even life. To have a hand in orchestrating all these components may be akin to the privilege one has in being a parent.

My first "parental" experience as a sole proprietor involved the expansion and renovation of a corporate travel consulting office located in a windowless space in a mall. The sequence of drawings and photographs that follow is my attempt to communicate that feeling of creating and nurturing and witnessing various phases of a project.

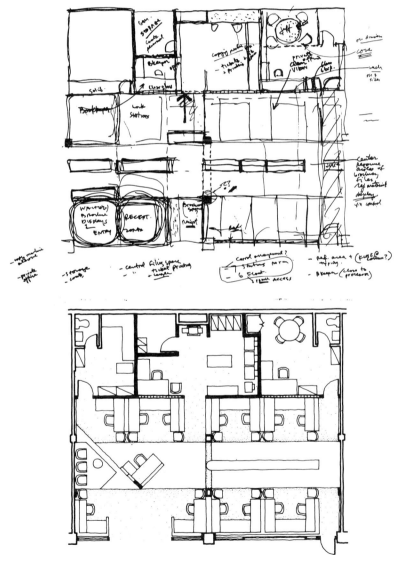

FIGURE 4-19   The topmost sketch illustrates the transition between bubble diagram and a more resolved plan. The bottom floor plan was presented to the client as the final layout.

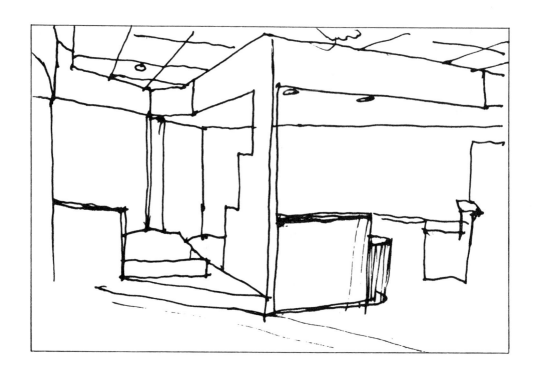

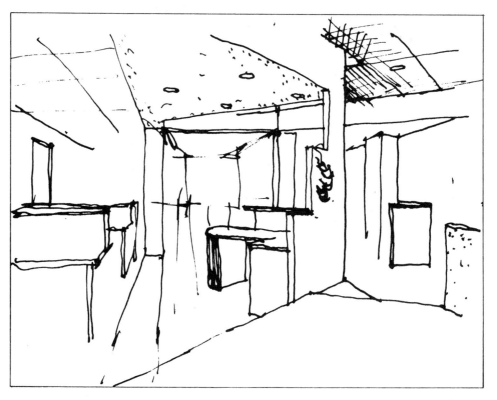

FIGURE 4-20 *Early perspective sketches of the angled reception desk and ceiling configuration.*

122

FIGURE 4-21 A view of the existing condition and the wall that will be demolished to expand the space.

FIGURE 4-22 Study model of chipboard and corrugated cardboard. (Note container of Elmer's glue in the background for scale!) I'm certain it was the model that sold the client on the design in this case.

FIGURE 4-23 Construction progress photo; note that the view is similar to that of study model. At this stage, I virtually felt the bold lines of the drawings coming to life.

FIGURE 4-24 (Top) Reception desk and waiting area; view upon entering the office. (Bottom) Diagonal orientation of reception desk directs clients toward workstations or waiting platform. Photos © Normal McGrath.

FIGURE 4-25 *View from waiting platform. The reception area is the focus for the design. Photo © Norman McGrath.*

FIGURE 4-26 *An image of the general contractor for the project as I first experienced him. Later, of course, our adversarial relationship gave way to one of mutual respect. Photo by the author during an early construction observation meeting.*

5

The Presentation

"You look mahvelous!"—Billy Crystal

Drawing by John O'Brien; © 1991 The New Yorker Magazine, Inc.

"Rather than imagining the audience or the client in underwear (which never works—never demean your audience), imagine them cheering you and bubbling with approval."—John S. Lyons, Ph.D., Associate Professor of Psychiatry, Psychology and Medicine at Northwestern University Medical School

"You never get a second chance to make a good first impression."—Voice-over from a dandruff . . . or was it a mouthwash television commercial . . . and equally valid commentary on architectural presentations. (Also quoted by Dorothy Lynn in *Architectural Record*, March 1983.)

"The process is communication.

"The objective is to project a fresh idea and have it acted upon.

"The name of the game is salesmanship.

"The techniques used . . . will vary considerably according to the nature of the idea and the audience to be reached."—Weld Coxe (from *Marketing Architectural and Engineering Services*, 2nd Edition, Van Nostrand Reinhold, New York, 1983).

"Communication among three categories of participants is needed to see a design project through to completion. . . . [1] the architect or designer, with colleagues, staff and consultants . . . [2] builders, manufacturers, fabricators, and tradespeople . . . [3] clients, financiers, competition jurors, enforcement officials, users, and the public."—Paul Stevenson Oles, A.I.A. (from *Architectural Illustration: The Value Delineation Process*, Van Nostrand Reinhold, New York, 1979).

In school, the audience for most presentations falls into Paul Oles' first and third categories listed above. Therefore, this chapter will focus primarily on presenting to juries comprised of faculty, invited professionals from outside the school, and typical (or simulated) building users and clients. Frankly, clients are probably the most important group to whom you will be communicating your work. These people are the decision makers and the likely source of your future income. So, avoid jargon-laden speech directed at the cognoscenti. Moreover, especially for the less sophisticated client group, *education* about architecture goes hand in hand with the presentation of your ideas (as well as operating throughout the design process) and is a natural extension of a professional's overall responsibility.

ANOTHER DESIGN PROBLEM

I always like to view the presentation of a project as another design problem. But then, I view almost every challenge in life as a design problem—that's one of those good and powerful side effects of an architectural education! You should be able to communicate your project visually and verbally in a manner that is consistent with the character of the design. *This requires planning and once again, TIME MANAGEMENT.* Time allotted to designing and executing the presentation *may* be mandated by your faculty. In any case, my guideline is to seek ways in which design time can be maximized without sacrificing the time and effort needed to produce the most compelling presentation possible.

One way to accomplish this latest scary-sounding goal is to make design tools and presentation tools or media the same. In fact, there is a personal and alluring quality to original drawings that can rarely be duplicated in a set of "presentation drawings" (see Figures 5-1 and 5-2). In many instances, it doesn't seem logical to redraw painstakingly—the results are sometimes sterile in feeling and, of course, take up precious time. With careful planning at the outset of projects, as elaborated in Supplement 5-1, it may be desirable to *make use of process drawings as a major presentation element.* Explore the various reprographic options available—for example, a blueline print of a design sketch can be experimented with, and rendered (using color pencils or markers) to read as a seductive presentation graphic. Similarly, xerography can offer more possibilities for translating the range of design sketches, from analysis diagrams to more elaborate perspective drawings, to an impressive and coherent presentation. Play with copying machines! Reduce, enlarge, try different papers, then experiment with rendering the copies (see Supplement 5-4). There is also an inherent beauty to pencil on yellow trace—witness many original design drawings being sold at galleries for enormous sums of money.

Returning to *designing* the presentation, a helpful tip is to block out all the drawings at small scale. A mini-set of presentation drawings will help to arrange (and size) individual sketches in the most effective sequence and produce dynamic

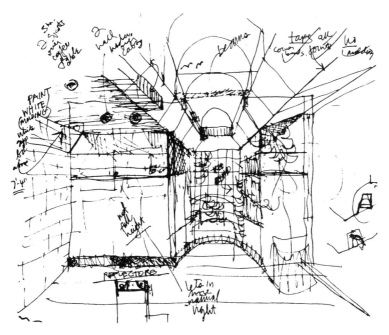

FIGURE 5-1   *This is a very early design sketch of a new family room that was eventually shown to the client as part of a preliminary design presentation. The basic elements of the design—barrel-vaulted skylight, splayed ceiling forms, and rounded glass block terminus—are all very loose but convey the overall intent. Design and drawing by the author.*

FIGURE 5-2 *Another quick and conceptual drawing, a newly exposed hip roof is revealed for a residential renovation, with lounge in foreground and mini-workstation beyond. This, too (in an enlarged form), was a helpful adjunct for the client presentation. Design and drawing by the author.*

layouts with focus and unity. Mock-ups like this are a common office practice regarding working drawings, and I believe the technique has great applicability for presentations as well.

> *SUPPLEMENT 5-1:* Ernest Burden, a New York–based architect, is an expert on design presentations and is one of the most prolific authors on the subject. Some of his books include *Architectural Delineation, Design Presentation, Design Communication,* the classic *Entourage: A Tracing File,* and his latest, *Grid Systems & Formats Sourcebook*. Mr. Burden was most frank in answering several very direct questions on the use of tracing files, maximizing design time, and producing professional-quality presentations.

AP: How can students improve presentation drawings while maximizing design time?

EB: The most obvious suggestion is that you do presentation drawings as you design, and vice versa because both tasks involve drawing. If the design is worked out in your conceptual thinking first, the drawing proceeds a lot more easily. The other thing, of course, is using design studies as presentation drawings, saving all of the sketches and conceptual drawings, overlays, and so forth, to be used in presentation manner, and thinking of them as one expression. The point is that you don't doodle your design, then sit down and come up with a totally different concept or arrangement for the presentation.

Unlike a lot of architects, Frank Lloyd Wright didn't consider renderings to be renderings as such that are executed after the design is done. In other words, they're part and parcel of the working-out process, the creative process.

AP: Could you make some suggestions on how to improve drawing skills through all phases of design?

EB: I don't think the schools put enough emphasis on drawing—they put so much emphasis on the models. Students should always draw from nature, sketching figures, trees, and so on. Take photos; study prints; study other drawings, and make drawing an integral part of the education instead of something that you do as just a hobby.

An alternative to the sketch is the design scroll. You take a piece of paper or a roll of trace and just keep on going. You don't tear it off—if you tear it off, then put on an overlay, you're working with the old idea. When you're going on a design scroll, the scroll disappears. So you've got your base plan underneath which you can use for the development of the next idea. This technique is an excellent way to start a series of design sketches that may not necessarily relate. One of the masters of this is Paolo Soleri; it's wonderful to follow the progression of ideas. Once the ideas are developed and turned into drawings, you have a combination of several things. You have the idea, the architecture, the drawing, the texture, the scale—all of the elements become part of the same composition. In other words, the elements within the drawing, the technique of drawing, now becomes part of the architectural expression. In a sense, there is a continuity and unity of purpose in development of drawings.

Finally, in presentation drawings, make sure that all the elements are there for a reason, that they all relate to the total creative idea.

AP: Use of entourage tracing files can save time and help drawings look accurate and professional. Should students take advantage of these files?

EB: Absolutely, I would suggest that students take advantage of them; why draw the same beautiful tree over and over again? You can get other ideas from looking at various species of trees that have already been drawn, and you can simply trace them and use a little bit more of the time saved toward developing the creative aspect of the rendering. And, of course, when you're using a tracing, you don't have to use it directly; you can always use it as an inspiration and draw over it in any manner that you want.

I actually did life figure drawings for years—every afternoon in the design school—and when it came time to put these figures in a rendering, I reverted back to the photograph not only because it was more accurate, but because it was quicker. Illustrators are apt to use their own interpretation of the figure. I would emphasize, though, that when you're drawing a realistic building, the figures must look realistic because if the figures are abstract or disproportionate, it detracts from the realism of the structure that you're portraying. After all, the object is to portray the building and the site or setting as accurately as possible. Therefore, if you've relied on photography to document the site and/or proposed building, you can also rely on photo-realism to create the entourage. The site of a building is actually part of the problem, and so in a rendering it is wise to include the context within which the building sits. I know that many architects would prefer to delete the surroundings, but that's definitely dodging the issue.

With all of my hours of figure drawing, I could not draw a figure in a rendering . . . fast enough. If you're the illustrator, you work on a figure to the point where you can actually see expression on the face. In an architectural rendering, it's quite different—you don't want the figures to be a distracting element.

AP: Is there anything else you would like to mention to students in support of creating successful presentations?

EB: What I have noticed in the schools is an emphasis on traditional forms of presentation and model building rather than a focus on visualization in three dimensions. These include ink-line drawings of plans, elevations, sections, and axonometrics (which show buildings first from one side, then from the other side). Axonometrics

FIGURE 5-3 *A sampling of material from Mr. Burden's* Entourage: A Tracing File *(2nd Edition). Figures, vehicles, plants, and trees can be reproduced, enlarged, copied same size, or interpreted as appropriate to match the character of a rough sketch or a refined rendering. Copyright © 1991 by Ernest Burden, published by McGraw-Hill.*

are nothing more than projections from the plan . . . you still don't get the sense of space, you still don't know what the building really looks like. And another observation I might note involves the inordinate amount of time that so many students spend on building perfect-looking models (they do look great). The students end up being nice constructors but still weak visualizers, because to visualize the space, you have to be inside it; sometimes, building a model places you on the outside. In other cases, I've seen some models built in pieces or sections where students *would* actually be able to study the inside of the building, and how this relates to the whole, and the drawings.

Another traditional way of showing a project includes rendering the plan within a site map where the plan is highly rendered and the map is kept subdued. This approach can also be used in the model form, where the model itself is highly developed and the background remains subdued.

There are many different approaches to the same presentation problem. I feel strongly that there should be at least a semblance of seeing how the project developed. With the more traditional methods mentioned earlier, often showing only the finished product, jurors or critics can't know how the project started and nobody knows where it went along the way. I have had to dig very hard to find evidence of how students thought these [finished] buildings through. Where did design ideas arise, and how were they translated into the final form?

Architects are famous for sketching—you should be drawing all the time. You don't design and then draw. You start to draw in the conceptual stage. Sketches don't have to be elaborate—they can be very simple—simple lines. Frank Lloyd Wright's economy of line was incredible! The technique is just as broad as there are people who can do them. The main thing is to keep it loose. These sketches can have much more dramatic impact than final renderings.

I've also noted that the scale and size of many student drawings are tremendous: 24 by 36, 30 by 40. When are these people going to get the *time* to fill-in and present information on this size piece of paper? The bigger the piece of paper, the more impressive they thought the presentation would be. But in fact, what happens is this: Two days before presentation, the work is only half finished. One obvious means of coordinating your ideas and concentrating graphic quality would be to use a smaller sheet of paper. I have a friend who could put so much detail into a rendering this big [gestures about $8\frac{1}{2}$ by 11], you could literally blow it up to the size of a wall and still see every leaf. It takes some training to be able to work at the smaller scale, but I think at the very least, an incredible amount of time is saved.

THE DOG AND PONY SHOW

Like a third-grader describing the family's summer vacation with a souvenir of the Washington Monument, you must do your homework. If you know what you're talking about, and can say it directly to your audience (i.e., with as much eye contact as possible), you will radiate confidence. Do not patronize visiting critics and outsiders by an exaggerated or simplified lecture; encourage any questions and respond with a level of detail consistent with the inquiry. John Lyons continues his commentary on student presentations. "The key to a presentation, whether it's before a small town client or the Congress of the United States, is to define what you want to say. One or two points should be identified, and those are the ones you amplify. More than this and most people tend to become ineffective and lose their audience. Present with confidence. Self-confidence is a most important metric of the effective presentation. The worst thing presenters do is to become their own audience, to get idiosyncratic. Stay basic, stay confident, and keep it brief. There will always be time to elaborate if that is called for." *The Take-Home Message is to project confidence if not charisma, express enthusiasm, "grab" the audience, and try to enjoy the experience!* View and convert any initial nervousness into excitement and enthusiasm for your work. Residual anxiety that can't be transduced or concealed will usually vanish as you become caught up in the momentum of the presentation and the response of the audience.

If you are presenting an incomplete project, be up-front about it. The conventional wisdom has always held that if you make a mistake, don't apologize, and at the same time don't be defensive. *Move on. Maintain a sense of humor.* A few years ago, I designed an upscale kitchen for a celebrity client who was always adding last minute changes. When construction was 90 percent complete, she informed me that her oversized computer keyboard didn't fit in the custom home-office casework I designed. I never knew anything about such an oversized component—so paraphrasing Frank Lloyd Wright, I advised her to get a smaller keyboard! We all had a good laugh (and I called my lawyer).

FIGURE 5-4 *Entourage makes this simple sketch come alive and tie it to its suburban site. New addition is on the right, with new second floor on existing house on the left. The bird is traced, perhaps a quirky preference of the renderer. The car, though, is dated—it must mean that the client is a collector of vintage automobiles. As Ernie Burden has said, "Strive to create continuity and a story within the rendering series." (The drawing was enlarged approximately 250 percent of its original size for the client presentation.) Design and drawing by the author.*

Try not to present at 5:00 P.M. Unfortunately, scheduling presentations is such that you may end up doing it at the end of the day—when attention spans of the jury are at a minimum and hunger is at a maximum. Be especially attuned to the audience's condition at this time and take action to prevent disinterest and discomfort resulting from sitting through a marathon session. Dorothy A. Lynn, a communications specialist, recommends (in *Architectural Record*, March 1983) speaking with varied cadence and volume, and maintaining high energy (don't slouch). Don't fidget, and maximally engage the group. Move as close as possible to your audience (don't be shy about striding away from a desk or lectern, and turning to face the group), and most important, maintain good eye contact.

Responding to Criticism

The title of this section may be somewhat misleading; it presupposes that the reader understands that life in the studio and in the design review is *not* singularly driven by critical unpleasantness. Criticism is very much a part of the process, but it should be pointed out very clearly that reviews and juries are by no means always tough, pressured events. A good portion of the time, the tone is relaxed, colleagial, and often absorbing.

However, it must also be said that a jury may indeed be tough and most unpleasant. This fact is sometimes prized; I once overheard a first-year graduate student tell a classmate that he chose the Blahblah School of Architecture "because of the criti-

FIGURE 5-5   *This is a typical but fairly relaxed final review where a student has just finished present-*
ing his scheme in front of a jury including faculty and other students. Professor Douglas Ryhn has the
floor. Photo © SARUP, University of Wisconsin–Milwaukee.

cal intensity." I was both incredulous and impressed—the student sounded the way
a novice fighter might if he were trying to learn about boxing by stepping into the
ring with the heavyweight champion . . . and at monthly intervals. On the other
hand, if this novice has some talent, motivation, and love of the game, and has the
capacity to duck, deflect, and most important, absorb a punch, he *will* learn the
game. He will draw upon the concentrated lessons, and each time he returns to the
ring, he will be better and better prepared.

Learning how to respond to the tough aspects of criticism is central to the ease
with which one returns to the critical forum. There are several truisms in this regard.
Perhaps the most often repeated one has to do with avoiding your natural propen-
sity for defending yourself: In a phrase, don't do it very often. If you find yourself
backed up against the ropes, there is probably a good reason for that position; try to
understand just what that reason is, carefully attend to every word the critic utters. If
there is any ambiguity in what you are hearing, form a hypothesis about what is
being said and try to restate the critic's comments. In this way, clarification is more
likely (the critic may soften and elaborate in valuable fashion), and you demonstrate your efforts at understanding and correction:

> *Critic:* As an object, your pavilion is well developed, but it may as well be
> dropped in from Mars.
> *Student:* [Staggers for a moment, shakes off the stinging jab, and speaks . . .
> clearly and thoughtfully] So, you are saying that I really haven't been sensitive
> enough to site issues?
> *Critic:* Yes, exactly! Why don't you take a look at Fay Jones' work, especially . . .

All this is not to say that you should always be unconditionally deferential and
subservient to criticism. Part of the educational value of presenting work to critics is
in preserving your individuality while being responsive to the judgments and sug-

gestions of others. Ultimately, this challenge is a preparation for the dialogues and transactions you will have with clients. So, as you struggle to understand and address your weaknesses, also try to discover and preserve your strengths.

If you feel a particular aspect of your project is exceptional, focus on it, and be sure to justify and support it clearly, from as many angles as possible. Be ready to take the offensive, but in a selective, measured, and graceful manner. Remember that it is *not* adequate to emphatically state that you "like" something. Critics and clients both need and deserve to know substantively why you have made each and every decision and why you have ruled out alternative schemes. This is not to suggest that every detail of a project should be identified and justified; it does mean that you must be prepared to field questions about any detail in order to show why it does not represent arbitrary thinking.

> *SUPPLEMENT 5-2:* Robert C. Greenstreet, Ph.D., is Dean of the School of Architecture and Urban Planning at the University of Wisconsin–Milwaukee, and has written extensively on presentation techniques and graphics. His recent book, *Architectural Representation*, is written in collaboration with James W. Shields.

THINKING AHEAD IN DEVELOPING A GOOD PRESENTATION

Despite their skills in drawing and delineation, architectural students and indeed many architects do not always present their designs in the most effective way. Considering the many hours that can go into developing each project, this is surprising, and yet often the final presentation of good schemes is marred by confusing or inadequate drawings coupled with an inarticulate or scrambled verbal accompaniment.

Claiming that a good design should be recognized without graphic gimmickry, or alternatively, that the drawings should speak for themselves is not good enough. Architects must compete in the marketplace to win clients, and their verbal and visual presentations are an important means of achieving a thriving practice through clear communication and, ultimately, persuasion. For architectural students, articulating their work to their faculty is no less important, and careful consideration should be paid to the planned presentation of each project.

When should this process start? Planning the presentation should begin right at the beginning of the design process, where making a few simple decisions can subsequently save much time and trouble. By answering the following questions, the presentation should grow naturally out of the design process, reduce wasted time and effort and hopefully, ensure the clearest, most impressive, final result.

1. *Will the Drawings Be Judged Alone, or with a Verbal Accompaniment?* If the designer has the opportunity to talk about the design, point to the drawings, and lead the audience through the scheme, ambiguities can be explained and details verbally embellished. Some designers, however, may not have the luxury of providing an additional explanation—in a competition, for example, or when the work is included in a portfolio—and the drawings will have to stand alone. In these cases, drawings need to be very clear in communicating the designer's intent and should be supplemented with clear information (scale, north point, title of each drawing, etc.), well-written text, or simplified concept drawings where appropriate. Some attempt to articulate the *process* whereby the designer reached the final scheme may also be useful in communicating the rationale of the scheme to the intended audience.

When planning a verbal accompaniment, the salient points of the presentation should be written out on check cards beforehand. This will clarify and order the ideas in the presenter's mind and provide points of reference in case he or she dries up in midpresentation. The drawings should be referred to throughout to integrate the verbal and visual materials, and practicing the overall presentation beforehand is advisable, perhaps to a group of friends who can be solicited for their suggestions and reactions.

Finally, the overall impact of the performance to the intended audience should be assessed. Personal appearance and delivery are both parts of the presentation, which can be impeded by inappropriate dress or incoherent mumbling into the drawings.

2. *What Should the Final Presentation Look Like?* Some basic decisions should be made during the early stages of design:

A. The type and mix of drawings to communicate the scheme adequately, which may include models, slides, video, and so on. The appropriateness of the selection should also be assessed. For example, hard-line exploded axonometrics may be too harsh a means of depicting a woodsy, vernacular scheme, while a watercolor wash or soft pencil sketch may be too vague to capture the technical precision of a highly technical building.

B. The style of the drawings. This affects both the media to be used in the final presentation and, no less importantly, the surface upon which they will be applied. Materials and equipment should be purchased as early as possible to ensure their availability and applicability, and should include enough extras and spares to take care of false starts, broken nibs, changes of mind, or accidents.

C. The need to reproduce, reduce, or print the final drawings. This will affect the method of delineation and the *timetable* for presentation. Print shops are usually only open regular hours and may be very busy, so should not be relied upon for last-minute printing. Some time for experimentation or for graphic additions to the prints may also be required, especially if the final visual effect was not exactly what was originally anticipated.

3. *Where Will the Scheme Be Presented?* Some thought should be given to the venue of the presentation. The lighting in the room should be checked out, in addition to available electrical outlets (for slide projectors) and the seating arrangement of the jurors/audience. If the conditions are not to the presenter's liking, some initiative may, in some circumstances, be appropriate by changing lighting levels and reorganizing the furniture to better advantage.

Pinable wall space should also be checked out. If there is insufficient space to mount the presentation, a free-standing exhibit may have to be planned, or a portable easel requested or, if necessary, provided.

If the wall surface is poor, badly defaced, or damaged, sturdy backing sheets should be used to pin behind the scheme so that the work can be viewed without distraction. Bear in mind, too, the density of the wall. Can pins easily be pushed into it, or will tape or nails be necessary? Come prepared with adequate tools and supplies to mount the scheme quickly and securely so that it doesn't drop or collapse during the presentation.

4. *How Will the Scheme Be Preserved?* Consideration should be paid to the future of the drawings beyond the presentation. Will the drawings be framed, for example, stored in a filing system or transferred to a portfolio? This decision will affect the size of the drawings, method of delineation, and any reproduction techniques that may be necessary to reduce or duplicate them.

QUICK TIPS

The following remarks may seem very obvious, but I have observed too many projects in which common sense standards have been neglected. The quick tips are intended to promote optimal communication and understanding of your design scheme.

• The site plan and floor plans should have the same orientation (north in the same direction), and include a north arrow. Drawings are read and appreciated far more easily when there is a standard orientation.

• Lower-floor plans should be at the bottom of the sheet with higher floors above, or lower floors at the left with higher floors to the right. Align the plans as they would appear in reality (i.e., a stair tower should appear in the same relative location on all plans, even if the shapes of the plans are all different).

• Show as much of the surrounding context as possible on *all* drawings and/or model. Set the building in a place, whether adjacent to other buildings or landscape, and include foreground and background where applicable.

• Include people and entourage as appropriate to the setting, season, and time—this certainly makes drawings more realistic. In a relevant essay in *Architectural Record* (May 1987), Tom Porter and George Dombeck caution about becoming overly stylized and standardized in "a strange drawing-board world . . . whose bleakness is occasionally punctuated by stereotype automobiles and mass-produced trees, and peopled by odd, balloon-shaped beings. . . . Students can lose contact with reality, and may later misrepresent their design ideas to lay people . . . ." Caren Connolly, at the University of Wisconsin–Milwaukee, has another valid point: "In a recent pinup, a student drew a beautiful perspective drawing with two trees on either side. I said to him, 'This is a minute point but you cannot put trees on the corners in the sidewalk in a major urban area—right underneath that sidewalk is this huge heating duct,' and he said, 'They're really not there, it's just to balance the drawing.' "

• Provide a sense of scale to the drawings—of course, include a graphic scale, but more, suggest a furnishings layout (in plan and section). It shows that you've thought about the specific functioning of the space, and it automatically gives a feeling of scale for nonarchitects.

• In general, attempt to draw plans, elevations, and sections at the same scale. It makes it easier to compare drawings. However, when time and space are very limited, or when a high level of detail is not required on a particular drawing, it may be appropriate to use a smaller scale. Although required scale will probably be assigned by the instructors, some latitude is likely to be permitted.

• Key-in all cross sections and elevations to the plans for easy reference.

• Be sure that any lettering is graphically consistent with the drawings. I've seen wonderful renderings that have obviously taken hours to draw ruined in five minutes by *awful* hand lettering! Hand lettering is a skill that takes time to mature. If you're not there yet, consider other options. (Practice lettering in everything you do: Letters to friends, taking notes in classes, and so on—your hand will become steady and consistent with experience.) Options: Use the computer (print out or photocopy on sticky-back sheets), use press-on letters like Letraset, or trace letters for freehand quality.

• Elevation labels usually refer to the cardinal directions of the compass (i.e., the east elevation faces east). Students occasionally incorrectly label the elevation as the direction in which they are viewing it.

• Sheet format—keep it simple! Don't take away from your design! You may want a border (a plain freehand or hard-line rule), and title block—again simple *(and small!)*—include name of project, name of drawing (why label a perspective, "Perspective"?—everyone knows it's a perspective—instead, indicate where the view is looking); scale (this may need to appear under separate sketches on the same drawing if there are differences in scale); north arrow; drawing number (i.e., 2 of 5—sequence is important); and don't forget your name and date of the presentation. I also recommend using the same sheet size for all drawings. Again, avoid overly stylized graphic or other idiosyncratic elements here (however closely or consistently you think they follow your design themes); they draw attention away from your *architectural* project, which defeats the purpose of presentation graphics. You don't want a jury discussing some obscure element at the expense of your design. I've seen this happen all too often.

• Employ a hierarchy of line weights to highlight (by contrast) more important elements (i.e., walls or edges are generally thick, furnishings are thin). They can also help to give a sense of depth: For instance, closer lines and section cut lines should be heavier; objects in the background should appear lighter. If everything is equally weighted and there is no hierarchy, nothing reads prominently.

• Use shade and shadow liberally! These qualities add depth, texture, and contrast to emphasize and animate forms, imbue two-dimensional drawings with a sense of reality, and help them to read better at a distance—where most juries sit. On occasion, grant yourself artistic license in developing shade and shadows to improve clarity, but be consistent within a set of drawings.

• In floor plans, use dotted lines to indicate space above (i.e., overhangs, balconies, floors, etc.). This again helps in comparing and reading plans and sections.

• *Suggest* materials. Partially render rather than draw every brick, for example. It not only saves time but can be just as effective. Concentrate the texture or value at the edges, and gradually diminish the density.

• Generally, provide more detail in the foreground, less in the background. Overlapping objects or cutting elements (only the upper half of a man is visible behind a counter) enhance the illusion of depth.

• If you're doing a precision drawing, be precise! Curves should flow into straight lines without a blotch, corners should be crisp—sloppiness can become a major issue for critics and clients alike. (You may have to embark on a preventive maintenance program for your Rapidographs!) Usually, the degree of precision is a function of the stage of design. Very preliminary design implies an ambiguity (freehand may be comfortable), and construction details imply high resolution (hard-line may be comfortable). This is not to say that you can't have a loose drawing stylistically that's not precise; in fact, the combination of freehand and precision drawing is sometimes desirable for schematic design and developing details.

• Consider cost. Paper, reprographics, and supplies can add up—be aware of your personal budget. At the same time, try not to skimp; remember, it is an investment in your education and future.

SUPPLEMENT 5-3: This is an interview with Iris Slikerman, Promotional Art Director for the Putnam/Berkley Publishing Group, Madison Avenue, New York. Ms. Slikerman applies her expertise and experience in the graphic art world to architectural presentations.

AP: We talked about the importance of creating a focus on each presentation board; what do you do about a board that has, say, two floor plans—equally weighted— how do you give that focus and make it an interesting layout?

IS: Try highlighting a certain element within each plan, for example, the circulation path. A gray tone, or perhaps some color with marker, pencil, tape, or film to show the underlying organization of the plan. It makes it easier to read—pops it out, and interesting graphically. If the project is a renovation, you could focus on the area to be renovated; render it more than areas to be left alone. Alternatively, key in to whatever it is that's particularly wonderful in plan (since we're talking about plans) and emphasize it graphically so that it becomes the focus.

AP: I've noticed a common mistake—a design theme (i.e., a stepped geometry) where "stepping" appears throughout a project (in plan and section) is carried through into the presentation graphics. It appears in things like borders and title blocks. To me, that's very annoying since it distracts from the building design. It's not the same thing as having a strong design concept that appears in details like the door pull.

IS: You have a good point, but what if the graphic translation is so subtle that you have pulled your viewer in just by a feeling you have evoked . . . consistent with your project's themes. The viewer may not even know why it's so appealing. What you're talking about is overkill—too much of a good thing—it can destroy the freshness of what you're trying to achieve. You have to be cautious in your use of design elements; I know it's cliché, but a little zip in the right place at the right time can go a long way.

AP: How do you feel about the use of color in presentations?

IS: Sure color is terrific, but only if it enhances your message. Its use shouldn't be arbitrary. You don't necessarily need to use a rainbow of colors—one or two might be most effective for any given presentation. And a *little bit* of color can have a **big** impact.

AP: I've seen site plans where all the trees and grass are colored in a grotesque green, and brown is supposed to represent dirt. Should students use restraint, or is that too inhibiting?

IS: Again, it all depends on what you're trying to achieve—there needs to be a rationale behind every move. If color is an integral part of your design, the presentation demands it. If however, you're showing something more subtle, like a certain species of wood or stone, the beauty of it might be in its muted tones—color would be inappropriate. Take direction from the specifics of your project.

AP: How would you summarize the function of graphics in presenting a design?

IS: Particularly in business, where selling is the name of the game, you want to distinguish your project; capture its essence and uniqueness. The package can count for a lot . . . at least initially.

AP: So your message is to underscore the importance of graphics and presentation in selling your design.

IS: Yes, but that is not to say that slickness and sheen are sufficient, especially in the profession of architecture. You can probably make a bad design look good with super graphics, but what's the point? You won't fool anyone in the long run. You can certainly make a good design look bad by not paying enough attention to pro-fessional quality in the presentation—that's a real waste—don't make that mistake twice! A great presentation of a good design can distinguish you from everyone else who has talent and enthusiasm.

AP: In your work, how do you deal with criticism?

IS: When a project is criticized or rejected in some form, and the artist is personally satisfied with it, I always tell the artist to think of it as another completely different assignment. It just shows that there are a hundred ways to approach a problem. Sometimes, and I really hate to admit this, I'm so glad I responded to the criticism because the project usually gets better.

AP: One issue I've noticed in studio is that some students spend too much time design-ing title blocks and logos. And in practice, I know of architects who design their own letterheads—and they're horrible!

IS: It does tarnish the professional image, not to mention wasting time. Graphic design is so polished today in just about everything we see—from flyers from the local Chinese restaurant to junk mail—that anything less than high polish appears glaringly bad. My advice to students (and practitioners) is, quite simply, to stick to what you do best—architecture! It's presumptuous to assume competence in another field, albeit related, without the requisite training or at least some good experience.

AP: Any quick graphic tips?

IS: Graphic elements should be emphasized differently—that is, there has to be a "hit" or focal point, along with a gradation of values. You don't want someone's interest to be diffused.

AP: Give me an example of an architectural design concept that influences or cues presentation ideas.

IS: Say that you have a tall building where the vertical lines are articulated. That may suggest a vertical orientation of drawings. Conversely, if you have a low, ram-bling suburban building, maybe you have a very wide format, accentuating the horizontality.

AP: What about presenting slides instead of drawings, or video?

IS: Depends on the situation. You certainly have more control in terms of sequence and maybe holding someone's attention with slides. For instance, you won't have a juror distractedly trying to balance your precious model on his/her knee while you're pointing to one of your boards. In general, slide shows work best on a big scale—when you've got an auditorium full of people. Then go all out with multiple images—use three screens!

Video has much potential—simulating a walk through of your building—and of course this kind of thing tied into computer animation is exciting. But it could turn out to be more of a gimmick, where attention is drawn to the medium and not the design. You should have a good reason for any medium you choose.

Art Supplies and Reprographics

The selection of graphic media, which involves the consideration of a range of art supplies and equipment, and perhaps the use of reproductions of sketches to reduce, enlarge, or render, is central to a coherent, efficient, and beautiful presen-tion. Often, the selection is a function of faculty requirements, available time, or the complexity of the project.

It is always useful and quite enjoyable to browse in a great art supply store to review what is appropriate and affordable for any given project. Similarly, a visit to a printing and copying establishment will help to clarify (and you will see firsthand) the quality of various reprographic processes. Experiment by bringing a few typical sketches, and ask for suggestions on how to achieve desired goals economically.

> *SUPPLEMENT 5-4:* One of the finest sources of materials for artists and architects is the Charrette Corporation, headquartered in Woburn, MA, with branches in many of the major educational centers. The first of this two-part Supplement is contributed by Blair Brown, President of Charrette. He has chosen to address the subject of "supplies" through a discussion of the architectural model—an application that relies on proper selection of materials.
>
> The second part is by Jim Maitland, who has served students of architecture for sixteen years, working in the retail stores, warehouse, and reprographics division of Charrette. He earned his B.A. at Amherst College. Mr. Maitland's superb review of reprographic technologies is the most informative and skillfully condensed treatment of the subject I have seen.

PART 1: SUPPLIES AND THE ARCHITECTURAL MODEL

Few tools that the architect uses have as much impact as the architectural model. Some believe that drawings, computer representations, or renderings cannot present as much information as convincingly as a three-dimensional depiction. There are several types of models: Study models, massing, and finished models. And all of these are done in several scales.

Small-scale models are very useful for site plans and massing studies and building location studies; large-scale models are quite useful for the examination of interior spaces. Large-scale models are also valuable in looking at building elevations and elevation details.

Small-Scale Models

Site plans and building location plans are usually shown at small scale, 50 feet to the inch or 100 feet to the inch. These models can show the contours of the land if the building is on a site that has significant elevation changes, and it can show the building location within a broader urban context.

Contour models are usually made from chipboard available in a variety of thicknesses. Chipboard is made from recycled newsprint and corrugated boxes. One-sixteenth-inch and one-thirty-second-inch chipboard are relatively easy to cut with a utility knife or a model knife, and the chip strata can be attached using a simple polyvinyl glue such as Elmer's or Sobo. One should use chip that is consistent in color. Eighth-inch chipboard would be an appropriate contour height, but this thickness is hard to cut in the irregular patterns necessary for a contour model. A Cutawl cutter is a useful tool under these circumstances, and may be available in the departmental shop.

Foam center boards such as Monsanto Fome-Cor, Bienfang Foam Board, or Charrette Cambridge Foam Board are also useful for making large-scale contour models. These materials are very easy to cut and their light weight means that a model depicting a dramatically sloping site need not be cumbersome or too heavy to carry. Some of these foam center boards are available with a Kraft surface paper, which many find useful in showing land contours. Make sure that the foam board that you use does not contain chlorinated fluorocarbons (CFCs), which are released into the atmosphere.

For siting buildings in an urban context, many have used "building elements" cut with a hot wire cutter from solid billets of foam. Several hot wire cutters are available on the market, including the Brownstone Hot Wire Cutter (see Figure 5-6). This method is a very fast, very useful way of making site models. Furthermore, because of their cavalier and rough-hewn nature, these models say "study model," which can serve in provoking dialogue and encouraging constructive "what if scenarios" while averting criticism of a "fait accompli."

Often, a diazo print can be mounted on a model base and the actual buildings placed on top of the drawing. A few elements, such as scale-model cars or trees (actually twigs of natural wildflowers such as yarrow), are usually enough to finish off the model.

Large-Scale Models

Building elevations are often studied at $\frac{1}{16}$ scale while interiors are often studied at $\frac{1}{8}$ inch or $\frac{1}{4}$ inch. Quarter-inch scale, often used in residential studies, leads to a model that is very descriptive and most useful both for the client, in understanding a specific job more fully, and for the architect, who must invest a model with quite a bit of detail and must reconcile various elements in three-dimensional form. While more demanding to make, these models are very useful and tell a lot about a specific project. They are often made of foam board or corrugated or white clear-through illustration board.

In large-scale models such as $\frac{1}{8}$ inch or $\frac{1}{4}$ inch = 1 foot, the diagram paste-down technique is most efficient. Wall element lengths are easily measured and the relationships between elements are clearly seen and understood. Often, representations or labels on the print are all that is needed to complete the model, and furniture or other elements need not be made.

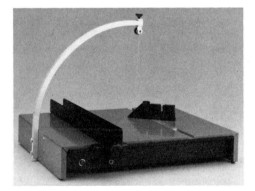

FIGURE 5-6   *The Brownstone Hot Wire Cutter is a professional model-making tool that can significantly enhance efficiency as described above. Its relatively high cost may require the investment of several students, who can then share its use throughout the studio. Photo courtesy of Charrette Corporation.*

PART 2: REPROGRAPHICS

Reprographics (a compound word encompassing all methods of reproducing graphic images) plays an integral role in the practice of architecture. Its primary function is to minimize redrawing time, an idea expressed in the old maxim "draw the line once" or, in today's computer-influenced parlance, "draw once, repro many." While a cost-conscious student may not want to take that advice too literally, no architect, student or professional, lives a repro-free life. Therefore, it is incumbent on all designers to "draw for reproduction" (i.e., learn and master the art of creating original drawings that can be reproduced effectively).

In this age of flourishing technology, reprographic methods abound. The four currently in widest use for reproducing architectural drawings are diazo printing, xerographic copying, photographic reproduction, and computer-based imaging. Students of architecture should begin experimenting with diazo printing and copying of their first major project drawings. Photographic reproductions are normally considered for portfolio preparation. Computer-based imaging of architectural drawings, such as plotting, depends on access to a CAD workstation and training.

Diazo Printing

For the student and professional alike, diazo printing is the least expensive and most accessible of these reprographic methods. Blueprinting, with its characteristic reversed-image white lines on a blue background, gave way to the positive-to-positive diazo printing process many years ago, although shops that offer diazo printing may still call themselves blueprinters and are listed in the Yellow Pages under that heading. To distinguish them from the older technology, diazo prints are sometimes called *whiteprints* because they produce dark lines on a white (or whitish) background. Most commonly, a diazo print is described by the color of its image, as in *blueline, blackline, or sepia*. As a benchmark for other large format materials and methods, a single 24-inch by 36-inch blackline print will cost about $2, with the price usually dropping for multiple prints done at the same time.

Like the photographic process, diazo printing involves exposure and development of a light-sensitive emulsion on a substrate material such as paper or film. The light-sensitive diazo material is first placed in contact with a translucent original, normally a drawing on trace paper, vellum, or Mylar, then exposed to ultraviolet light. Light passes through the background or nonimage areas of the translucent original, "burning off" the diazo emulsion, and is blocked by the drawn image, leaving the diazo emulsion under it intact. Original and diazo material are separated. When the diazo material is then developed in a mixture of ammonia and water vapor, the print is ready. Depending on the print machine used, the entire process may take less than a minute to several minutes per print.

In generic terms, the fact that light passes through the original during exposure makes diazo a transmission process, as opposed to the reflection process of xerography, in which light is reflected off the surface of an original in reproduction. The quality of any transmission process print is largely dependent on the opacity of the image. Drafting ink is far more opaque than graphite. Consequently, drawings done in ink make better diazo prints than those done in pencil. The possibility of making a good, legible print of a pencil drawing is greatly enhanced if a relatively soft lead (2H or softer) is used by a firm, decisive hand.

Diazo prints fall into two basic substrate categories: Opaque and translucent. The most frequently used and inexpensive of all diazo prints—blacklines and bluelines—have an opaque bond paper substrate. Many architects prefer blackline to blueline, for aesthetic reasons. Black is more neutral if a print is to be colored. Black also reproduces better if a print needs to be copied or photographed later. Blacklines are used throughout a project's life—prints of preliminary sketches, prints for presentation, progress check prints, bid sets, construction plans, shop drawings, and as-builts.

Designers often enhance blackline prints for presentation by coloring them with pencils, pastels, markers, or translucent color overlays such as Pantone adhesive-backed film. Because of their porosity, blacklines usually aren't watercolored, but if a print is first mounted on a rigid substrate such as foam board, watercolors can be applied successfully. Blacklines can also be used to simplify model making. After making prints of the project's site plan and elevations in the required scale, mounting (adhering) the prints to a rigid material such as foam board precedes cutting and assembly.

Within the opaque diazo print category are higher-quality, higher-cost papers typically used for presentations. Options might include heavier weight, smoother or rougher surface texture for improved workability with various coloring media, and higher-contrast emulsions capable of producing denser solids with whiter whites.

In the second basic type of diazo print, an original drawing is reproduced on a translucent diazo material so that the translucent print can be used as a second or duplicate original, suitable for additional drawing and printing. Prints of this type are often called *intermediates*. Students and professionals choose to have an intermediate made when certain basic information on a drawing—topographic lines, floor plan, existing conditions, and so on—is to be included on other drawings. A translucent print of this type is either a "sepia" [diazo-coated vellum which when exposed and developed shows a sepia-colored (reddish-brown) image] or a "diazo Mylar" (diazo-coated drafting film). Sepias and diazo Mylars are usually printed "reverse-read," with the image on the back of the print to permit new drawing on the front without disturbing the basic information. If changes need to be made, diazo images can be removed from sepias and diazo Mylars with eradicating fluid, or, in some cases, with a rubber eraser.

Xerography

The second technology frequently used by architects is xerography. For sketches and studies smaller than 11 inches by 17 inches, the average office copier can be an effective and inexpensive repro tool. Since most architectural drawings exceed 11 inches by 17 inches, large-format copiers that handle 36-inch-width materials both in and out are indispensable. Unlike diazo print machines, sophisticated large-format copiers are capable of reproducing an opaque original and of changing its size. If an architect begins a project with existing conditions expressed in supplied blackline or blueline prints, there is no quicker, more cost-effective way to convert those plans into draftable originals than to make a large format copy on vellum from the diazo prints, perhaps converting them to a preferred scale at the same time. The common scaling range of most large-format copiers is approximately 45 through 200 percent of original size. Having this control over the size of a drawing enables a designer to cut, paste, and recopy reduced drawings to show multiple views or design evolution in one composite. When preparing a model from drawings that are out of scale, a large-format copy usually solves the problem quickly. Reducing drawings for a portfolio is also possible on a large-format copier, although drawings larger than 18 inches by 24 inches usually require multiple reduction steps, which may affect line quality. Like a standard copier, large-format copiers tend to darken lines in the reduction mode, a tendency compounded by multiple-step reductions.

Large-format copies are available on bond paper, vellum, Mylar, and depending on the repro shop, premium presentation-grade papers. Although these materials are comparable to diazo materials, large-format copies tend to be more expensive. A same-size copy on vellum at 24 inches by 36 inches is usually in the $8 to $11 range. However, for jobs involving scale changes, large-format copies are the least expensive option, running about half of what a photographic reproduction costs.

Photographic Reproduction

Despite its higher cost, there are some situations in which photo reproduction is worth it. This is especially true with reductions of large originals for paste-up or portfolio preparation. The advantage of photo over large-format copying is that most reductions can be made in one shot without significant loss of line quality. Many repro centers specializing in architectural drawings have cameras capable of reducing a 40-inch by 60-inch drawing to fit any portfolio size. Within the photo family are direct positive "stats," a.k.a. "p.m.t.s," which create a high-contrast black-and-white reproduction without a film negative and cost $7 to $15 per original. Stats tend to be the least expensive photo option. At the upper end of the cost scale, a lab can shoot a copy negative of a drawing, then make photographic prints at any size from the negative. An 8.5-inch by 11-inch copy negative and print will cost about $20 to $30 combined. For black-and-white reproduction, this option affords the highest quality available.

Color Reprographics

To this point we've discussed monochrome reprographics (i.e., methods that are meant to reproduce "black-and-white" drawings). For reproducing color originals in color, there are both xerographic and photographic options, although students should be aware from the outset that full-color reproduction is often significantly more expensive than black-and-white for large-format originals. The best value in full-color reprographics currently available is the color laser copy, which is quick, high in quality, moderately priced, and versatile enough to handle slides, chromes, and flat art. Prices and quality can vary widely for color laser copies, but should be less than $5 for a standard 8.5-inch by 11-inch size.

Unfortunately, the size limitations of most color laser copiers (maximum original and copy size is 11 inches by 17 inches) require some adjustments for architects working with large-format originals. For reductions of colored diazo prints, there are two options. The expensive option, $20 to $50 per original, is to have a color photographic or Bubble-Jet color copy reduction made at a photo lab or repro center. In the less expensive option, architects shoot slides of their own originals for copying on the Canon CLC500 with film scanner. If images are ganged on one roll of film, this method can save more than half of the color lab cost. Of course, as with all reprographic methods, the quality of the copy depends on the quality of the original slide. Making good slides of original artwork is itself a skill. Proper film and lighting are essential if the end product, a color copy, is to be satisfactory. Shooting slides of original art is also a service offered at many reprographics centers and photo labs, usually at a cost of around $12 per original.

Evaluate Benefits and Costs

Properly used, reprographics allows one drawing to serve many purposes without redrafting. To maximize this effect, an original drawing should be considered a master for reproduction, never to be seen by teacher or client other than in print form. Of course, cost is a factor, especially for students who, unlike professional architects, aren't usually reimbursed for their reprographic bills. Impecunious students may choose to put more sweat equity into their work by redrafting rather than make another trip to the repro center. One thing to remember when having a repro job done—always get a sense of what it will cost before placing the order.

THREE-DIMENSIONAL VEHICLES

Nancy Hubbard, Ph.D., an Assistant Professor at the University of Wisconsin–Milwaukee and a principal of her own firm in Chicago, once told me that if she had only one type of presentation vehicle for her clients, it would be a series of colorful *perspective* renderings. For me, it would probably be a *study model*. The point is this: An accurate three-dimensional representation is worth a thousand two-dimensional drawings. Communication of the design scheme is quite simply much easier to understand, and for many clients, essential. Plans and sections are not easy to read—it takes considerable effort and time to coordinate and assimilate the different pieces of information. The three-dimensional drawing or model puts it all together. Marc Hinshaw of Holt Hinshaw Pfau Jones, quoted in *Progressive Architecture*, June 1989, states: "The model is there to comfort the client so that the drawings can reach for a higher level of understanding about a project. It is like a one-two punch."

A major disadvantage of a formal presentation model is the time required to fabricate it. Simulations of materials and visible construction details can be startlingly close to reality. Basswood is a common model material—it is relatively hard and thus produces crisp edges, but it is difficult to work with. There may be a rare occasion to build one of these when an especially fine model is required, and every student should probably have the experience at least once (but only once).

I believe that a good cardboard study model augmented with graphics, in general, comprises a well-balanced communications attack. As always, try to appreciate the client's point of view (this is not always easy, especially as your level of competence and sophistication keep growing). If you get in the habit of graphically expressing ideas for the nonarchitect (i.e., realistically, three-dimensionally), communication is invariably enhanced. Better design more than likely follows from improved dialogue between architect and client.

> *SUPPLEMENT 5-5:* Norman McGrath is one of the finest architectural photographers in the world. His work has been published in every major architectural publication in the United States and Europe. Here Mr. McGrath gives advice on photographing models. (See also his Supplement 6-5 on photographing buildings.)

MODEL PHOTOGRAPHY FOR PRESENTATION

Do not attempt model photography without a good-quality single-lens reflex (SLR) camera. Even with a reflex camera it's not easy. You should try to get close to your subject, particularly if you wish to simulate the look of a real building. Keep your backgrounds simple. A roll of no-seam paper as a backdrop will create a mini-studio for your model. Put the model on a table or support so that you can approximate ground-level views.

FIGURE 5-7   *Peter Pfau provided one of his firm's (Holt Hinshaw Pfau Jones Architecture) presentation drawings. This demonstrates how a combination of talent and effort can produce a stunning "visual" (ink with dot screen overlays).*

Shooting outside to take advantage of sunlight can be great, with good, sharp shadows, but watch out for those backgrounds. It is easier, however, to work with reflector spots (or floods) in a room where you can control the light. If you use tungsten or incandescent lights, use a type B film if you're doing slides. With color negative, even a daylight film can be corrected when prints are made. For aerial views, you can tilt the camera down, but for ground-level shots, try and keep it level and your vertical elements will remain vertical. Removable parts of your model may permit you to get in closer with your camera. Your lens, of course, will have to have close-focusing capability. For added depth of field or sharp focus, you will have to stop the aperture of the lens down as much as possible and use a longer exposure, so the camera must be firmly mounted (on a tripod or tabletop stand) and use a cable release. A blue background may suggest sky, but gray may also work. Controlling the lighting of the model as well as the backdrop will create different effects. Don't be discouraged if you don't achieve your objectives the first time. Get advice or help if possible. Good luck!

AN ADDENDUM ON JURIES

I don't think most of the learning about design occurs at final design reviews. The environment of a review is subject to variation and may be a function of the specific jury makeup and other factors, but it is often charged with academic and emotional intensity. This extreme is not usually the most conducive for reflective learning. However, I do think reviews can be excellent exercises for improving presentation of your work in front of groups of people. This is, of course, a very important part of the process. Kathryn Anthony's book (*Design Juries on Trial*) is a fine source for much additional information on this enduring phenomenon of architectural education.

Take time after each final review to think about the criticism of your project and that of others as well. Take a few specific notes on what was said immediately after your presentation. See if the comments apply in the cold light of the next morning. If the criticism was not crystal clear even after your best efforts to achieve clarification, approach a juror for a follow-up: What specifically could have been done differently to improve the project? There shouldn't be too much of a mystery assuming that you've had critiques in class during the course of the project. If you were a little shaky, it may also be a product of inexperience. You cannot expect perfection from yourself when starting out.

A few words on "emotional trauma." As in any intense and sometimes emotionally demanding experience, you will occasionally feel somewhat drained, beat-up, even hurt in the wake of a rough review. The best way to roll with the punches is through talking, both to faculty members and to your peers. Ventilate and express how you feel. You will surely be comforted by the relief that comes from talking, and strengthened by the understanding and support of allies. Moreover, you will marvel at how healing for you it will be to provide a warm and sympathetic ear for others who are temporarily down-and-out.

6

The Future

"There is no room now for the dilettante, the weakling, for the shirker, or the sluggard."—Sir Winston S. Churchill

Example of a dilettante, weakling, shirker, and sluggard who survived design studios and became an architect.
Photo credit: Peter Pressman.

Building a model out of mat board, using an X-Acto knife. Things going smoothly. After a half-hour, realization that the knife penetrated through the cardboard and ruined the custom laminate work surface. . . .

Penciling-in changes on a sepia drawing using eradicator fluid, then look away for a moment, turn, and knock over the bottle of fluid which spills over the entire drawing. The presentation deadline will not be met, or at least this drawing will not be part of it. . . .

Using the blueprint machine on a Saturday when nobody else is in the office to run some copies of drawings for personal portfolio. The machine jams, and the original drawing gets stuck and rips. Can't get it out of the machine. . . .

The summer job or coop experience coupled with the tolerance and patience of the involved architectural firms truly help the fledgling architect bridge the worlds of school and professional practice. Most practicing architects, as professionals, take their responsibility of helping and advising interns seriously, and it is of course now mandated by law via the Intern Development Program in all states.

I always enjoy visiting architects' offices. They usually express unconsciously and self-consciously something of the collective personality of the firm and the quality of design produced. Sometimes there is real experimentation going on, sometimes slickness to impress clients, and rarely can one say that offices are mundane. A former classmate of mine was hired by a New York City firm after graduating, just blocks away from the firm where I was working. It was incredible to see the environment in which he worked: It felt like a time warp back into the 1950s, complete with institutional green walls, "elder" draftsmen (no women) with green eyeshades, and sandpaper for sharpening pencils. It was no wonder they had commissions renovating prisons in New Jersey. Not that this was a bad internship experience—in fact, it may be valuable for those who are undecided as to specialty interest and type of practice to work in a diversity of office settings.

Many smaller offices have a large space for staff workstations, with private offices only for firm principals, and meeting rooms. Expect to be out in the open!— not too much space and not too much privacy.

As you contemplate searching for a job, take a look at the A.I.A. brochure entitled, "Graduating into Architecture" (telephone or write A.I.A. National Headquarters in Washington, DC). This nineteen-page publication contains particularly useful information on requirements for initial registration. Other valuable tidbits, addresses, lists, and a brief discussion of the Intern Development Program (IDP) lie among the usual public relations material.

GETTING IN THE DOOR

Start thinking about summer job prospects during winter break. Begin to formulate a list of firms to approach, block out a résumé, and make sure that your portfolio can come on-line at a moment's notice (and is flexible enough to accept any relevant current work).

FIGURE 6-1   *The New York City loft offices of Robert A.M. Stern Architects skillfully combine low budget with high-style Postmodern elegance. Photograph © 1987 Peter Aaron/Esto.*

Try to look out for any personal contacts, possible referrals from faculty or colleagues, notices on department bulletin boards, names of practicing alumni, and classified advertisements. Barring a windfall from one of the preceding sources, contact the local A.I.A. chapter as a starting point to develop your list of firms to research and approach. Many chapters publish annual directories of all architecture firms in their particular region or state. Typical listings include firm size and specialty, contact persons, principals, examples of projects, awards, and some even include "firm philosophy." This is a great way to narrow down the field and limit the randomness of your initial possibilities. Consult the A.I.A.'s *ProFile* (available in many libraries and local A.I.A. chapters), which covers some of these data nationwide—although, depending on the edition, may not be as up-to-date as the local version.

My personal preference for initial inquiries is via a letter and accompanying résumé. Make certain that the letter is tailored to the target firm at least to some degree. You might mention your school experience and the way in which it aligns with the work of the firm. If you have some compelling attraction to a firm's geographic locale, this may translate to a distinctive and valuable bit of information.

FIGURE 6-2 *NBBJ headquarters in Seattle is planned around a cascading five-story stair. Conversion of this old warehouse displays design talent to prospective clients far in excess of the standard promotional material. Photograph © Dick Busher 1987.*

When you are eventually called for an interview, refer back to the firm's directory listing, and commit the information to memory. Try to visit one of the typical projects listed. If none are listed, check all indexes in the library (for the architecture journals as well as any trade magazines related to the firm's specialty) to learn about their work. This will help you to make a more educated decision and will be quite impressive in your discussions with firm personnel.

Line-up potential references. Prepare packages of material for your faculty "mentors," including a résumé and possibly some selected portfolio inserts—make sure that you obtain first-rate reproductions. Arrange a brief meeting to discuss your plans, leave the package, and consider requesting a letter of recommendation. You might want one or two letters to strengthen the résumé you review at your job interviews to really distinguish yourself. Be sure to follow-up with news about job outcome (good or bad) to all references—it is not only the correct protocol but common sense—your reference undoubtedly spent time on your behalf and deserves to be kept informed.

FIGURE 6-3   *This now-defunct San Francisco branch office of what was The Ehrenkrantz Group occupied renovated space in a historic coffee bean warehouse. The striking, sculptural, and inexpensive gypsum board insertions define workstations, yet preserve the visual integrity of the existing structure. Photograph copyright Peter J. Henricks.*

SUPPLEMENT 6-1: Norman Rosenfeld is the founding principal of Norman Rosenfeld, A.I.A. Architects, a New York City-based architectural firm, since 1969, specializing in the programming, planning, and design for health care, education, and commercial projects. Mr. Rosenfeld has lectured widely and taught hospital planning and design courses for graduate students and architects.

IN PURSUIT OF A JOB

The decision by a firm principal as to which young architect to hire is frequently more visceral than quantifiable. We're looking for the bright-eyed and energetic next generation. Grade-point average is a superficial indicator but not a clincher, nor is an advanced degree. Degrees from certain schools may offer better promise, but school reputations are often cyclical. Broad interests, a good hand, an inquisitive mind, a poised personality, professional potential, and the right fit for the office all count.

The Résumé

Of course, the résumé is an important calling card—presentation counts! A Mac résumé gives you the opportunity to show your computer skills, your graphic sensitivity, your good design sense, and that you consider it important to present yourself well and professionally. Poorly presented résumés will be left aside for the third- or fourth-round review, if that ever happens. After all, everyone knows you can and often do "tell a book by its cover"; at least you may buy it and begin to read it before you put it down. You do want the reader to read on.

The content and style of résumés are important. How an intern applicant presents his/her minimal experience will indicate a certain initiative and imagination—not dissimilar to architects who submit their credentials for a new project for which they may have no special qualifications. Clients and potential employers may look past slim experience if other things present well. Often, personal recommendations from respected colleagues, or staff, are the best door opener. Getting the interview is what you want!

The Interview

First impressions count! Show up on time. Dress generally to match the office's style. Some minor quirky statement may be useful to impress. I often annotate a résumé during an interview with lots of facts and impressions but also may note the interviewee's unique eyeglass frames or tie as a future memory trigger—you may think you are unique, but all those bright faces do sometimes blur.

Always have an extra copy of your résumé. Résumés have a way of getting buried in other papers, preventing easy recall and causing me some embarrassment while rummaging. Help me with a fresh copy—gently proffered. The résumé undoubtedly contained something of interest—that's why you were invited to the interview. Be prepared to answer questions about school, job experience, and other skills if you are light on architectural office experience. CAD and Mac skills are very appealing to prospective employers and a good entrée to an office. CAD proficiency is a modern-day substitute for tracers who did the routine drafting. Mac skills are valuable in the graphics/presentation efforts of an office.

The Portfolio

Presentation counts! One assumes that the substance and content of intern architects is limited to school work. Graphic quality, organization of project material, as an adjunct to the interviewee's discussion of the material will demonstrate a sense of design and an ability to express verbally unique aspects of the development thought process or project presented. I often silently review the portfolio, but will concurrently ask several searching questions to determine if the interviewee understood what was drawn, and has an agile mind and verbal presence to respond to questions from left field. These attributes can turn adversity into success and then point my questions in another more fruitful direction.

Closing the Hire

I enjoy interviews that are a two-way street. After I have reviewed the portfolio and asked my questions, I welcome the interviewee who poses questions to me. Not about fringe benefits or office vacation policy, but unanswered professional questions—perhaps about what the office does or how it does it. While I try to cover this ground during my introductory discussion, I encourage questions that will give me insight into what interests the interviewee and how the mind and spirit work. It may be questions on our built work—which I will likely have shown those who have lasted through my early questioning, or it may be how the office is organized and staff assigned—finishing with what employment opportunity is available. The outcome of this exchange may be when I sense the interviewee has great potential and could be a valuable addition to our staff. I may then mentally create a new job position on the spot as I am talking. It has truly happened.

Salary is best left to the end and is usually the least difficult hurdle to address—except when you choose to interview with those firms who believe their experience opportunity is so valuable that it is a privilege to work there, at no salary. You know who they are. Everyone else knows what a hiring wage is, or should be, with some relationship to your level of contribution. The commitment to hire is rarely done at the first interview, but the sense to hire is usually established. I may have other interviews scheduled, partners to meet with, and scheduling to consider, but positive messages can be given and a time frame for decision committed to. A follow-up short letter from the interviewee, again as we do with new client prospects, is a nice touch and a good reminder that you are interested.

IN THE TRENCHES

Once you have the job, the Take-Home Message is to be a good soldier. The whole point is to learn about professional practice; get exposed to as many diverse tasks as possible. And in contrast to the old army wisdom, volunteer for everything!

A general student concern is whether the tasks assigned will be boring. The fear is that while school studio focuses on design and is incredibly stimulating, a summer office experience will require nothing but getting coffee and doing everyone else's most unpleasant leftovers. To some extent that is true; however—make the most out of whatever opportunity is presented. You *are* qualified to do some design-related work, and firm principals know this. For example, you are asked to develop a tile layout for a toilet room. Adopt the attitude that these relatively mundane tasks can be transformed into an *intriguing design challenge* (which **is** true). It is precisely this attitude that ultimately produces better results, and ostensibly, satisfaction. What kind of interesting floor/wall pattern can be developed? Can you propose a small band of color tile? Can you propose using a couple of different sizes of tile? Can you use a few tiles along the wall to create an interesting accent or mosaic? Actors say, "There are no small parts, only small actors." The same applies to architectural projects: The designer has the power to make the most seemingly insignificant projects into something very special that has an impact. That's why, in my own practice, I rarely turn down small-scale projects that have practically no budget. In fact, I *want* these types of projects! I actively seek them out (begging can be a very effective marketing strategy, but that is beyond the scope of this book). You'd be amazed at the gratefulness of clients not to mention enormous publicity that can result from attentiveness to a small problem, and a clever and sensitive response. Another benefit is that it keeps the architect in touch with *reality* . . . dealing with some of the most basic issues of daily life. When you are relegated to bathroom details as an intern, or when you become a "star" architect and have your own practice, remember this point. (See Figures 6-4 and 6-5.)

Your First Job

The following three Supplements written by an intern, an architect from a large practice, and two small-firm practitioners characterize starting-out from their respective points of view. Common to all is the thinking that there is a great diversity

FIGURE 6-4 *This is an example from my practice of a "mundane" kitchen renovation project in Chicago that was budgeted at $8000 (construction cost, not architectural fee). We went through the entire process of programming, analyses, and even built a study model. It was a satisfying experience for both client and architect, and what we didn't receive in fees, we more than made up with publication in* Popular Science, The Washington Post, *and* Qualified Remodeler. *This is not to say that we turn down or don't want larger-scale projects—it's just to demonstrate that an attitude of service for clients who present with "everyday" projects can be quite rewarding. Design and drawing by the author.*

not only within a specific job, but within the profession itself. Also expressed is the theme that the design of buildings does not constitute a singular effort—typically, many people contribute within the firm in addition to outside consultants.

> *SUPPLEMENT 6-2:* Intern architect Michael Sobczak worked throughout his undergraduate studies and was a teaching assistant in the design studio during his graduate studies. He has been honored with scholarships and his designs have been recognized by The Wisconsin Society of Architects. He currently works with Plunkett Raysich Architects in Milwaukee.

FIGURE 6-5   *Another "ordinary" project for which the thought of hiring an architect would not even occur to most people. Back rooms like this can offer architects challenges involving lighting, space planning, ceiling forms, color, and casework. This one in Princeton, NJ, functions as playroom and occasional guest suite with bathroom. Total construction cost including new bathroom: $12,000. Total architect's time (design through construction administration): 35 hours. Design and drawing by the author.*

SCHOOL AND PRACTICE—A BALANCING ACT

In the field of architecture, like most professions, there is a great difference between school and practice. Training in school or studio focuses on the development of conceptual and critical thinking skills. Designs are too often executed in this ideal setting with no budgets, clients, or thorough attention to the practical issues of technology. And, in school, one student orchestrates *every* aspect of a project.

Unlike the school studio, a design is the product of many people, not a single author. These may include planners, project managers, architects, draftspeople, consultant engineers, interior designers, and field supervisors. To many new interns, this division of the job is a very new idea and the seemingly small role that each may play can be a shock. Many interns spend numerous hours laying out room elevations, doing door schedules, and making drafting changes (a process called "picking up red marks"). Although the school and practice experience may be quite different, they are, nonetheless, both parts of what an architect is about; a certain complementary balance exists between the acquisition of basic skills in the ideal studio and how those skills are tempered and applied in professional practice.

The intern architect should approach the first job with open eyes and a willingness to learn new things. During an internship you will learn about construction techniques and drawings, shop drawings, construction administration, budget, programming, client presentation, and marketing. The intern should observe the process in the office and develop a feel for where he or she would like to specialize (i.e., as project manager, field supervisor, or designer). Do not neglect to communicate your preferences to management. If you happen to be in school while simultaneously holding down a part-time job, you can also focus on aspects of your curriculum that will support the attainment of your goals.

The intern should take responsibility for professional development by letting principals know his/her aspirations. Take professional development classes and attend seminars. This professional "take charge" attitude will help develop your strengths and will be appreciated by employers.

In conclusion, an intern should view school as a place to learn design in its purest form, and practice as a place to make it reality. Architects are constantly compromising between the ideals they aspire to and the realities of practice. This dichotomy not only characterizes practice but leads to creative solutions. Finally, an intern must be patient with the apparently slow progress in learning the skills inherent to the practice of architecture. These new skills will combine with and balance the idealism of school to produce an effective and efficient architect.

SUPPLEMENT 6-3:   Lawrence J. Schnuck, A.I.A., is a design architect with the fifty-two-person Milwaukee firm Kahler Slater Architects. He is a member of the Committee on Design of the American Institute of Architects. As an Adjunct Assistant Professor in the School of Architecture at the University of Wisconsin–Milwaukee, Mr. Schnuck is in a unique position to observe students make "the transition" from the design studio to the office environment of the typical large firm.

YOUR FIRST JOB—THE TRANSITION

As you complete your studies in architecture and begin to pursue a job in the architectural field, you should conduct a certain amount of research into each firm with which you become interested. Each firm tends to specialize in various "types" of architecture, and this aspect should be illuminated. As an example, if your focus in school was housing and you wish to continue to develop this building type, try to identify firms that specialize in housing. Many firms pursue more than one building type and you, as a prospective employee, should appreciate this as you begin to create your own inventory of a firm's strengths and weaknesses. This may sound somewhat judgmental and even premature; however, it is always wise to try to achieve a thorough understanding of the situation you hope to enter.

It is also important to find a firm that will support you and is committed to the Intern Development Program (IDP) as established by the National Council of Architectural Registration Boards. The IDP program will be required for architectural registration beginning in 1993 in all states. The IDP program is an excellent format, as it requires an Intern's involvement in all phases and aspects of architecture and provides a well-rounded background for your professional development.

Not all of you will work in a traditional architectural office setting, as there are numerous jobs related to architecture, such as corporate architecture and facilities management, to name but two. Within these alternative fields along with the more "traditional" route in practicing architecture, the most significant change, as you make the transition into your new job, will be the concept of teamwork. You will no longer be the sole individual responsible for a project as you were in the studio. Rather, you will be one of a group of talented professionals to whom a range of tasks will be delegated. Among those tasks that at first glance may seem less than exciting are running prints, building models, and picking up red lines on drawings. When running prints, look at the way projects go together, how details are drawn. This gives you a better understanding of what it takes to develop a project and also helps you learn something about the various consultants. A senior staff member will have reviewed the project drawings for conformance to program and quality assurance. Any deficiencies will be marked up or "red lined." It will be your job to transfer the notes and correct the drawings as marked. Picking up red lines gives you further opportunity to take a close look at the construction documents—an excellent educational exercise, and one that provides firsthand participation toward learning how materials go together.

As you develop a better understanding of how the office operates and begin to hone your skills, you will be assigned to a team within the office to work on a specific project. You will become an integral (junior) member of that team. Your tasks will probably be to provide assistance to a senior member of your team in the development of a specific element of the project, such as working out a lobby space for an office building or producing schematic plans for a housing complex. Your work will be critiqued by other members of your team and refinements suggested. It is inevitable that you will be asked to provide additional schemes for aspects of your project; some of this work may seem unchallenging and trivial, but it does pay off in learning. Your opinion is very important to the successful completion of the project. Over time, you will be called upon to take greater responsibility in projects and eventually lead teams. But remember, you never stop learning!

SUPPLEMENT 6-4: Ordway-Kousoulas Architects of Bethesda, MD, is a small architectural and exhibit design firm. The principals, Fred Ordway and George Kousoulas, offer another glimpse of reality from the trenches. They reiterate that there is a broad range of job opportunities, and with experience and self-awareness, you can continue to grow professionally and ultimately avert any midlife crises!

YOUR FIRST JOB—WHAT TO THINK, WHAT TO EXPECT

In many ways, your first job will be an experience not far removed from starting architecture school. An entry-level position in architecture is certainly another beginning. There is a big learning curve, and a honing of creative talents as well. There is rising responsibility. Then there is more; you begin to acquire a stature in the profession and in the community, and of course, you are earning a living.

The modes of earning a living in architecture and the kinds of organizations offering design services have multiplied in the last twenty years. An intern today might work for a city planning agency, a corporation's facilities management department, or an interior design firm. The traditional path, of course, is through firms that design buildings for others, but even in this mode there is variety. There are large national design firms, regional production-oriented firms, and many small sole proprietorships and partnerships. The many options make it more advantageous than ever to be focused and informed in your search for a first job. Concentrated efforts (i.e., doing your homework) in the smallest and most manageable universe of possibilities will probably yield greater chances for success.

Study your personal and professional goals. Aside from making money (the magnitude of which may be a function of the particular direction you choose), assess what you really want to accomplish in the profession, and think about the arena in which you are likely to feel most comfortable.

Study your strengths and weaknesses. Are you design oriented, technically inclined, maybe you enjoy monitoring and controlling the progress of a job (i.e., telling other people what to do!), or does being a jack-of-all-trades appeal to you?

Study the jobs. In discussions with other architects, including prospective employers, make an effort to know what is really behind the standard job descriptions, with an eye toward understanding the range of available positions and their growth potentials. Then try to match them with your own style and interests. Compare and contrast work done by private firms, corporate departments, and government agencies. Examine all the variables, including location and office size. Excited by the prospect of some new, exotic place? What about working in a small office? You would most likely be involved in all aspects of a project, although the scale of projects tend to be smaller.

The differences between school and the office are what make the first job both more difficult and more exciting than school. The nature of the work varies with offices, but some of the challenges include working with real clients (who are very concerned about money)—the client is not another studio professor, and in all probability not someone who will use the building (this definitely adds a unique dimension); junior staff can be assigned to a project and taken off at any time; major decisions will be made by others, such as a principal of the firm, an associate, or the client, often outside the office (don't feel left out and don't take it personally); schedules in the office have none of the clarity and finality of those in school [the authors assume you have read the section on time management in Chapter 1]; projects can unravel in midstride with a whimper and inexplicably restart months later; the ones that are completed may be done so with a charrette, occasionally more chaotic than those of architecture school. Still interested?

A comment on interviews. Some are nerve-wracking affairs with little obvious reward except that they are soon over. Others become fascinating intellectual adventures that reinforce the belief that you have made the right career choice. If at first you don't land a job, be patient and remain positive. It may not seem obvious at the time, but a series of interviews provides valuable experience and practice in the ability to present yourself and your work to others. You may also have made a professional contact that may prove important at a later date.

Whatever your professional interests, working for the the best firms and the best people will ensure that you will learn and grow professionally. In the future, good experience coupled with the talent, service, and credibility you offer clients will be the basis of your success and fulfillment in architecture.

CONTINUING EDUCATION AND DEVELOPMENT

Even if you find yourself without a summer job, stay in touch with the profession in some manner. Equipped with the most compelling of portfolios and recommendations, sometimes you are just not at the right place at the right time. This is no reflection on you or your capabilities; rather, work patterns in architecture are often cyclical and are vulnerable to fluctuating economic conditions.

Some schools and some local A.I.A. chapters have "mentoring" programs where practicing professionals are paired with students. The mentors act as advisors, give office tours, and generally help the student gain a sense of the nature of practice and the economic climate. Approach a local firm if such a program does not exist, and propose a monthly meeting (for the summer) with a principal. The contact could be important for future full- or part-time work, and it will broaden your network and chance for potential referrals. The Faber College (of *Animal House* fame) dictum, "Knowledge is good," applies here. Go out and get it.

Travel

Travel is another architectural tradition . . . and for good reason. If at all financially feasible (and you may need a wealthy relative), take advantage of vacation times—summer, between semesters, spring break—to visit architecturally significant works. During recessionary times, when it is not so easy to find work, this is one way to keep growing and learning professionally. As stated previously, there simply is no substitute for studying buildings firsthand. Moreover, many school programs have optional foreign study programs. You may never have another opportunity for this kind of extended travel time, with a minimum of personal responsibilities.

To get the most out of your travels, study and record the built environment. Prepare well ahead of your visit by developing an itinerary, researching plans, photos, and contexts of buildings you plan to see. Slides are a great means to record what you see on the road; they are a personal resource that can be treasured and referred to often, and you can bore insufferable relatives (especially the ones who financed your trip).

SUPPLEMENT 6-5: As noted previously, Norman McGrath is one of the finest architectural photographers in the world. Here Mr. McGrath comments on developing a personal collection of photographs, a means of recording images from travel experiences. I recommend his widely acclaimed book, *Photographing Buildings Inside and Out*, which is clearly the definitive source on the subject.

Some people look without seeing. The would-be architect must develop a keen eye to analyze and evaluate "architecture" and thus encourage the evolution of a sense of good taste. This is not something one inherits, but it is essential to the production of high-quality work. Learn to recognize good design when you see it. Observe, read, experience. When you discover something you like, try to reason why. Your favorites may become role models for your own work later.

To develop a useful reference library of personal images, you must first decide on a convenient format. 35mm slides are great for projection but are not that easy to view in the hand. You may find that simple, small color prints are easier to refer to and handle. Either way, you should first establish a good filing system, so that you can find a particular photograph when you want to. Some cameras nowadays will imprint dates or numbers on the original, preferably optionally. There are times when you may not want this information on a print or slide, but it can be useful.

Economics will play a major part in determining what equipment you purchase. If you can't afford a 35mm single-lens reflex (SLR) with removable lenses, you will at the very least need a "point-and-shoot" camera with a wide-angle lens, 35mm focal length or shorter. This will give you snapshot capability but not much more. The ultimate 35mm camera would be an SLR with perhaps a wide-angle zoom lens, 24 to 50 or 28 to 70mm, and, if you're really extravagant, a perspective control (PC) lens (35 or 28), which is what the pros use. For interiors, you will need a tripod for longer exposures. If you are a real beginner, you should enroll in a crash course in basic photography. Workshops of a day or so to a week or more are widely available for different levels of expertise.

Travel sketches are also an architectural tradition, not necessarily a substitute for slides. Just as with sketching details of a building site, sketching details of some master work of a piazza can instill a sense of proportion that lasts a lifetime.

FIGURE 6-6   *This is an example of a terrific travel sketch—a Mosque in Istanbul—by Robert S. Oliver on a trip around the world. It is excerpted from his book* The Sketch, 1979, *with permission of Van Nostrand Reinhold, New York.*

Portfolio

Everyone should have an impressive portfolio. *Flexibility* is the operative word for portfolio format. Develop or select a means of showcasing your work that can (1) evolve as your work improves through the years—you may want to substitute old projects for recent work that shows current capabilities or evidence of growth, and (2) tailor projects that would be of specific interest to your audience (i.e., for a particular firm or client). A binder or folder that has plug-in or removal ability would be ideal.

Avoid overkill! Do not feel compelled to show every piece of design work that you produced since the first grade! People to whom you will be showing your work will unquestionably have limited time, so *edit* appropriately.

Aim for a balance of your best design work and practical examples. Perhaps include a series of process sketches for a single "best" project. This provides your prospective employer with a window into *how* you work. In terms of the more "practical," if you have had previous job experience or have taken a course in architectural detailing (or design development), include *full-size* reproductions of this work. Perhaps it is an entire sheet itself, or single drawings from a larger sheet, translated to your portfolio format. In this way, you leave no doubt about your ability to draw, draft, letter—whatever the actual product.

As Bob Greenstreet mentioned in Supplement 5-2, consider, during the course of the semester, how you will eventually incorporate studio projects into the portfolio. This may have an impact on selecting your presentation media. For example, line drawings are less costly to reduce and reproduce than those with gray tones or color.

But this should only be *one* factor (and not necessarily the most important) in developing presentation graphics. Color may be added after reductions, independent of original project graphics, or as part of the overall portfolio format.

Jorge Silvetti, Professor of Design at Harvard University, has stated: "Students at the graduate level are interested in having a good portfolio so they can get a good job. That means they're not going to try things and be experimental." Do not let the idea of a practical/economical portfolio unduly influence the way in which you approach projects in the studio and diminish the quality of how problems are creatively engaged.

Once again, view the portfolio as a design problem. Conduct research: Study the journals themselves for examples of layout strategies. Although you will not have photographs of buildings, you may have photographs of models or perspective renderings. Note the graphic focus, and the relative sizes of the elements: Site plans, floor plans, sections, three-dimensional representations, and their relationships. Also note page format—look for how continuity is achieved for each project and for all editorial sections. These magazine formats are certainly very different from the presentation formats designed for large group viewing at your final reviews.

There is one note I would like to add, and this is personal. I have committed, and continue to commit a large amount of resources (both time and money) to documenting my design projects. *And this is not always easy!* However, I believe it is a most worthwhile investment on at least two levels: in helping to solidify how I view my architectural work, and in potentially educating prospective clients and the public in general about architecture. In other words, I would advise you not to skimp on executing this perhaps final phase of a project. In your portfolio, try to match the excellence of the work itself.

Define Your Role

As I set out to conclude *Architecture 101: A Guide to the Design Studio* with some speculation about the role of the architect, I pledged to avoid two extremes. One extreme, an almost foolish idealism, essentially holds that we all ought to be saving the world daily. The second, equally myopic extreme might best be personified by the insulated prima donna who never thinks about anything but high art and high income.

What *can* be said is that the actual range of possible roles is broad and dynamic, and amenable to individualization. Perhaps the most exciting aspect of this discussion is the way in which self-definition is continuously fine-tuned. As opportunities arise in experience and in the enrichment of continuing education, new possibilities are framed, and one or two of these may end up defining your special niche.

The reference to a myriad of possibilities rests on the solid bedrock of something called professional service. Stressed throughout this book is the primacy of certain qualities of interaction with clients, colleagues, consultants, and constructors. These are qualities such as listening, striving to understand, helping, being flexible and open-minded, educating . . . in other words, *serving in the context of highly educated and well-trained expertise*. This model of service plus expertise is the theoretical common denominator for all professionals, and the most fundamental and enduringly gratifying aspect of your role.

Appendixes

Appendix A

Reading List

BOOKS FOR A PROFESSIONAL COLLECTION

This kind of collection is one that will be *used* throughout your student and professional careers. Books are obviously expensive and the following list is not recommended lightly. These are books that are full of architectural wisdom. If you are unable to purchase your favorites, know where they are in the library stacks; you will want to refer to them frequently.

Allen, Edward and Joseph Iano. *The Architect's Studio Companion: Technical Guidelines for Preliminary Design*. New York: Wiley, 1989.

Allen, Edward and Joseph Iano. *Fundamentals of Building Construction: Materials and Methods*, 2nd Ed. New York: Wiley, 1990.

Burden, Ernest. *Entourage: A Tracing File*, 2nd Ed. New York: McGraw-Hill, 1991.

Cullen, Gordon. *The Concise Townscape*. New York: Van Nostrand Reinhold, 1961.

Greenstreet, Robert and James W. Shields. *Architectural Representation*. Englewood Cliffs, NJ: Prentice Hall, 1988.

Halprin, Lawrence. *Cities*, Rev. Paperback Ed. Cambridge, MA: MIT Press, 1972.

Lechner, Norbert M. *Heating, Cooling, Lighting: Design Methods for Architects*. New York: Wiley, 1991.

Lockard, William Kirby. *Design Drawing*, Rev. Ed. New York: Van Nostrand Reinhold, 1982.

Lynch, Kevin and Gary Hack. *Site Planning*, 3rd Ed. Cambridge, MA: MIT Press, 1984.

Patterson, Terry L. *Construction Materials for Architects and Designers*. Englewood Cliffs, NJ: Prentice Hall, 1990.

Peña, William with Steven Parshall and Kevin Kelly. *Problem Seeking: An Architectural Programming Primer*, 3rd Ed. Washington, DC: AIA Press, 1987.

Simonds, John Ormsbee. *Landscape Architecture: A Manual of Site Planning and Design*, 2nd Ed. New York: McGraw-Hill, 1983.

BOOKS FOR REFERENCE

The following books may be found readily and consulted in the library. At some point, you may decide to add one or all of them to your personal collection as specific interests and needs emerge.

Brown, G. Z. (Illustrations by V. Cartwright). *Sun, Wind, and Light: Architectural Design Strategies*. New York: Wiley, 1985.

DeChiara, Joseph and John Callender. *Time-Saver Standards for Building Types*, 3rd Ed. New York: McGraw-Hill, 1991.

Fletcher, Sir Banister and John Musgrove, Editors. *A History of Architecture*, 19th Ed. London: Butterworth, 1987.

Hoke, John Ray. *Ramsey/Sleeper Architectural Graphic Standards*, 8th Ed. New York: Wiley, 1988.

Lam, William M. C. *Perception and Lighting as Formgivers for Architecture*. New York: Van Nostrand Reinhold, 1977 (reprinted 1992).

Lockard, William Kirby. *Drawing as a Means to Architecture*. New York: Van Nostrand Reinhold, 1977.

McGrath, Norman. *Photographing Buildings Inside and Out*. New York: Amphoto/Watson-Guptill, 1987.

McHarg, Ian L. *Design with Nature*. New York: Wiley, 1969 (reprinted 1992).

Moore, Charles, Gerald Allen, and Donlyn Lyndon. *The Place of Houses*. New York: Holt, Rinehart and Winston, 1974.

Panero, Julius and Martin Zelnik. *Human Dimension and Interior Space: A Source Book of Design Reference Standards*. New York: Whitney/Watson-Guptill, 1979.

Assessing Architectural Photographs

Charles D. Linn, A.I.A., Editor at Large of *Architectural Record*, concludes his message to students with a brief essay on critically assessing architectural photographs. His specific point of view is that of a lighting expert, and of course lighting is a key factor in documenting space.

Most students spend more time looking at the various design magazines than actually visiting the grand spaces. This is almost a necessity for students who don't go to school in the major urban centers. These magazines do afford an excellent means of taking a monthly field trip to important new and old buildings, even buildings that don't exist any more. But students must learn to be critical of the lighting they observe in architectural photographs, because photographers use multiple exposures, filters, fill-light, and other tricks to make their photographs acceptable.

These can significantly alter the way a space looks in a photo, adding shadows and bright spots where they do not appear in real life. Photographic film does not "see" light the way the eyes see it—making it difficult for photographs to render color accurately, especially when multiple types of light sources are used. Fluorescent light looks sickly next to perfectly rendered incandescent light when photographed together. Daylight and electric light are also difficult to photograph side by side.

It takes some study to tell if photographs accurately depict a lighting situation, especially if the observer cannot visit the space personally. But here are some tips:

• If the ceiling plane is brighter than the floor plane, and there appears to be no source of uplight in the room, the photographer has probably added fill-light.

• Watch for harsh shadows that don't seem to belong. Why would the shadow of a picture frame appear above the picture unless the light is coming from knee level?

• Watch for bright streaks of light on walls and floors that originate behind sofas, chairs, and potted plants. Sometimes, though seldom, these exist permanently in the interior. More often than not, they are added by the photographer.

• Think about whether the lighting system shown in the room would deliver the sort of light you see. A downlight close to a wall, for example, should project a corresponding scallop of light on the wall. If it is absent, the downlight was probably turned off when the picture was taken. A ceiling full of black holes may mean all of the lights in the room were off when the photograph was taken.

• Multiple sources probably mean either multiple exposures, or filters, were used. For example, sometimes rooms with large windows are photographed twice on the same sheet of film. During the day, the exterior scene is exposed. At night, filters are added to the camera lens or placed over the light sources themselves to balance them. Then a second exposure is made.

To a certain extent, there is nothing wrong with photographers manipulating the light in a room to get a picture. Photographs are simulations of reality, and rendering these simulations as accurately as possible is the photographer's art. It is seldom that even the best illumination can be photographed without some manipulation.

But sometimes photographers go beyond simulating the actual lighting and take it upon themselves to "create" the lighting environment that appears in published photographs. If the designer of the space's lighting has done a poor job, the photographer may have no choice. If students notice these characteristics in photographs they are studying, it may be as instructive for them to analyze why the lighting had to be supplemented as it is for them to look at projects that required no help from the photographer. The main thing that students should always remember when looking at photographs is that their eyes should not be believed.

Index

A

Aalto, Alvar, 80
Abstract problems/thinking, 12, 84
Accessibility, 26–30
    Americans with Disabilities Act, 27, 29
Acoustics, 118–120
Advice, 13–16
    Erickson, Arthur, 15–16
    Jacobsen, Hugh Newell, 14–15
    Jahn, Helmut, 13–14
    Moore, Charles, 16
Aesthetic issues, 79–81
    contrast/blending, 81
    focus, 81
    light and shadow, 80
    ornament, 81
    perspective, 80
    proportion, 80
    rhythm, 81
    scale, 80
    symmetry/asymmetry, 81
    variety, 81
    visual coherence, 81
Air conditioning, *see* Mechanical systems
Albers, Joseph, color theory, 104
Allen, Edward, 25. *See also* Foreword
All-nighter, 5
American National Standards Institute, 27, 28
Americans with Disabilities Act, 27, 29
Analysis and interpretation of information, 19, 30–34, 56

B

Ando, Tadao, 60
Anthropometrics, 80
Approach, 12. *See also* Procession
Architect/client dialogue, 18, 21, 147. *See also* Interviewing techniques; Program
The Architect's Handbook of Professional Practice, 18, 19, 56
Architects' offices, 152–155
    Ehrenkrantz Group, 155
    NBBJ Headquarters, 154
    Stern, Robert A. M., 153
Architect, as team captain, 105, 120
Area:
    gross, 19
    net, 19
Art supplies, 141–143. *See also* Equipment
Axonometrics, 85, 131–132

B

Barker, Rinker, Seacat & Partners, 47
Barragan, Luis, 79, 104
Barrier-free design, *see* Accessibility
Blueprints, *see* Reprographics, diazo printing
Brainstorming tips, 82–83
    confidence, success, enjoyment, 83
    conflicts, resolution of, 82
    editing, 82
    failure and mistakes, embracing, 82
    if frozen, 82
    ideas, openness to, 82
    problems as assets, 82

Brainstorming tips (*Continued*)
    starting over, 82
    trial, error, and refinement, 82
    user perspective, 82
Brown, Blair, models, 142–143
Bubble diagrams, 31–34
    refinement of, 74
Building codes and standards, 25–27
    exit requirements, 25, 26
    preliminary design, related to, 25
Building system integration, 73, 74, 75,
    104–105
Burden, Ernest, presentations, 130–132, 133

C
Cantor, Marvin, building codes and
    standards, 25–27
Cartwright, Virginia, daylighting, 60–62
Central space, major, 74, 77
Charrette, *see* All-nighter
Charrette Corporation, *see* Brown, Blair;
    Maitland, Jim
Circulation systems, 31, 73–74, 140
Client/user perspective, 18, 40, 82. *See also*
    Environment/behavior factors
Climate, 46, 52
Color:
    in architecture, 103–104
    in presentations, 140
Common mistakes, 83
    arbitrary decisions, 83
    ideas:
        infatuation with, 83
        too many, 83
    insecurity, 5, 13, 83
    losing the big picture, 83
    obscure references, 83
    outdoor space, left over, 83
    perfection, search for, 83
    precious features, 83
Community, 43
Computers, 90–92, 93. *See also* Design tools
Concept development, 19, 35–36, 44, 46
Conklin, William, 105
Connolly, Caren:
    criticism, 4
    daylighting, 60
    presentation tip, 138
    site model, 65
Conservation, 42, 45. *See also*
    Environmentally conscious design;
    Landscape architecture

Construction costs, 23–24, 94, 99
    vs. creativity, 24
Construction technology, 92–101
    constructors, working with, 93–95,
        98–101
    design impact, 35, 97
    detailing, 95–98
        issues of, 95
        visual power, 97
    field experience, 95, 99
    as stylistic movement, 94, 97
    teamwork, 93–95, 100
Constructors, 94
    trade secrets of, 99
    working with, 98
Context, 44, 47–48, 50–54, 59, 65
Contours, 62–63, 64. *See also* Slope
Contrast/blending, 81
Costs, *see* Construction costs
Coxe, Weld, 128
Criticism, 3–4
    response to, 3, 134–136, 141, 149
    seeking, 3
Cross section, 76
Cullen, Gordon, 56

D
Daylighting, 60–62, 112, 113–117
Deadlines, 5–6. *See also* Time management
Design, 71–125
    collaboration, multidisciplinary, 44, 60,
        98, 104–105, 120
    construction technology, 92–101
    definition, 72
    diagrams, 75
    engineering consultations, 104–120
        acoustics, 118–120
        lighting, 113–117
        mechanical systems, 110–113, 114
        structures, 105–110
    instinctive, 72
    methodology, 72–73
    orchestration of, 120–125
        first experience, 121
    process, 12
    synthesis, 72–73, 105
Design facilitation, 72–83
    aesthetic issues, 79–81
    brainstorming tips, 82
    common mistakes, 83
    history, 76–79
    organizing elements, 73–74, 77

three-dimensional considerations, 74, 76, 78, 147
Design studio, 2–13
  competitiveness, 3–4
  completing projects, 6
  content, 2
  dialogue, 3
  experience, 2
  resources, 3–4
  responsibilities, 2–6
  rewards, 11–13, 128, 165
Design tools, 84–92, 93
  computers, 90–92, 93
    conceptual design, 91, 93
    presentation, 92
    resolving design ideas, 91–92
    simulation of reality, 92
    visualization and evaluation, 92
  drawings, 84–87, 130–132
    axonometrics/isometrics, 85, 131–132
    freehand *vs.* hard-line, 85
    interior perspectives, 85, 86
    as learnable skill, 87
    massing sketches, 85
    stylized rendering, 86
  models, 62, 65, 66, 87–90, 115, 142–143, 147–149
    building technique, 88
    experimenting with, 88
    exterior massing, 65, 66, 89
    interior, 88, 89, 90
    materials, 88, 142–143
    for perspective drawing generation, 88–89
  scale, selection of appropriate, 84
Desk crits, 7
  pluralism in, 7
Detailing, 95–98
Diagrams, 31–34, 55–58, 59, 74–75
Diazo printing, 129, 144–145. *See also* Reprographics
Drawings, 84–87, 130–132. *See also* Design tools

E
Edge City, 48
Electrical systems, 112. *See also* Lighting
Elevations, 76, 79, 80
Enclosure, 76
Energy efficient buildings, 49–50, 51, 110–113, 114
Engineering, *see* Design, engineering

consultations
Entry sequence, 58–59, 64
Environment, 42–45. *See also* Landscape architecture
Environmentally conscious design, 48–50, 51, 110–113, 114
Environment/behavior factors, 37–40
Equipment, 10–11. *See also* Art supplies
  drafting, 11
  model making, 11, 88
  sketching, 10, 84
  work surface, 10
Ergonomics, 80
Erickson, Arthur, 15–16, 46, 113
Exit requirements, 25, 26. *See also* Building codes and standards

F
Favoritism, 9
Focus, *see* Aesthetic issues; Presentation
Foster, Norman, 18, 98
The Fountainhead, 3
Friedberg, Paul, landscape architecture, 44–45
Future, 151–165. *See also* Jobs
  continuing education and development, 162–165
  defining role in, 165

G
Gibbons, Heidtmann, and Salvador, 47
Globalization of architecture, 65–69
  Kohn, Eugene, 67–69
  metrication, 66–67
Goldberger, Paul, 73, 76–77
Gordon, Scott, client perspective, 18, 40
Grades, 9–10
Graphics, *see* Design tools; Presentation
Greenstreet, Robert, presentations, 136–137
Grid, 74, 76, 108–110
Gross area, *see* Area

H
Halprin, Lawrence, landscape architecture, 42–44
Harmony, 42, 56, 59
Harner, Jeff, daylighting, 60
Heating, *see* Mechanical systems
Heery, George, construction technology, 95
History, 76–79
  design studio, relevance in, 78–79
  Gropius, Walter, 79

History (*Continued*)
  Kahn, Louis, 77
  McKim, Mead & White, 76–77
Holt Hinshaw Pfau Jones Architecture,
  147, 148

I
Indoor/outdoor transitions, 62, 101
Information gathering, 19–30
  primary data, 19–21
    collaborators, 21
    personal contact, 20
    simulations of clients, users, and
      consultants, 20
    social factors, 20
  secondary data, 22–23
    biographical data on architects, 22
    building typologies and specific
      buildings, 22–23
    historic styles, 22
    indexes to journals, 22
    technical references, 23
Initiation, 1–16
Intern Development Program, 152, 160
Interviewing techniques for clients/users,
  20–21
Interviews for jobs, 154, 156–157, 162

J
Jacobsen, Hugh Newell, 14–15
Jahn, Helmut, 13–14
Jobs, 152–162
  "everyday" projects, 157, 158, 159
  expectations, 157–162
  intern perspective, 158–160
  interview, 154, 156–157, 162
  large-firm perspective, 160–161
  portfolio, 6, 156, 164–165
  references, 154
  résumé, 155–156
  seeking, 152–157, 161–162
  small-firm perspective, 161–162
Jofeh, Chris, structures, 105–106
Johnson/Burgee Architects, 76, 98
Jones, Fay, 46
Journals, 6–7. *See also* Information
    gathering, secondary data
  benefits of, 6
  indexes to, 22
  limitations of, 7
Juries, 134–136, 149
  emotional trauma, 149
  follow-up, 149

K
Kahn, Louis, 60, 77
Kallmann, McKinnell & Wood, 73–74
Kaplan/McLaughlin/Diaz, 31
Keeley, William, construction and
    business, 98–101
Kohn, Eugene, 67–69
Kohn Pedersen Fox Associates, 48, 67–69

L
Lam, William, 87–88, 114–116
Landscape architecture, 42–45
  Friedberg, Paul, 44–45
  Halprin, Lawrence, 42–44
  open space design, 43, 83
  related to building design, 42
Larson, Kent, computer for design and
    presentation, 91–92, 93
Lechner, Norbert, mechanical systems,
    111–113, 114
Library resources, 22–23
Lighting, 113–117. *See also* Daylighting.
  as applied perception psychology, 116
  architectural photographs, related to,
    171–172
  fixtures, 117
  models for, 62, 115
Light and shadow, 52, 60, 80
Linn, Charles:
  all-nighter, 5
  lighting, 116–117
  photographs, assessing architectural,
    171–172
  pinups, 8
Lockard, William Kirby, 85, 87
Lusher, Ruth, accessibility, 27, 29–30
Lynch, Kevin, 51, 56, 63
Lyons, John:
  presentations, 128, 132–133
  rewards, 11–12

M
McDonough, William, 48–50, 51
McGrath, Norman, photography:
  presentation models, 147–149
  travel, 163
McKim, Mead & White, 76–77
McMullan, Denis, structures, 106–108
Maitland, Jim, reprographics, 142, 144–147
Materials, 101–103
  interior finishes, 101
  properties of, 102

selection criteria for, 101, 102
visual implications of, 102
Wright, Frank Lloyd, use of, 102–103
Maxman, Susan, 18
Mechanical systems, 110–113, 114
Media selection, 129, 141–142. *See also*
    Design tools; Presentation
Meier, Richard, 62
Mentors, 9, 154
Metrication, 66–67
Models, 62, 65, 66, 87–90, 115, 142–143,
    147–149. *See also* Design tools.
    photography:
        for perspective generation, 88–89
        for presentation, 147–149
Moore, Charles, 16
Mumford, Lewis, 42

N

Nagle, Hartray & Associates, Ltd., 97
Natural light, *see* Daylighting
Nature, 42
NBBJ, diagrams, 55, 75
Net area, *see* Area
Noise, 47. *See also* Acoustics
Novitske, Raymond:
    building codes, 25
    construction costs, 24
    construction technology, 96, 97

O

Oles, Paul Stevenson, 128
Oliver, Robert, travel sketch, 164
Ordway-Kousoulas Architects, small-firm
    perspective, 161–162
Organizing elements, 73–74, 77
    central space, major, 74, 77
    circulation systems, 31, 73–74
    grid, 74, 76, 108–110
    radial, dispersion, doughnut, and
        hierarchy, 74
Ornament, 81

P

Parking, 63–65
Patterson, Terry, materials, 101–103
Pawley, Charles Harrison, 48
Pei Cobb Freed & Partners, 46–47, 81, 84,
    98
Pelli, Cesar, 42
Peña, William, programming graphics, 33
Perspective:
    as aesthetic issue, 80

drawing, 85, 88–89
Photographic reproduction, *see*
    Reprographics
Photography:
    assessing architectural, 171–172
    model, 88–89, 147–149
    site, 51, 52
    travel, 163
Pinups, 8. *See also* Presentation
Place making, 39, 42–45
Plumbing systems, 112
Polshek, James Stewart, 37, 72, 79
Portfolio, 6, 156, 164–165
Portman, John, 74
Predock, Antoine, 44
Presentation, 127–149. *See also*
    Reprographics; Juries.
    audiences, 128
    color, use of, 140
    criticism, response to, 134–136, 141, 149
    as design problem, 128–130, 136–137
    design scroll, 131
    design studies, use of, 129, 130
    focus, 140, 141
    incomplete, 5, 133
    mock-up drawings, 129–130
    plan rendering, 132, 140
    preservation of, 137
    process drawings, 32, 129, 136
    scheduling, 134
    size of drawings, 132
    three-dimensional vehicles, 147–149
    tips, 138–139
        context, showing, 138
        cost, 139
        detail, 139
        elevations, labeling, 139
        keying drawings, 138
        lettering, 138
        line weights, 139
        materials rendering, 139
        orientation, 138
        people and entourage, 138
        plan alignment, 138
        precision drawings, 139
        scale, sense of, 138
        shade and shadow, 139
        sheet format, 139
    title blocks, 139, 141
    tracing files, 131, 133
    verbal, 132–137
Pressman, Peter, interviewing techniques,
    20–21

Process drawings, 32, 129, 136
Procession, 58–59, 64
Professional service ethic, 4, 13, 37, 128, 165
Program, 17–40
    approach to, 18–19
    CRS tradition, 33, 39
    definition, 18
    diagrams, 30–34
        for final presentation, 32, 129
    discussions with clients and users, 18,
        19–21, 30
    forms, 18
    site fit, 56, 58, 59
Programming phases:
    analysis and interpretation of
        information, 19, 30–34
    concept development, 19, 35–36, 44, 46
    information gathering, 19–30
Project delivery, constructors' view of, 98
Proportion, 80, 163

R
Rapport with clients, 18, 21
Reading list, 169–170
    books for a professional collection, 169
    books for reference, 170
Reprographics, 129, 141–142, 144–147
    color, 146
    cost/benefit evaluation, 146–147
    diazo printing, 129, 144–145
        rendering, 145
    photographic reproduction, 146
    xerography, 129, 145–146
Résumé, 155–156
Reviews, *see* Juries; Pinups
Revisions, 3, 83
Rewards from design studio, 11–13, 128, 165
Rhythm, 81
Richardson, H. H., 81
Roche, Kevin, 74
Rosenfeld, Norman:
    bubble diagrams, 34
    job seeking, 155–157
Ryhn, Douglas, structures, 108–110, 135

S
Sanborn maps, 50
Scale:
    as aesthetic issue, 80
    for selecting with design tools, 84, 138
Scheduling, for programming, 35. *See also*
    Time management

Schnuck, Lawrence, large-firm perspective,
    160–161
Schweitzer, Josh, 47
Seismic factors, 54
Shepley Bulfinch Richardson and Abbott,
    47
Siebein, Gary, acoustics, 118–120
Signage, need for, 73
Simonds, John, 52, 56, 57–58, 59, 82
Singleton, Robert, 95–96
Site, 41–69
    alternatives, 56
    characteristics, 42
    context model and drawings, 65, 66
    contours, 62–63, 64
    diagrams, 55–58, 59
        alternatives, 56
        napkin sketch, 59
        with program elements, 58
    globalization, 65–69
    harmony, 42, 56, 59
    indoor/outdoor transitions, 62, 101
    inventory, 50–55
        big picture, 50–51
        context, immediate, 51
        history, 51
        regional issues, 50
        spirit/"karma", 50, 51
    preparation, 52
        available documentation, 52
        photography and sketching, 52
        site plan copies for field notes, 52
    recording data, 52–55
        existing building, renovation of,
            54
        existing objects, materials, and
            public works, 53–54
        microclimate, 52
        miscellaneous, 55
        noise and smells, 54
        slopes, 52
        subsurface conditions, 54
        vegetation and wildlife, 53
        views, 52
        zoning, 54
    landscape architecture, 42–45
    parking, 63–65
    program fit, 56, 58, 59
    relationships, 56
    visits, 44
Site analysis, 55–58
Site influences on design, 46–49

climate:
  rain, 46
  sun, 46
  wind, 46
context, 47–48
good views, 47
noise, smells, and bad views, 47
slope, 46–47
sociocultural context, 48
traffic, 48
vegetation, 46
Slikerman, Iris, presentations, 140–141
Slope:
  flat, 46
  steep, 46–47
Smells, 47
Sobczak, Michael, intern perspective, 158–160
Social responsibility, 37–38
Sociocultural context, 48
Solar path diagrams, 53
Soo, Lydia, history, 78–79
Sound, *see* Acoustics
Structures, 105–110
Strunk and White, 79–80
Sun, *see* Climate; Daylighting; Solar path diagrams
Sussman, Deborah, color in architecture, 103–104
Symmetry/asymmetry, 81
Synthesis, of design, 72–73, 105

T
Teamwork, *see* Design, collaboration; Construction technology, teamwork
Three-dimensional considerations, 74, 76
  cross section, 76
  diagrams, 76
  enclosure, 76
  presentation vehicles, 147–149
Time management, 4–6, 84, 128
  all-nighter, 5
  bar chart/timeline, 6
  chip away at tasks, 5
  as design problem, 5
Topography, 46–47, 50, 52, 62–63, 64

Tracing files, 131, 133
Traffic, 48
Travel, 163–164
  photographs, 163
  sketches, 163–164

U
U.S. Geological Survey, 50
Universal design, *see* Accessibility
Users, building, 18, 19–21, 40, 82. *See also* Environment/behavior factors

V
Value engineering, 94, 99–100
Values, 13–16, 165. *See also* Professional service ethic
Van der Rohe, Mies, 74, 81, 104
Variety, as aesthetic issue, 81
Vegetation, 46
Venturi, Scott Brown & Associates, 73, 78
Views:
  bad, 47
  good, 47
Visual coherence, 81
Vocabulary, architectural, 3, 6

W
Weisman, Gerald, environment/behavior factors, 38–40
Wish list, 18, 20
Woolever, Mary, library resources, 22–23
Worley, Raymond, construction technology, 93–95
Wright, Frank Lloyd:
  humor, sense of, 133
  materials, use of, 102–103
  renderings, 130, 132
  site, design with, 62

X
Xerography, 129, 145–146

Z
Zoning ordinances, 25, 50, 54
Zoning of space, 56, 74